The New Middle Ages

Series Editor
Bonnie Wheeler
English and Medieval Studies
Southern Methodist University
Dallas, TX, USA

The New Middle Ages is a series dedicated to pluridisciplinary studies of medieval cultures, with particular emphasis on recuperating women's history and on feminist and gender analyses. This peer-reviewed series includes both scholarly monographs and essay collections.

More information about this series at
http://www.palgrave.com/gp/series/14239

Nicholas Ealy

Narcissism and Selfhood in Medieval French Literature

Wounds of Desire

Nicholas Ealy
University of Hartford
West Hartford, CT, USA

The New Middle Ages
ISBN 978-3-030-27915-8   ISBN 978-3-030-27916-5   (eBook)
https://doi.org/10.1007/978-3-030-27916-5

This Palgrave Macmillan imprint is published by the registered company Springer Nature Switzerland AG.
The registered company address is: Gewerbestrasse 11, 6330 Cham, Switzerland

ACKNOWLEDGMENTS

The seeds of this project were planted in a graduate seminar I took at Emory University with Claire Nouvet. It is here I was introduced to the myth of Narcissus, a tale whose complexity has not ceased fascinating and challenging me. I will always be grateful to Claire, whose instruction pushed me to question and explore the endless puzzles this myth and its legacy pose regarding the human condition. Special thanks also go to Lori Walters, whose graduate seminars at Florida State University cultivated my love for medieval literature. It is with her I first read some of the texts that shape the argument for this book. I must also thank those teachers of mine who served as mentors, for their instruction continues to influence my teaching and scholarship: Cathy Caruth, William Cloonan, Jean Dangler, Raymond Fleming, Michael Gerli, Jean Graham-Jones, Mark Jordan, Dalia Judovitz, and Elissa Marder. Jennifer Heneghan-Paquette and Iliana Mankin, both of whom are unfortunately no longer with us, deserve recognition for instilling within me a lifelong passion for languages.

While writing this book, many friends lent their support along the way. Primary thanks go to Karen Tejada-Peña and Sarah Senk, my two academic spouses, who read and commented upon parts of this manuscript while letting me talk through my ideas in countless conversations. I am also grateful to Aimee Pozorski for her comments on drafts of the last two chapters and to Stéphanie Boulard and Jenny Davis Barnett for their help with some of the translations contained herein. Additionally, I hold dear those friends who have lent their support at various times throughout this project: Geillan Aly, Jeff Blanchette, Lauren Cook, Deidra Donmoyer, Cyril Ghosh, Cécile Guillaume-Pey, Kasturi Gupta, Carmen

Hernández-Ojeda, Erica Hughes, Lillian Kamal, Robert Lang, Kate McGrath, Kenny Nienhusser, Zee Onuf, T Stores, Elizabeth Trelenberg, Charles Twombly, and Paul Watt. I also must recognize my friend Juanita Garciagodoy, taken from this world too soon—her words of advice and encouragement live on within me, continuing to direct me in my scholarly endeavors.

I thank my students at the University of Hartford, Wesleyan College, and Emory University, from whom I have learned so much through many discussions. I thank my colleagues in the Department of English and Modern Languages at the University of Hartford for creating such a friendly work environment and for the opportunity to teach the English Capstone on "Love and Illness" in 2017, where I was able to discuss with those students many of the issues raised in this book. I thank the University of Hartford, which granted me a sabbatical in Spring 2015, during which some of this project was completed.

I am grateful to the editorial staff at Palgrave for supporting this project from the start and to my anonymous reviewer there, thanks to whom this is now a stronger book. Parts of Chap. 4 have appeared in *Fifteenth-Century Studies* as my article "The Poet at the Mirror: René d'Anjou and Authorial Doubling in the *Livre du Cœur d'Amour épris*." I thank Camden House for the permission to use it here. I also thank the Bibliothèque nationale de France and the Österreichische Nationalbibliothek for permission to use images from their collections.

I thank my siblings, through biology and marriage, Taisia, Bill, Gregory, and Miho, for their encouragement, as well as my four beautiful nieces, Hannah, Emma, Nino, and Mila, who have brought endless joy to my life. Finally, I cannot express enough love and gratitude to my parents, John and Barbara, for their constant support and for always giving me a place to call home. I dedicate this book to you.

CONTENTS

LIST OF FIGURES

PART I

Narcissism and Selfhood in Context

CHAPTER 1

Introduction: Narcissus and the Wounded Self

In the twelfth-century Occitan composition "When I See the Lark," Bernart de Ventadorn, one of the most influential poets during the High Middle Ages, sings of the devastating longing he feels for his lady:

> Ai, las, tan cuidava saber
> d'amor e tan petit en sai,
> car eu d'amar no·m posc tener
> celeis don ja pro non aurai.
> Tout m'a mo cor e tout m'a me
> e se mezeis e tot lo mon,
> e can se·m tolc, no·m laisset re
> mas dezirer e cor volon.

> Alas! I thought I knew so much about love, but really, I know so little. For I cannot keep myself from loving her from whom I shall have no favor. She has stolen from me my heart, myself, herself and all the world. When she took herself from me, she left me nothing but desire and a longing heart.[1]

Bernart here thus finds, as is the case in numerous medieval erotic songs from southern France, that his desire has profoundly changed him. For, driven by an alienating passion, he struggles to grasp the reality that, in his lady's absence, any acknowledgment he might have expected to receive from her will never be forthcoming. Losing his self due to isolation and

© The Author(s) 2019   3
N. Ealy, *Narcissism and Selfhood in Medieval French Literature*, The New
Middle Ages, https://doi.org/10.1007/978-3-030-27916-5_1

solitude, losing who he thought he was because his self *has been stolen from him*, he thereby undergoes a transformation, experiencing a shift that destabilizes his entire identity in how he sees himself and his place in the world.

With this realization, Bernart emerges as a subject enmeshed in and undone by his frustrated longing, a process that, in this move from supposed knowledge to ignorance of love, *happened* to him at a certain point in his desiring state. Bereft of hope, he can only now look back and, in the song, attempt to work through this disaffecting selfhood that *has already occurred*.[2] Though, what has taken place in his transformation, in this new understanding of his selfhood? What constitutes and defines such a process? The aim of this book is to examine such questions regarding selfhood, questions that, we might say, do not simply affect Bernart but rather speak to a phenomenon that could be seen as central to the human experience. We all, for instance, move through life as a self—both introspectively and in our dealings with others and the world around us. At the same time, though, we are not born with an awareness of our selfhood, and our memories only extend back so far before there is nothing to remember about "our self."[3] How then does selfhood happen? Is it stable or, as Bernart's song implies, something that shifts and is lost or reconfigured due to external circumstances? And, most importantly for this study, how might literary texts, like Bernart's song, approach an understanding of selfhood from which we might gain explanations that inform our own selfhood as well?

My objective here is to attempt an answer to these questions by examining the construction of selfhood that comes to the fore in medieval literature, a construction that has contributed a dominant model for how selfhood is considered, even today, in the Western tradition. My inquiry begins in France during the twelfth century with a group of poet-singers—known as troubadours in the Occitan-speaking South (where Bernart resided) and trouvères in the French-speaking North—who begin to compose love songs where a unique understanding of the self emerges. Taking their name from the Occitan verb *trobar* and the French verb *trouver* (from the Latin *tropare* for composing tropes or musical verse), the ambition of these poet-singers becomes one of finding—the secondary meaning of *trobar* and *trouver*—new means of expressing the self. Such new means involve, as a first step, joining the poet-singer to the *lyric I*, the first-person pronoun at the center of these songs who speaks in the poet's voice and declares his point of view. As we see with Bernart, the singer, thanks to this *lyric I*, can assume an identity in his own work, casting himself not simply as the composer of the lyric, but as its subject—as its *self*—as well.[4] In and of itself, the creation of a singular identity from two separate entities (singer and literary persona) may not seem extraordinary, but if we examine the implications of this *lyric I*, we can see such a move is nonetheless quite revolutionary in how notions of selfhood come to be understood in Western European culture.

For this innovative *lyric I* does not arrive alone, but appears alongside a certain representation of *love*—referred to as "courtly love" in English and *fin'amor* ("refined love") by the troubadours and trouvères—that structures the ways in which it develops. Before exploring the relationship between love and selfhood though, we must first take a step back and seek to comprehend what constitutes this love. Scholars have long understood *fin'amor*, albeit an ambiguous term, to embody an ethical framework of amorous behavior situating the *lyric I* in relation to several distinct qualities—*mezura* (self-discipline), *cortesia* (courtesy), *joven* (generosity) and *joi* (joy)—all of which dictate how the *lyric I* should act and treat his beloved.[5] In this ethical framework, which Sarah Kay calls a "matrix of desire," the lover's identity comes forth, not as an autonomous individual, but as a result of the interplay between his deeds and emotions—*as a desiring self*—and those of his lady—*as his desired other*. The matrix of desire, due to this exchange between poet and lady, is consequently the place where "participants [in this poetry] are located and defined," where the lover's *lyric I*—his selfhood—emerges *in relation to and dependent upon the other*.[6]

Bernart's "When I See the Lark" perhaps best illustrates this emergence of selfhood within the matrix of desire, for we can see the poet turn to his longing, manifested in the pain he endures for his lady, as a way of exploring *who he is*. Initially this desire, defining Bernart's subjectivity, opens him up to a longing for fulfillment, to a fantasy that fulfillment might be possible. Simultaneously though, it makes him vulnerable to the reality this may never happen. For, Bernart's song is not simply about how desire shapes his selfhood, but rather is a composition revealing how his sense of self comes to be *under attack* by his longing. At a certain point, for instance, his passion takes a turn and, as his *self-as-desire* emerges in this relationship with the beloved lady, he realizes the desire now defining him may also be what is destroying him:

> Anc non agui de me poder
> ni no fui meus de l'or' en sai
> que·m laisset en sos olhs vezer
> en un miralh que mout me plai.
> Miralhs, pus me mirei en te,
> m'an mort li sospir de preon
> c'aissi·m perdei com perdet se
> lo bels Narcisus en la fon.

> Never have I been in control of myself or even belonged to myself from the
> hour she let me gaze into her eyes: that mirror which pleases me so greatly.
> Mirror, since I saw myself reflected in you, deep sighs have been killing me.
> I have lost myself just as the beautiful Narcissus lost himself in the fountain.[7]

Attempting to find satisfaction and put a stop to his endless longing, Bernart tries to look into his beloved's eyes. Rather than a welcoming glance from her, however, he finds her eyes have become mirrors, a discovery that pleases him at first but, in a radical turn, then alienates him from her and, most surprisingly, from his own self. For he ceases to be himself once he directs his gaze toward these eyes. The boundary one might expect to find between this desiring self and desired other has collapsed and, in the search for this lady, he instead encounters his own reflection in a mirror that he addresses *in place of her*. And it is this moment, as Bernart recognizes his own reflection, that leads to his destruction as deep sighs sap away his life force.

The precarious selfhood coming forth in Bernart's song, a selfhood created in its own destruction, raises a few more questions. Why, in this quest for erotic fulfillment, does Bernart find an image (here his own), instead of the lady, as the object of his desire? Why, in this confusion of self and other, does the poet find his *self* through desire, only to be killed by the same desire? Answers begin to take shape at the end of the stanza where Bernart, describing his death before the mirror, compares himself to Narcissus, that young boy who suffers a similar fate when he gazes at his own reflection, falls in love with it, and dies. For Narcissus's tale, from Book Three of Ovid's Latin work *The Metamorphoses* (8 C.E.), comes to serve as *the* narrative structuring *fin'amor*, not simply in Bernart's verses, but in much of French literature during the Middle Ages, where the self emerges as *narcissistic* in its design.[8] And it is this comparison Bernart and others make to Narcissus that warrants further exploration, for with this mythological figure a host of tensions stemming from the desire imposed upon the self comes to the fore, tensions, to which I now turn, that will guide my argument throughout this book.

1.1   Selfhood and the Myth of Narcissus

From its start, Ovid's myth of Narcissus establishes itself as a narrative about the emergence of selfhood and, as we see in Bernart's poem, about the perils of what such a selfhood might imply. It is here the tale introduces Tiresias, the blind prophet of antiquity, who informs Narcissus's mother, when she comes seeking her son's fortune, that he will live to see old age only "si se non noverit," if he does not *know himself*.[9] This move from not having a sense of self to cognizance of one's selfhood takes place in two ways as the myth unfolds—acoustically through spoken language and visually through reflected imagery—and these two modes of discourse, the linguistic and the imaginary, inform the emergence of Narcissus's selfhood. First, Ovid presents the discourse on language when Narcissus—now sixteen years old—encounters the nymph Echo, who has viewed him from afar and fallen for his beauty. Punished by Juno, she cannot, however, generate any speech and, true to her name, is only capable of repeating what she hears. Longing for Narcissus, she begins to echo back to him his words whenever he speaks and he, believing to hear the speech of another, remains unaware that what he hears is, in truth, his own speech returning to him.[10] Failing the test of self-recognition through speech, Narcissus rejects Echo and, soon afterward, approaches a fountain where he falls in love for the first time, not with a person, but with his reflection upon the water's mirrored surface:

> adstupet ipse sibi vultuque inmotus eodem
> haeret ut e Pario formatum marmore signum.
> spectat humi positus geminum, sua lumina, sidus
> et dignos Baccho, dignos et Apolline crines
> inpubesque genas et eburnea colla decusque
> oris et in niveo mixtum candore ruborem
> cunctaque miratur, quibus est mirabilis ipse.

And he gazes in dismay at his own self; he cannot turn away his eyes; he does not stir; he is as still as any statue carved of Parian marble. Stretched out along the ground, he stares again, again at the twin stars that are his eyes; at his fair hair, which can compare with Bacchus' or with Apollo's; at his beard-less cheeks and at his ivory neck, his splendid mouth, the blood-red blush on a face as white as dazzling snow; in sum, he now is struck with wonder by what's wonderful in him.[11]

Despite the popular interpretation that Narcissus falls in love *with himself,* the young man is not, as Ovid makes clear, the same as the blood-red and snow-white image (*umbra* or "shadow" in the original Latin) cast before him. Becoming enamored with an image, nonetheless, signals two errors befalling him, for he does not realize what he sees is his own reflection, nor does he realize what he sees is *not alive,* mistaking it for another person. Believing the *umbra* to be real, he tries to reach out and speak to it thinking, because it mimics his actions, that it must long for him in return:

> spem mihi nescio quam vultu promittis amico,
> cumque ego porrexi tibi bracchia, porrigis ultro;
> cum risi, adrides; lacrimas quoque saepe notavi
> me lacrimante tuas; nutu quoque signa remittis
> et, quantum motu formosi suspicor oris,
> verba refers aures non pervenientia nostras.
> iste ego sum! sensi; nec me mea fallit imago[.]

Your gaze is fond and promising; I stretch my arms to you, and you reach back in turn. I smile and you smile, too. And, often, I've seen tears upon your face just when I've wept, and when I signal to you, you reply; and I can see the movement of your lovely lips—returning words that cannot reach my ears. Yes, yes, I am this! [*Iste ego sum!*] I've seen through the deceit: my image cannot trick me anymore.[12]

Identical to the way in which Bernart encounters his lady's mirrored eyes, the image in the fountain holds any chance for reciprocal fulfillment at bay, acting as a permanent barrier to Narcissus's realization of his desire. When, however, he understands that what he sees is just an image, the resulting exclamation of *iste ego sum*—"I am this"—establishes a central understanding of how selfhood emerges from the tense interplay with something *other.* For, although *iste ego sum* can be read as reassuring, serving as "the confirmation of a rather classic definition of the subject that maintains a clean separation between the 'I' [ego] and the image," its secondary interpretation shatters any notion of a stable and unified selfhood:

> Understood literally, "Iste ego sum" [I am this] confirms that Narcissus's error is not singular: the "I" [ego] can be confused with an image [imago] because it is itself an image. The "I" is simply this, "*iste*" [...]. Narcissus is originally this "other" from which he thinks he can distinguish himself. He is other because he is alienated from the start, formed only by absorbing the "other" that is the image.[13]

Caught between his hopeless love for a non-existent entity and his frustrated desire for erotic satisfaction, Narcissus comes to understand two fateful things: (1) his desire, the result of the image, can never be realized, as he is left to endure the lacking qualities it represents in its incapacity to reciprocate affection and (2) his desire defines his selfhood, which, in turn, embodies the lack housed in the reflected image, this external and lifeless "other." Narcissus's self comes forth due to the lack constituting his desire, not as a unified whole, but forever divided and frustrated in his inability to achieve fulfillment, a simulacrum of the image, *as an other*, alienated to his very self. Mourning his own demise, he attempts to undo these disastrous effects by joining himself to the image while simultaneously destroying it. The sole way to accomplish this, however, is to annihilate the self that the image reflects, the self only possible *because* of the image:

> dumque dolet, summa vestem deduxit ab ora
> nudaque marmoreis percussit pectora palmis.
> pectora traxerunt roseum percussa ruborem,
> non aliter quam poma solent, quae candida parte,
> parte rubent, aut ut variis solet uva racemis
> ducere purpureum nondum matura colorem.

> As he laments, he tears his tunic's top; with marble hands he beats his naked chest. His flesh, once struck, is stained with subtle red; as apples, white in one part will display another crimson part; or just as grapes, in varied clusters, when they ripen, wear a purple veil.[14]

Bemoaning the impossibility of libidinal satisfaction, and, overcome by the heat of his passion, he dies through liquefaction, like "igne levi cerae matutinaeque pruniae/sole tepente solent" [blond wax will melt near a gentle fire, or frost will melt beneath the sun].[15] As his tale ends, his sisters cannot find his body, but instead—in his place—the flower bearing his name.

Although I raise the salient points of Ovid's account of Narcissus as a means of introducing the issues of imagery, language, desire, and selfhood that I explore in relation to the myth throughout this book, part of my aim is to make clear that the tale has nothing to do with the arrogance or selfishness shaping our contemporary understanding of narcissism. If anything, Ovidian narcissism presents the opposite perspective of a self, not "full of itself," but one rendered vulnerable as an impossible yearning for an image assaults the self's *notion of its own self*. Stemming from Ovid's legacy, such notions of narcissistic selfhood and desire based upon imagery remain central to the Western tradition in what Giorgio Agamben refers to as the "phantasmatic conception of love," where love is structured, not around desire for a flesh-and-blood person, but rather an ephemeral reflection (or phantasm) of the beloved.[16] For these images—as we see with Bernart and Narcissus—"emerge [...] as origin and object of love, and the proper situation of eros is displaced from the sense of sight to the phantasy."[17] The lover of this literature can only approach his beloved through the fantastical qualities of the image, which maintains its presence in memory and permanently stands in for the physicality of the "real" person it reflects. First imprinted on the eye, which acts as an aquatic mirror, the phantasms are reflected into the thoughts of the seer, who, recalling them in daydreams or nocturnal visions, increases his desire for and fidelity to this object of affection.[18] As such, the medieval literary lover discovers what Narcissus learns when he looks at his image: the beloved does not occupy a space in the tangible world, but rather always already exists within the realm of memory and illusions from which it derives its strength. The image of the desired person, inhabiting the thoughts of the one who longs for it, will always supersede the physical, giving way to a tradition that is, for Agamben: "one of [the] most fertile legacies [of the Middle Ages] in Western culture [where love is conceived] as an essentially phantasmatic process, involving both imagery and memory in an assiduous, tormented circling around an image painted or reflected in the deepest self."[19] For this reason, Narcissus becomes the model for two opposing viewpoints regarding love, both the refined love of *fin'amor*, where the image causes the delicious torture of a lover's unending desire, and its opposite in *fol amour* or mad love, which attempts to reify the image, break the phantasmatic process and seize the image as if it were real.

The narcissistic paradigm of the phantasmatic process thereby becomes *the* means of exploring selfhood through desire for the troubadours and trouvères as well as their literary descendants. By the twelfth century,

Ovid's tale of Narcissus—along with the entire *Metamorphoses*—had become quite popular as an increasing number of authors employed the figure of Narcissus in order to examine selfhood through imagery as the paradigm for human love and subjectivity. Probably the best known example of such an examination in the French tradition comes from Guillaume de Lorris's *Romance of the Rose* (*Roman de la Rose*) (c. 1270), where a dreaming Lover enters a garden, encounters the fountain where Narcissus died, sees roses reflected upon its water's surface (one of which will serve as a double for the beloved), and falls in love:

> Ou mireor entre mil choses
> Quenui rosiers chargez de roses
> Qui estoient en un destor
> D'une haie clos tout entor,
> Et lors me prist si grant envie,
> Que ne leissase pour pavie
> Ne por paris que n'i alasse,
> La ou je vi la greignor masse.

In the mirror, amidst a thousand other things, I spied some rose bushes full of roses in a secluded place, completely surrounded and enclosed by a hedge, and a desire so great took ahold of me, that I would not have left that place where I saw this most important flowerbed for either Pavia or Paris.[20]

Here, an image of the rose representing the beloved woman appears, housing the Lover's desire in a way that will create a circularity of frustrated longing while allowing him to revel in the sweet agonies of his predicament. The fact that the Lover sees his beloved's reflection instead of his own, however, is not in opposition to Ovid's tale, where Narcissus sees his own reflection, but rather expands, in perhaps even starker terms than Bernart's song, our understanding of the relationship between self and other. For, in the *Romance of the Rose*, the beloved other who "appears where the self should appear," in truth stands in for the self, making it into a "glorious figure" where the Lover can admire, thanks to the reflection, "the image of [his] self, not as [he] is, *but as [he] desires to be*"—in other words, the perfected image of a seemingly stable longing, endlessly reciprocated between "self" and "other."[21] Such are the reasons why Bernart confuses his lady with a mirror and why the Lover of the *Romance of the Rose* sees the rose bushes in place of his reflection. And, in this collapse of self and other, a *labyrinth of desire* emerges, where the Lover finds himself caught within a host of tensions—joy and sadness, pleasure and pain, satisfaction and denial, dominance and oppression, life and death—situating the self's fragile existence, consistently coming-into-being through desire while consistently under threat because of it.

The fact that desire puts the self under threat comes from the lack of reciprocation that the image, which will always deny satisfaction, imposes upon the self. In this manner, the literary mirror of *fin'amor* does not simply serve to "elevate the value of the [beloved other] by putting up conventional obstacles to its attainability," but, more fundamentally, it serves to "conceal the inherent impossibility of attaining the object."[22] As such, the mirror creates a secondary illusion in addition to the presence of the image: that without it to act as a barrier, the beloved other *"would be directly accessible,"* fulfillment would appear possible, and the lover could achieve certainty of his self as stable and whole.[23] Because the mirror denies satisfaction though, as evident with Narcissus and Bernart, the alienation the self experiences from its own desire renders it vulnerable, tearing it between the endless pain of longing and the endless hope for fulfillment. And it is in this rupture that the language of wounding—a central focus of this book—finds a space to emerge within the literature of *fin'amor*.

1.2   Selfhood and Wounding

To explore the implications of this language of wounding, let us look once again at Guillaume's *Romance of the Rose* where, after the Lover looks into the fountain and notices the roses, Love personified, who has been following him with a drawn bow, shoots him in the heart through the eye. Stunned, the Lover falls into a faint, awakening to find that the arrow draws no blood. Able to remove its feathered shaft from his body, he cannot, however, remove the tip. In agony, he seeks some remedy for his wound and, drawn to the roses, looks to them for some relief. Then, Love shoots a second and third arrow, causing a wound so deep and wide the Lover faints again. A fourth arrow follows, making him swoon three more times, and finally a fifth arrow with a tip like a razor's edge which, this time, spreads an ointment throughout the wound:

> Ceste flesche a douce costume:
> Douceur i a et amertume.
> J'ai bien santi et coneü
> Qu'el m'a aidié et m'a neü:

Il ot angoisse en la pointure
Si me rasouage l'ointure;
D'une part oint, d'autre part cuit,
Einssi m'aide, einssi me nuit.

This arrow has a pleasant characteristic: it joins together sweetness and bitterness. I certainly felt it and realized all too well that it helped and harmed me at the same time. Its sting caused me torment, but the ointment brings me relief. On the one hand it brings me solace, while on the other it burns me, this is how it helps me and how it harms me.[24]

The relentlessness with which Love assaults the Lover appears to border on outright torture, as he does not know if he will survive the blows. Able to pull out the shaft of each arrow, five tips nonetheless remain in him, irremovable and fixed in place. Repeatedly shot by Love, he now becomes a permanent vessel for these weapons, carrying a wound that bears the mark of an attack he must perpetually endure, a wound calling out for healing only to be iteratively undercut by renewed pain.[25]

So far, I have given a definition for selfhood as it emerges through desire and in conjunction with an other, or, more specifically, with an image-as-other. What is most pertinent for this study, however, is how such a definition can theorize selfhood as fundamentally *wounded*. As evident in the *Romance of the Rose*, the wound locates the self at the nexus of pain and pleasure, illness and health, suffering and cure. What may not be immediately evident, however, is how this drama plays out in the disconnect between the forces of desire and the construct of love. For, even though desire and love seem to have the same aim, the two, as Erin F. Labbie posits, operate against one another, opening a space where fulfillment is frustrated and the self permanently *wounded*:

The presence of love is always inadequate to the fulfillment of desire, such that a dehiscence between desire and love is evident in the perpetual longing for the object of desire. In *love* the poet thinks he should be fulfilled; however, because his desire is always for that which is beyond his reach, the presence of love is necessarily an imposition on the fantasy of the scene of the love relationship.[26]

In this manner, love fails to contain and quell the surplus of desire, even if desire looks to love in the hopes that it can solve such excesses. *Love* and *desire*, in other words, are not the same, and the confrontation between the two causes a dehiscence, to use Labbie's term, rupturing the wound of selfhood. However, given their close conceptual relationship, there is a fair amount of slippage in their usage, evident in troubadour poetry and the literature it inspires. This, I would argue, is not simply due to the fact that they *seem* to describe the same phenomenon but that there is a longing within this literature for them *to describe* the same phenomenon, a hope love could, in fact, lead to the fulfillment of desire. Narcissus, for instance, experiences this uncoupling of love and desire at the fountain in his attempts to call out to and embrace the boy he believes to see. Thinking there are signs of recognition coming back to him from the reflection, he hopes it will confirm and reciprocate his appeals. This expectation for love, though, reveals itself to be based on a fantasy, and Narcissus experiences his desire, his very selfhood, as split between longing for the image and the denial it can only grant "in return." Fascinated with his likeness, Narcissus tries to capture and conform to it at any cost, even to the point of self-sacrifice, to ensure the "oneness" he craves. When he beats himself, staining his skin crimson with blood, the alienating division originally imposed upon him by the image now appears as physical marks—as wounds—upon his body. And these wounds, as Claire Nouvet argues, "literalize the wound that the reflection inflicted upon him," rendering him an "I" that "appears as originally wounded, cut off from an identity with itself that it never enjoyed [dont il n'a jamais joui]."[27]

That the Lover of the *Romance of the Rose* finds himself similarly wounded, marked as a wounded "I"—a direct descendant of Ovid's Narcissus—is not out of place in the Middle Ages, for, as Larissa Tracy and Kelly DeVries attest, wounds and references to wounds are ever-present within medieval society. Appearing upon battlefields and in medical and legal discourse, hagiography, secular and religious iconography as well as literature, wounds gain such prominence in the Middle Ages precisely because they *speak to what it is to be human*, "open[ing] the body to investigation and inquiry [...] test[ing] the boundaries of mortality, and [... serving as] something that people lived with and from which they often died."[28] And, as we see with Narcissus and the Lover of the *Rose*, such inquiry into the effects of desire and the consequences they impose upon our humanity were not simply emotional or mental processes, but instead transform themselves into physical marks, bruises and apertures—into wounds—upon the surface of the body. How then are we to understand the ways in which this wounding operates? And how might courtly literature help us to theorize the wounded self, to theorize selfhood as a *lived performance of this wounding*? To attempt some initial answers to these questions, let us look again to the Lover of the *Rose* for whom the wound represents a physical and temporal indication that his body has been attacked—here in an assault Love has lodged against it with five arrows. This wound first indicates that his body has undergone an acutely felt injury and that Love, no longer simply abstract, has transformed it into a site that has been weakened, opened, separated, and sundered—in short, *violently altered*. To these ends, his wound, which *will never heal*, also denies him any wholeness or fulfillment he may have believed to have, something that, in truth, symbolizes the perpetual longing constituting him and all courtly lovers. Resulting from a series of arrows that puncture and distress his body's liminality, the Lover's injury has also broken down barriers between oppositions, as the barbed tips, once external, now come to be lodged within his heart, reflecting and heightening the unrequited desire he already felt when he looked into the fountain. In this manner, what was internalized can now come forth from the Lover through the wound, now the locale where "the external boundary of the body [...] begins to externalize, objectify, and make sharable what is originally an interior and unsharable experience."[29] The Lover's wound, in other words, puts inside and outside into communication with one another, destabilizing the confines of a permeable body where contraries such as self and other—the makeup of narcissism—collapse.

From the wound emerges *a language* directed toward speaking about the sentient experience of the injury and of this corporeal site where love and desire, integrity and vulnerability, creation and destruction, all come together to play out the drama of *fin'amor*. The wound becomes *the place* where the self attempts to understand itself, to grapple with the conse-quences of the fact that it is wounded, and has emerged as such, within a narcissistic matrix of desire. And the discourse—the literature—coming forth with the self becomes, as Labbie posits, the "symptom [of] and the solution" to this dehiscence.[30] It is in this space opened up by the wound that the literature analyzed in this book attempts to come to terms with the injured self, to find a language externalizing through narration the internal pain felt from narcissistic alienation.

1.3   Overview of This Book

I find this language of the wounded self to emerge in five texts from the Middle Ages that may at first seem disparate in nature, content, and time period, but it is the mark of Ovid's myth, their indebtedness to *fin'amor*, and the resulting discourse of how the wounds of desire shape selfhood that holds them together. My goal in choosing these texts is to demonstrate that such a corpus reflects the wide-ranging influence of this myth that, in turn, sparked an exploration of selfhood by generations of writers working across a variety of literary genres. For, as Emmanuèle Baumgartner posits, this myth's prominence extends across the entirety of the High and Late Middle Ages in France as authors, appropriating its flexibility, wrote new versions of the tale and wove recognizable allusions of it into their works.[31] Nonetheless, I do not intend to portray an "evolution" of the myth's use over time, and for this reason the chapters of this book do not progress chronologically but thematically, as I envisage them to encompass three distinct yet interconnected parts, each one dealing with a different aspect of the wounded self.

Containing Chaps. 1 and 2, Part I ("Narcissism and Selfhood in Context") comprises this introduction as well as an examination of the *Lay of Narcissus* (*Narcisus*) (c. 1160), an adaptation of Ovid's tale into Old French. Here, I continue to work through the language of wounding, begun in this introduction, and its effects upon the selfhood of the lay's central characters while establishing much of the psycho-physiological framework used in the book's subsequent chapters. Because narcissism deals with the wounded self, concepts emerging in medieval literature related to wounding—mourning, melancholy, trauma, and testimony—have an intimate bond with narcissism, expounding upon it in numerous ways. As such, these discourses play a prominent role throughout the remainder of the book because each speaks a unique language directed toward understanding the sentient experience of the wounded self. For instance, mourning is codified as an exploration of grief within the "plaint," a poetic genre in the Middle Ages seeking to close—through a meditation upon language—those wounds caused by desire and loss. Melancholy, conversely, thought to be the result of too much black bile within the body, comes to be congruent with lovesickness in pre-modern texts, a condition advocating for an opening of the wounds caused by unrequited desire.[32] Together, they form the framework for "Selfhood and the Open Wound," Part II of the book (Chaps. 3 and 4). In this manner, Alain de Lille's Latin cosmographical allegory *The Plaint of Nature* (*De planctu Naturae*) (c. 1168), the focus of Chap. 3, seeks, I argue, to close the wound of human subjectivity, evident due to its sinful nature, through the work of mourning. On the other hand, the central character of René d'Anjou's allegorical romance, *The Book of the Love-Smitten Heart* (*Livre du cœur d'Amour épris*) (c. 1457), as explored in Chap. 4, quests to maintain his wound's opening, reveling in the sweet melancholy his desire brings. Building upon the discourses of closing and opening wounds, trauma and testimony form the framework for "The Wounded Self as Witness," Part III (Chaps. 5 and 6) of the book. Trauma, ever-present in pre-modern literature, relates to its etymology from the Greek for "wound" within a medieval context, something which, in turn, speaks to the physical lacerations wrought by violence, as well as by the violence of desire, upon the body.[33] Testimony, an attempt to respond through language to the wounds trauma inflicts, finds itself across a host of medieval texts where lovers feel compelled to bear witness to the damaging consequences of their desires. As such, Chrétien de Troyes's chivalric romance *The Story of the Grail* (*Le Conte du Graal*) (c. 1181), the focus of Chap. 5, provides an opportunity to examine the phenomenon of a repetitive wound inflicted in a series of traumatic piercings that call into question the stability of its central character's selfhood. Finally, Chap. 6 serves to analyze the testimonial speech put forth by the lover in Guillaume de Machaut's narrative poem *The Fountain of Love* (*La Fontaine amoureuse*) (c. 1360) as he attempts to understand the wounds of his desire.

In each chapter, this book interprets the archetype of Narcissus's wounding as a model for selfhood where the human subject is frustrated by unfulfillable desire for an image (phantasm or *other*). The experience for the human subject within the medieval literature under examination, along with the related discourses of mourning, melancholy, trauma, and testimony, forms part of a larger tradition of humanistic thought regarding the wounded self that begins in the European classical world, moves through the Middle Ages, and continues to shape discourse within the humanities. It is for this reason I put the medieval texts under examination in this book not solely in conversation with ancient texts, but also explore how medieval literature informs psychoanalytic theory, a mode of discourse that correspondingly seeks to understand the human condition. I want to emphasize that my aim in using psychoanalysis is not an attempt to force a retroactive theoretical reading onto medieval literature. Rather, I examine how the structures at work in psychoanalytic discourse are already prefigured in the texts analyzed in this current study. I intend to demonstrate, therefore, through close readings (on the level of linguistic, symbolic, and thematic analysis), how these five medieval texts treat notions of narcissism and selfhood in a way that prioritizes their own psycho-physiology, to the point where they can be said to represent a corpus of *pre-modern psychoanalysis*, the legacy of which has come to influence psychoanalytic thought.

The main reason I am able to use psychoanalytic theory as an analytical lens is because the troubadours and trouvères, as well as their literary progeny, create a notion of the self that is desiring and destabilized by its desires. This notion is quite close to the constructs of selfhood postulated by Sigmund Freud and Jacques Lacan, constructs that are, I would argue, *medieval* in nature. A deliberate move against the philosophy of René Descartes, the field of psychoanalysis opposes his famous dictum "I think, therefore I am" ("cogito ergo sum" in Latin) which, serving as the dominant model of the self in Enlightenment thought, upends pre-modern concepts of selfhood by presenting the notion of a stable human self convinced of its own cognitive and subjective integrity.[34] Definitely not the wounded, desiring self of narcissistic *fin'amor*, the "Cartesian cogito, based as it is on the need for certainty, attempts to close the gaps, ruptures and fissures of subjectivity [...] by postulating at its core a subject which is whole, seamless and constant."[35] Anti-medieval from the start, the philosophy of the cogito goes against Freud's insistence that the ego, something that "cannot exist in the individual from the start" but rather "has to be developed," is linked to repression and resistance, navigating—and resulting from—unconscious desires rendering the *self unknowable to its own self*.[36] And the phantasms of troubadour poetry that imprint themselves within memory find their psychoanalytic counterpart at the heart of Freud's theories on repression and resistance, as he places the wounded and desiring self, haunted by images and shades, at the center of his writings on mourning, melancholy, and trauma. Building upon Freud, Lacan presents a theory of the self revolving around the phantasm that is nearly identical to the wounded subject emerging in Ovid's myth and the literature of *fin'amor*. For in his essay on the "Mirror Stage," he outlines how the "I" gains its identity by viewing in a mirror its image that it mistakes for the self. The mirror image, misunderstood as the place of the self, represents for Lacan a fundamental misrecognition (*méconnaissance*) that, in turn, frustrates the emerging self's desires while creating for it a fantasy of corporeal stability.[37] Freud and Lacan, subsequently, present selfhood, not as an exemplar of wholeness but, like the literature of *fin'amor*, as an entity existing in relation to images that imbue it with doubt and unfulfilled longing, in other words, something *narcissistically wounded* in its makeup.

Narcissism thus becomes in psychoanalysis, as in the medieval literature under examination in this book, an exploration of the self wounded by desire, a concept that might arguably serve as its most fundamental claim. As a theory of desire, psychoanalysis marks itself as a rightful heir of *fin'amor*. And this has not been ignored by scholars of the Middle Ages, for, as Simon Gaunt observes, the subject emerging from the narcissistic paradigm of self and other in medieval courtly literature is "foundational in the 'invention' of the modern subject."[38] To these ends, scholars whose work focuses on the intersection of medieval literature, narcissism and psychoanalysis (Giorgio Agamben, L. O. Fradenberg, Simon Gaunt, Claire Nouvet, Slavoj Žižek), trauma (Cathy Caruth, Dominick LaCapra) and testimony (Shoshana Felman) will prove to be important voices in an analysis of these concepts here.

NOTES

1. Bernart de Ventadorn, *The Songs of Bernart de Ventadorn*, ed. Stephen G. Nichols (Chapel Hill: University of North Carolina Press, 1965), vv. 9–16, 166–68.
2. Stephen G. Nichols refers to this song as having "define[d] lyric subjectivity for the troubadour canon." See: "The Early Troubadours: Guilhem IX to Bernart de Ventadorn" in *The Troubadours: An Introduction*, ed. Simon Gaunt and Sarah Kay (Cambridge: Cambridge University Press, 1999), 68. Jean Frappier claims "il apparaît [...] comme le principe [...] d'une connaissance de soi" [it appears to aim for a knowledge of the self]. See: "Variations sur le thème du miroir, de Bernard de Ventadour à Maurice Scève," *Cahiers de l'Association Internationale des Etudes françaises* 11 (1959), 154, my translation.
3. See: Richard Sorabji, *Self: Ancient and Modern Insights About Individuality, Life, and Death* (Chicago: University of Chicago Press, 2006), 17–53.
4. Stephen G. Nichols, "The Old Provençal Lyric" in *A New History of French Literature*, ed. Dennis Hollier (Cambridge, MA: Harvard University Press, 1989), 31–32.
5. For more on *joven* and *mezura*, see: Glynnis M. Cropp, *Le Vocabulaire courtois des troubadours de l'époque Classique* (Geneva: Droz, 1975), 413–25. For more on *joi*, see: Jean-Charles Huchet, *L'Amour discourtois: la 'fin'amors' chez le premiers troubadours* (Toulouse: Privat, 1987), 203–16.
6. Sarah Kay, "Desire and Subjectivity" in *The Troubadours: An Introduction*, ed. Simon Gaunt and Sarah Kay (Cambridge: Cambridge University Press, 1999), 221.
7. Bernart, *Songs*, vv. 17–24, 166–68, translation modified.
8. For a discussion on Narcissus in troubadour poetry, see: Marie-Noëlle Toury, *Mort et fin'amor dans la poésie d'oc et d'oïl aux XIIe et XIIIe siècles* (Paris: Honoré Champion, 2001), 283–95.
9. Ovid, *Ovid's Metamorphoses, Books 1–5*, ed. William S. Anderson (Norman: University of Oklahoma Press, 1997), v. 3.348, 97.

10. Despite Echo's importance here, she is almost systematically removed from medieval versions of the story. See: Christopher Lucken, "L'Echo du poème ('ki sert de recorder che k'austres dist')" in *Par la vue et par l'ouïe (Littérature du Moyen Age et de la Renaissance)* (Fontenay-aux-Roses: E.N.S. Editions, 1999), 25–58.

11. Ovid, *Metamorphoses*, vv. 3.418–24, 98; Ovid, *The Metamorphoses of Ovid*, trans. Allen Mandelbaum (New York: Hardcourt Brace, 1993), 94, translation modified.

12. Ibid., vv. 3.457–63, 99; Ibid., 95, translation modified.

13. Claire Nouvet, *Enfances Narcisse* (Paris: Galilée, 2009), 104. My translation of: "la confirmation d'une définition plutôt classique du sujet qui maintient une nette séparation entre l'ego et l'image."; "Entendu à la lettre, '*Iste ego sum*' confirme que l'erreur de Narcisse n'en est pas une: l'ego peut être confondu avec une *imago* parce qu'il est lui-même une *imago*. L''ego' n'est que ceci, '*iste*' [...]. Il est originellement cet 'autre' dont il croit pouvoir se distinguer. Il est autre, car aliéné, et ceci dès l'origine, de ne se constituer qu'en absorbant l'autre' qu'est l'image." Nouvet translates "iste" as "ceci" or "this," and this is the translation I will use throughout my study. "Iste," as a masculine pronoun, can also mean "he," rendering the alternate translation "I am he."

14. Ovid, *Metamorphoses*, vv. 3.480–85, 100; Ovid, *Metamorphoses*, 96.

15. Ibid., vv. 3.488–89, 100; Ibid.

16. Giorgio Agamben, *Stanzas: Word and Phantasm in Western Culture*, trans. Ronald L. Martinez (Minneapolis: University of Minneapolis Press, 1993), 82.

17. Ibid., 82.

18. On the philosophical context for phantasms, see: Karine Descoings, "Fantasma d'amore: quand la bien-aimée vient hanter son poète (Antiquité et Renaissance)," *Camenae* 8 (2010).

19. Agamben, *Stanzas*, 81.

20. Guillaume de Lorris and Jean de Meun, *Le Roman de la Rose*, ed. Armand Strubel (Paris: Librairie Générale Française, 1992), vv. 1612–20, 128. English translations are mine.

21. Nouvet, *Enfances*, 144, my emphasis. Based on my translation of: "L'aimée apparaît à la place où le moi devrait apparaître parce qu'elle en tient lieu et en donne la glorieuse figure. [...] On peut aimer dans l'autre l'image de soi, non tel que l'on est, mais tel que l'on désire être."

22. Slavoj Žižek, *The Metasteses of Enjoyment: On Women and Causality* (London: Verso, 1994), 94.

23. Ibid.

24. Guillaume de Lorris, *Rose*, vv. 1870–77, 142.

25. For more on the connection between Love and the lover's heart, see: Christopher Lucken, "L'imagination de la dame: fantasmes amoureux et poésie courtoise," *Micrologus* 6 (1998).

26. Erin Felicia Labbie, *Lacan's Medievalism* (Minneapolis: University of Minnesota Press, 2006), 127.
27. Nouvet, *Enfances*, 131. My translation based upon: "Les blessures que Narcisse s'inflige ne font que littéraliser la blessure que la réflexion lui infligea. Le 'je' apparaît originellement blessé, amputé d'une identité à soi dont il n'a jamais joui."
28. Larissa Tracy and Kelly DeVries, "Introduction: Penetrating Medieval Wounds" in *Wounds and Wound Repair in Medieval Culture*, ed. Larissa Tracy and Kelly DeVries (Leiden: Brill, 2015), 21.
29. Elaine Scarry, *The Body in Pain: The Making and Unmaking of the World* (New York: Oxford University Press, 1985), 15–16.
30. Labbie, *Lacan's Medievalism*, 127.
31. Emmanuèle Baumgartner, "Narcisse à la fontaine: du 'conte' à 'l'exemple'" in *Cahiers de recherches médiévales* 9 (2002), 131. For a discussion of how the myth, and Ovid's *Metamorphoses* as a whole, had a more direct influence on Medieval French literature, see: Miranda Griffin, *Transforming Tales: Rewriting Metamorphosis in Medieval French Literature* (Oxford: Oxford University Press, 2015).
32. Cropp discusses melancholy as a central element of troubadour lyric. See: *Vocabulaire courtois*, 275–316.
33. Wendy J. Turner and Christina Lee, "Conceptualizing Trauma for the Middle Ages" in *Trauma in Medieval Society*, ed. Wendy J. Turner and Christina Lee (Leiden, Netherlands: Brill, 2018), 8.
34. René Descartes, *Discourse on Method and Meditations of First Philosophy*, trans. Donald A. Cress (Indianapolis: Hackett, 1998), 18.
35. Patrick Fuery, *Theories of Desire* (Melbourne: Melbourne University Press, 1995), 11.
36. Sigmund Freud, "On Narcissism: An Introduction" in *The Standard Edition of the Complete Works of Sigmund Freud, Vol. 14*, trans. and ed. James Strachey (London: Hogarth, 1964), 76–77; Freud, *The Ego and the Id*, trans. Joan Riviere (New York: W. W. Norton, 1960), 3–10.
37. Jacques Lacan, "The Mirror Stage" in *Ecrits* (New York: W. W. Norton, 2006).
38. Simon Gaunt, *Love and Death in Medieval French and Occitan Courtly Literature: Martyrs to Love* (Oxford: Oxford University Press, 2006), 33.

References

Agamben, Giorgio. 1993. *Stanzas: Word and Phantasm in Western Culture*. Trans. Ronald L. Martinez. Minneapolis, MN: University of Minnesota Press.
Baumgartner, Emmanuèle. 2002. Narcisse à la fontaine: du 'conte' à 'l'exemple'. *Cahiers de recherches médiévales* 9: 131–141.

Bernart de Ventadorn. 1965. *The Songs of Bernart de Ventadorn*. Ed. Stephen G. Nichols. Chapel Hill, NC: University of North Carolina Press.

Cropp, Glynnis M. 1975. *Le Vocabulaire courtois des troubadours de l'époque classique*. Geneva: Droz.

Descartes, René. 1998. *Discourse on Method and Meditations on First Philosophy*. Trans. Donald A. Cress. Indianapolis, IN: Hackett.

Descoings, Karine. 2010. Fantasma d'amore: quand la bien-aimée vient hanter son poète (Antiquité et Renaissance). *Camenae* 8: 1–53.

Frappier, Jean. 1959. Variations sur le thème du miroir, de Bernard de Ventadour à Maurice Scève. *Cahiers de l'Association internationale des études françaises* 11: 134–158.

Freud, Sigmund. 1960. *The Ego and the Id*. Trans. Joan Riviere. New York: W. W. Norton.

———. 1964. On Narcissism: An Introduction. In *The Standard Edition of the Complete Works of Sigmund Freud, Vol. 14*. Trans. and Ed. James Strachey, 73–102. London: Hogarth.

Fuery, Patrick. 1995. *Theories of Desire*. Melbourne: Melbourne University Press.

Gaunt, Simon. 2006. *Love and Death in Medieval French and Occitan Courtly Literature: Martyrs to Love*. Oxford: Oxford University Press.

Griffin, Miranda. 2015. *Transforming Tales: Rewriting Metamorphosis in Medieval French Literature*. Oxford: Oxford University Press.

Guillaume de Lorris and Jean de Meun. 1992. *Le Roman de la Rose*. Ed. Armand Strubel. Paris: Librairie Générale Française.

Huchet, Jean-Charles. 1987. *L'amour discourtois: la 'fin'amors' chez les premiers troubadours*. Toulouse: Privat.

Kay, Sarah. 1999. Desire and Subjectivity. In *The Troubadours: An Introduction*, ed. Simon Gaunt and Sarah Kay, 212–227. Cambridge: Cambridge University Press.

Labbie, Erin Felicia. 2006. *Lacan's Medievalism*. Minneapolis, MN: University of Minnesota Press.

Lacan, Jacques. 2006. The Mirror Stage. In *Ecrits*. Trans. Bruce Fink, 75–81. New York: W. W. Norton.

Lucken, Christopher. 1998. L'imagination de la dame: fantasmes amoureux et poésie courtoise. *Micrologus* 6: 201–223.

———. 1999. L'Echo du poème ('ki sert de recorder che k'austres dist'). In *Par la vue et par l'ouïe (Littérature du Moyen Age et de la Renaissance)*, ed. Michèle Gally and Michel Jourde, 25–58. Fontenay-aux-Roses: E.N.S. Editions.

Nichols, Stephen G. 1989. The Old Provençal Lyric. In *A New History of French Literature*, ed. Denis Hollier, 30–36. Cambridge, MA: Harvard University Press.

———. 1999. The Early Troubadours: Guilhem IX to Bernart de Ventadorn. In *The Troubadours: An Introduction*, ed. Simon Gaunt and Sarah Kay, 66–82. Cambridge: Cambridge University Press.

Nouvet, Claire. 2009. *Enfances narcisse*. Paris: Galilée.

Ovid. 1993. *The Metamorphoses of Ovid*. Trans. Allen Mandelbaum. New York: Harcourt Brace.

———. 1997. *Ovid's Metamorphoses, Books 1–5*. Ed. William S. Anderson. Norman: University of Oklahoma Press.

Scarry, Elaine. 1985. *The Body in Pain: The Making and Unmaking of the World*. New York: Oxford University Press.

Sorabji, Richard. 2006. *Self: Ancient and Modern Insights about Individuality, Life, and Death*. Chicago: University of Chicago Press.

Toury, Marie-Noëlle. 2001. *Mort et fin'amor dans la poésie d'oc et d'oïl aux XIIe et XIIIe siècles*. Paris: Honoré Champion.

Tracy, Larissa and Kelly DeVries. 2015. Introduction: Penetrating Medieval Wounds. In *Wounds and Wound Repair in Medieval Culture*, ed. Larissa Tracy and Kelly DeVries, 1–21. Leiden: Brill.

Turner, Wendy J. and Christina Lee. 2018. Conceptualizing Trauma for the Middle Ages. In *Trauma in Medieval Society*, ed. Wendy J. Turner and Christina Lee, 3–12. Leiden: Brill.

Žižek, Slavoj. 1994. *The Metastases of Enjoyment: On Women and Causality*. London: Verso.

CHAPTER 2

Narcissus and Selfhood: *The Lay of Narcissus*

I begin with the anonymous *The Lay of Narcissus* (c. 1160) which, in addition to serving as the earliest text from the Middle Ages this study will treat, is the most complete stand-alone adaptation of Ovid's tale in Old French literature we have to investigate the theme of selfhood within a discourse of narcissistic wounding. Contemporaneous with the troubadour and trouvère poets of France, the lay reflects these writers' exploration of *fin'amor* and search for a lyric voice capable of speaking to the pleasures and tortures of their longing. These poets, however, were not to get "carried away" with the power love might have over them, ideally adhering instead to *mezura* (balance or self-discipline), one of the main tenets of *fin'amor*, which encapsulated that equilibrium between reason and emotions.[1] For, if *mezura* can be kept in check, a lover will not become *unbalanced*, falling into wayward desire or foolish love (*desmezura* or *fol amour*) where passion leads to self-destruction. Of course, Narcissus in Ovid's account falls into this latter camp of lovers, as his waywardness leads to a tragic death caused by what can be considered an irrational longing for a shadow. In this retelling of the classical tale, the lay, with one eye toward Narcissus's fate, ponders at its start whether it is possible to love without being wounded by negative repercussions. Can *mezura* be kept in check if a lover prioritizes reason over passion? Can it, in other words, serve as protection for the self *against* the sundering effects of love? Appearing to respond affirmatively to these questions, *Narcissus* begins

© The Author(s) 2019

N. Ealy, *Narcissism and Selfhood in Medieval French Literature*, The New Middle Ages, https://doi.org/10.1007/978-3-030-27916-5_2

with a stern injunction to its readers concerning the dangers of *fol amour* (foolish love) by establishing an analogy between love and seafaring, an undertaking potentially as dangerous as love, by positing that nobody would dare set sail without the assurances of a strong wind for successful navigation. As such, the text suggests, similar precautions should also be taken by those setting out to explore their libidinal impulses:

> Ausi qui s'entremet d'amer
> Et par savoir se veut mener,
> Bien doit garder au comencier
> Qu'il ne s'i laist trop enlacier,
> Car des que s'en est entremis
> Et il en est auques aquis,
> Puis n'est il pas a son plaisir[.]

Anyone who gives himself over to love and wants to behave wisely must, at the start, be careful not to let himself get too tied up, for as soon as he begins to love and is more or less conquered, he is no longer his own master.[2]

This warning is essential, for careful lovers might lose control over themselves, allowing passions to dominate to the detriment of all logic and reason. Though, sometimes it is not always up to lovers to manage their passions; foolish love might also arise, not as the result of overwhelming desires, but rather from their beloved's failure to reciprocate their amorous inclinations. Because reciprocation is necessary for love, those who dismiss it, the narrator insists, commit such a grievous error they should either be burned or hanged. With this stern injunction, *Narcissus* confronts its audience with a dual command: one must not only love wisely, but one is obligated to accept love whenever it presents itself. To love becomes an unavoidable imperative even if how one does this (honorably or foolishly) might still be left up to the individual. The message, then, is simple: one either loves or suffers annihilation. The notion that love is never an option, that one *must love*, thereby becomes the fundamental way in how the lay defines the notion of "selfhood." For the self, in texts such as this, is always constructed and directed by one's desires, by the ways in which "my" longings come to shape my existence and interaction with the world around me. With this, *Narcissus* stages itself as having witnessed the lethal consequences of those who fail to love—of those who, in other words, *fail* in their selfhood:

De maintes gens avons veü
Qu'il lor en est mesavenu.
Narcisus, qui fu mors d'amer,
Nous doit essanple demostrer.
Amors blasmoit et sa poisçance,
Ki puis en prist aspre venjance:
A tel amor le fist aclin
Dont il reçut mort en la fin.

We have seen numerous people who have known love's misfortunes. Narcissus, dead for having loved, should serve here as an example for us. He scorned Love and his power, who then carried out his terrible vengeance against Narcissus by making him submit to such a love that in the end he died from it.[3]

Ultimately, Narcissus becomes the primary illustration of what *not to do*, of how not to betray one's own self, for in this failure to love, he is forced to love—and tragically so. Along with Narcissus, though, there is another character, Dané, who, like Echo in Ovid's myth, tortures herself with the love she holds for this young man.[4] Similar to her mythic predecessor, Dané does not reject love, for, hit with an overwhelming passion for Narcissus, she burns with uncontrollable desire. In this story of frustrated love, the lay thus raises questions regarding love's inevitability, the agency of the desiring self, and the text's own ability to witness, not simply to tragic cases of wayward desire, but also to honorable love. Caught in this tension between the reasonable and foolish modes of love, *Narcissus* examines the extent to which the individual self has autonomy over its ability to love, the autonomy the individual self has, in other words, over its own "selfhood."

2.1   THE IMAGE OF THE SELF: VISION AND TRUTH (*VEOIR* AND *VOIR*)

Such explorations of autonomy over one's selfhood find themselves at the start of *Narcissus* when, after its directives regarding refined and foolish love, the text begins with the mother of its titular character, who, concerned with her son's future, brings him as a baby to the soothsayer of Thebes and poses to him the same question her Ovidian counterpart asks of Tiresias—will her child live to old age? Whereas the Latin tale indicates

Narcissus will survive only if he does not know himself ["si se non noverit"], here the seer issues an altered warning, professing that the boy will indeed live into his advanced years, but only if his mother can assure that he never set eyes upon himself ["il ne se voie mie"].[5] In this slippage from self-knowledge to self-seeing, the lay establishes the course for its entire narrative: this will be a tale, not initially about love and selfhood (as the prologue might suggest), but rather about vision, vision's connection to notions of an autonomous selfhood, and the lethal consequences of such a pairing. For, if the reader is to take the soothsayer at his word, the confrontation between vision and selfhood is, like love, a life-or-death situation.

Despite the doubts of Narcissus's mother, who laughs upon hearing the fortune, the text attests to the truth of its own chronology by alluding to its conclusion, already here at the start, hinting that her son *shall* meet an untimely death that will retroactively confirm the soothsayer's prophecy. The lay then goes one step further, for if not enough proof exists within these opening words, it takes great care to emphasize that the predictions given by this man are always *voir*—true and verifiable: "Uns devins ert, de Tebes nés,/Qui de voir dire ert esprovés./[…] K'il deïst onques se voir non" [There was a soothsayer, a native of Thebes, who was known for the truth of his predictions. He never said anything other than the truth].[6] And this is so because Narcissus, as the story reveals, *does* look upon a reflective surface and perishes, the interdiction against which the auger professes two times: "Gart bien qu'il ne se voie mie:/Ne vivra gaires s'il se voit" [be careful that he never sees himself, if he sees himself he will not live for long].[7] This recurrence of truth and sight at the start of the lay— *voir* and *veoir* respectively in Old French—establishes an iterative and homophonic connection between the two terms that successively influences the entire direction of its narrative structure.[8] For, to see something, the interplay of these words implies, must mean it is true, as the text's own conclusion affirms, fulfilling the prophecy and internal drive of the lay's plot. Veracity and vision, in other words, go hand in hand. Such a reading appears valid, except for the fact that even a cursory understanding of the lay (not to mention its source material in Ovid's myth) reveals that Narcissus does not see himself, but rather views his *reflection* upon the intermediary surface of the fountain's waters. Seeing one's reflection, though, is not the same as seeing the self, for this lifeless projection is something *other* than a self; it is not a self at all. It would appear, then, the prophecy is flawed, despite the text's insistence to the contrary, and the soothsayer's inability to foresee such a discrepancy between a self and a reflection subsequently poses a serious problem within the plot's logic. The relationship established between truth and sight, between *voir* and *veoir*, is not as straightforward as *Narcissus* purports. Seeing—especially as it shall occur at the fountain—does not reveal authenticity, but rather the confusion of this person with his reflection, two things appearing to be rather separate entities.

To address this tension between truth and vision, it is necessary to start with the few available clues regarding Narcissus's identity. For instance, the lay's narrator curiously omits the name of this central character, referring to him solely in context to his mother as "un sien enfant" [an infant of hers].[9] Lacking an independent existence, Narcissus, from the text's inception, is linked to an *other*—his mother in this case—who provides an otherwise absent identity for him. And such a substitution is necessary, for the boy at this point is preverbal—an *enfant* (infant)—a word whose etymology, from the Latin for "not talking" (*infans*), marks him as incapable of expressing any individualized desires or expectations within a community of speakers. In this mute state, Narcissus is barred from participation in society as his mother maps her desires onto him and speaks in place of him, acting as a proxy for her son who has nothing to say, precisely because he *cannot* say anything.[10]

Given that the child at this stage lacks a self-identity and the ability for self-expression, it is more than a bit puzzling when the soothsayer in his prediction refers to Narcissus as a *self* (*se* in Old French), apparently believing the infant has a self he can reference and use as part of his prophecy.[11] His interdiction to this (non-)self, represented twice by the pronoun *se* (himself) and coupled each time with a form of the verb *veoir* (to see), carries a warning against its recognition, against its very existence— because to see and witness the self as a self shall result in an unavoidable death. The moment this foundational identity reveals itself, will have revealed itself, the repetitive prophecy goes, Narcissus will "not live for long"; seeing the self, the moment it is recognized *as such*, shall strangely coincide with its simultaneous destruction. The teller's prediction though, taken at face value, seems to hold that the (non-)self before him is uncomplicated and uncontaminated, an identity that simply "is." Even the reiteration of *se* (himself) within his words can be read as a possible affirmation of this integrated subjectivity, for Narcissus's mother must make sure that her son never sees *himself* because he will not survive if he sees *himself*. Located in the somewhat awkward phrasing of this clairvoyance, the self-

hood of the mute (non-)self—in the linguistic repetition of "himself," of
se—goes, however, from zero to two, from nothing to a duality, with no
apparent intervening step. The need to reiterate within the prophecy the
viewing of the self suggests that selfhood, in its emergence, necessitates a
repetition; and this makes sense, for a visual duplication must exist so the
infant can "see himself," a projected image read *as the self*. The doubling
is therefore not between two "selves," as the prophecy proposes, but
rather between the self and its double, a "something other" outside the
self but nonetheless recognized as such. In the binary structure of self and
other, such an other will *stand in* for Narcissus, as the visual manifestation
of his "self," providing him an identity just as his mother now does, as she
speaks and acts in place of her preverbal child. It is for this reason the
qualities of his infancy—evident by a definitive *lack of self*—will strangely
remain with Narcissus throughout the entire lay, even after he reaches
adolescence.

In order though for a reflection to render this duplication possible, a
model to be reflected must first exist. Whereas Ovid has his readers wait
for the reflection, unveiled only when Narcissus looks into the fountain
and sees the iteration of this model, the lay introduces it after the auger's
fateful prophecy. In a precursor to what the infant will behold upon the
surface of the waters, the narrator gives a detailed portrait of his beauty,
the direct result of Nature's exemplary work, who has:

> [...] i mist toute s'entente
> Au deviser et au portraire,
> [...]
> Car tant i mist de la biauté
> Q'onques ne pot rien porpenser
> K'iloeuques ne vausist mostrer.

> Deployed all her effort in designing and fashioning his features, for she put
> so much beauty in him that there is nothing she could have imagined that
> she did not already want to show in him.[12]

Exhausting the limits of her capabilities, Nature has constructed the most
perfect of human beings, so handsome that "[o]nques si bele creature/Ne
fu mais nee ne si gente" [never had such a beautiful creature, so full of
charm, been born].[13] Even Love himself can find nothing to criticize in
this work, astonished at how well Nature has made the boy. And yet,
despite that nothing—it would appear—can supplement the excesses of

her work, Love discovers something he *can add* to the fullness of what she has already done. For, although she may have fashioned the most attractive of all creatures, she has failed to consider how his beauty will affect others, and so, Love steps into this void to lend his assistance. Narcissus's eyes, which Nature creates first, are "vairs" [shining], but it is Love who assures the boy has a "doç regart" [sweet gaze], capable of "tot le mont esprent et art" [inflaming and burning everyone].[14] Sending itself out in glorious luminosity, this vision will draw others with unavoidable desire to the boy. For, just as loving is inescapable, so is loving Narcissus, whose eyes serve as the origin and maintenance of erotic longing, a longing that will overtake his onlookers from without and burn them with an uncontrollable passion. The performative gaze Love gives him is a necessary supplement to Nature's work, introducing into the text the notion that the amorous process is one structured by a duality (or longed-for duality) of vision. For the doubling of sight—of the gaze the desiring subject projects onto others in the hope that they will send their gaze back in return—will prove essential to the genesis of desire in the lay. Desire then, like the notion of selfhood contained in the soothsayer's warning, goes from nothing, from a non-existence, immediately to a dual structure between self and other. And this is no accident, for the lay is an exploration of the synchronous emergence of selfhood *and* desire, as they bring one another forth—most centrally with Narcissus at the fountain—into a mutual and symbiotic existence.

The structure of doubling regarding desire and selfhood that will happen to Narcissus in the interaction with his reflection—this move from zero to two—is already present within Nature's and Love's roles needed for his creation as an a priori duality between cosmic and libidinal forces. The binary at work in the construction of his beauty, however, sustains a precarious dichotomy, for while Love imbues the boy with properties causing heat and fiery passion, Nature endows him with features drawing upon cold, frozen, and static imagery. In addition to his luminous vision, for instance, Love bestows upon Narcissus's mouth such ardent sweetness that any woman who feels it will burn with fiery passion, while Nature makes for him teeth as white as snow and cheeks clearer than ice or crystal. In this fragile tension between hot and cold, Narcissus is not only on the verge of causing injury to others from the unavoidable passion he instills, but of doing inevitable harm to himself as well if this dichotomy—this *mezura* (balance)—is not kept in check. And it does not stop, for whereas the first part of his fashioning stems from a balance of fire and ice, Nature finishes by adding qualities that heighten this fusion of oppositions as she finishes the boy—like a sculptor putting the final touches on a stone she has hewn:

> Par le viaire li espant
> Et par le face qu'il ot tainte
> Une color qui pas n'est fainte,
> Ki ne cange ne ne se muet:
> Tant ne fait bel ne tant ne pleut,
> Ne se desfait en nule fin;
> Tes est au soir com au matin,
> Mesleement blance et vermeille.

She spread out over his entire face and on his still pale cheeks a color that contains nothing artificial and that never changes or alters. In beautiful weather or rain, it is not altered. It is the same in the evening and the morning, a mixture of white and red.[15]

Akin to an ivory or marble statue painted with a red flush, Narcissus transforms into a pale and petrified body—which might as well be lifeless were it not for the trace of crimson blood, of *life*, running through him.[16] Nonetheless, this infant made by Nature—an incorruptible figure bordering on the godlike—ironically appears to exceed any notion of what might be considered "natural." His eyes glow, his hair is brighter than gold, he dons a polished chin, his lips remain parted, and the coloring of his skin cannot fluctuate. His being seems to contradict the coupling of *voir* (truth) and *veoir* (vision), as to see him is to behold something not entirely authentic, but rather a statuesque human whose glance transforms those it touches. The duality of hot and cold in him joins further contraries—those of permanence and fragility, of life and death, of an entity always on the brink of self-annihilation. This is the image upon which Narcissus will gaze at the fountain, a reflection serving as a life mask *and* a death mask that will—in one move—give birth to and destroy the self it projects. Nonetheless, the boy's image is not only a personalized reflection, but rather contains universalizing properties affecting all others as well. As such, the text takes care to state that his face is more radiant than *glace*, which, coming from the Latin for hardness and rigidity (*glacia*), signifies ice *and* mirror in Old French; the boy's godlike portrait will thereby serve as a looking glass, freezing all those unavoidably trapped in its haptic gaze.

Anyone who looks into this icy mirror of all-inclusive selfhood and unrestricted desire will now come to see his or her own image precariously frozen in a fiery passion from which any escape proves impossible.

2.2   Wounding Images: Inside and Outside (*Dedenz* and *Dehors*)

Love may instill the potential for unavoidable desire within Narcissus's makeup, but it first manifests itself in the lay with Dané, daughter of the king of Thebes, who finds herself trapped within the boy's icy mirror when she spies him one day passing her window after hunting. Immediately attracted to his handsome body, she is transfixed, unable to move or think while he stays within her line of vision—and yet she cannot discern what it is about him she finds so appealing. At this moment though, Love, detecting Dané's hesitation, gives the princess the push she needs and hits her with an arrow of such beguiling force that it fells her to the ground. Overcome with pain, she removes her upper garment and, attempting to come to some understanding of this torment, searches her naked chest for the physical imprint caused by the assault. She is left, however, bewildered; unable to find any torn or pierced flesh, she nonetheless feels that *something*—however visibly undetectable—has just wounded her.

Within this scene of *innamoramento*, the text examines a fundamental dichotomy—extended throughout the remainder of its narrative—between the simultaneous internal and external forces Love imposes upon its victims. Dané, incapable of comprehending what has just occurred to her, "[p]laie cuide trover *dehors*" [expects to find a wound *on the outside*] from the arrow, unaware that it has invisibly penetrated her, something she can already feel "*dedenz* le cors" [*within* her body].[17] This juxtaposition of outside and inside (*dehors* and *dedenz*) during love's inception establishes the dual structure desire assumes within *Narcissus*, as erotic inclinations, evident with Dané, will always inhabit a wounded space fraught with the tension of these oppositions. The wound caused by desire metaphorically tears the flesh, opens up a passageway where the boundaries of the human body break down, where *inside* and *outside* lose their distinctive qualities, where the external rushes in to infect the internal in an unavoidable cataclysm of overwhelming passions. Due to this aperture, the victims of desire are propelled toward a struggle both extremely personal (Dané knows this is what *she* wants, she "feels" it internally) and disaffecting (she remains unable to grasp what *is happening to her*). Her yearning for Narcissus, for instance, appears at first to originate from within her; she catches sight of him, and, in an act that seems to place her as the *subject* of her "own" desires, directs her gaze toward the *infant* with libidinal intent. This internal longing, however, is overtaken by an external force, physically manifest in Love's gaze and his resulting arrow, which strikes her from without, rendering her the *object* of his attack. Each aspect of this bilocational desire is real for Dané—she instinctively experiences the blow of the arrow upon her chest from Love's gaze as well as the internalized longing for union with the handsome *infant*. At the same time though, this desire is beyond her control, as she cannot simply decide to turn her attention from Narcissus and *not* find him attractive, nor can she disrupt the trajectory of Love's weapon and deflect it from its inevitable target. It hits her with such force that, under its power, she has no choice but to be its object, experiencing this onslaught from without as it intensifies her longing from within. That this yearning presents itself as external signals Dané's longing for union with something outside her physical body—in other words, her *desire to be desired* "externally" by Narcissus and to be the object of *his* affection, for him to project his gaze onto her with the same intensity with which she looks upon him. Love's arrow, therefore, not only symbolizes the longed-for reciprocity Dané hopes to receive from Narcissus, but is also a manifestation of his failure to glance in her direction. For, were he to reciprocate this desire from without, she would have no reason to suffer anything, the wound inflicted upon her would be healed, and the physical and psychological harm of his failure to return affection could be brought to naught. Due to this logic, the arrow represents the fundamental *absence* of reciprocity that Dané undergoes in her non-existent relationship with the young hunter, a non-existence she nonetheless feels as fully present in a torturous reality of unshared longing. Consequently, the erotic fulfillment for which Dané hopes will only come through a mutual exchange of gazes, as if in a mirror, between her and the statuesque figure she finds so beguiling. And so, Dané *may* have a reason to be optimistic, since this is the type of love the lay praises as worthy in its prologue, where the narrator posits:

> Amors ke Nature consent,
> Dequ'ele a anbedeus se prent
> Et de tout est a lor plaisir,
> Est bien loiaus a maintenir.

> The Love that Nature authorizes, as soon as it is shared and agreed upon by both lovers, should be honestly maintained.[18]

Might such reciprocity in love be the answer to her problem? To answer this question, it is necessary to explore the ways in which the lay presents the nature and structure of desire in this first episode of unrequited eros. For instance, the opposition in Dané's yearning, coming to her from without as an external force while simultaneously felt from within her body, presents itself as something *divided* and *wounding* in its inception, as something not completely in her possession. Her desire, removed from her being in a manner that is strangely alienating, is something to which she has had to submit herself—and to such a point that in its immutable alterity, one must question as to whether it can still be referred to as "her" desire. For this is "her" desire and yet is a desire controlling her. And, in the thick of this tense estrangement and troubled excitement, Dané remains incapable of sleep, pondering the malady that has struck her so unaware:

> Or ai el cors ne sai quel rage
> Qui si m'escaufe mon corage.
> [...]
> Or reveul a celui penser
> Que je vi ier par ci passer.
> K'ai ge a faire de ce vassal?
> C'est la riens qui plus me fait mal
> Quant me menbre de sa biauté.

I do not know this heat that I have that sets me all aflame. I only want to think about him whom I saw pass by here yesterday. But what do I have to do with that man? This is the thing [*la riens*] that causes me the most torment when I remember his beauty.[19]

In such anguish, Dané's thoughts are driven by her memory of Narcissus's handsomeness, that *thing*—the *riens*—troubling her most during her nocturnal restlessness. What drives this wakeful obsession is not the physical presence of the fair *infant* she saw earlier, but rather his *absence* and, in this absence, a desire to recollect his handsomeness in her fevered memory. Directing her thoughts to an obsession over what she remembers, Dané's overwhelming drive recalls what Agamben refers to as the phantasmatic process of love which, as I explain in Chap. 1, outlines the way in which a lover can approach the beloved solely through imagery. For the image of the beloved, existing within memory and fantasy, becomes the focus of her attention, increasing her desire to appropriate it, as if it were real, and satisfy her longing.[20] Dané has thus unknowingly discovered what Narcissus will soon learn when he looks at his image, that the beloved other derives its power precisely because it is an illusion. Given the mental processes involved in such phantasmatic desire, the princess's use of the term *riens* is quite revelatory, for in Old French this word is a contranym signifying "(some)thing" (from the Latin *res*) as well as its opposite, as in the modern French *rien*, "nothing." Aflame with passion for an elusive image, Dané has claimed her fidelity to a *some/no-thing* seemingly so real it hits her and takes up residence in her thoughts, a *some/no-thing* estranging her from the comprehension of her own desires. And she not only loves this *riens*, this image that has wounded her, but yearns to conform to it, believing she can see her idealized self with it as she waits by her window hoping to catch sight of it again so it can feed her fantasy. It has, quite literally, formed her being, a being-as-wounded, a wounding she readily embraces despite the torture it causes her. For it is precisely the *some/no-thing* that gives her the greatest amount of pain, declaring this happens most "quant me menbre de sa biauté" [when I remember his beauty].[21] Due to the ambiguity in the term *menbre* (remember), a near-homonym with Old French *membre* (limb, member), however, Dané's words indicate that she *remembers* his allure and that the handsome image of this *some/no-thing* "re-members" her, constantly holding out the promise to heal her wound and render her whole even as it tears her body asunder.[22] Knowing nothing about Narcissus, she constructs a scenario regarding their non-existent relationship that only heightens her desire for the *some/no-thing*, solidifies her belief in a realistic future with him, and emboldens her will to confront him. Because of his beauty, she decides that he must be a good man from a noble family, that they must be of similar backgrounds, ages, and appearances, and that she desires him more than any man her father could choose as her husband.

Seeing (*veoir*), it would appear, does not bring about truth (*voir*), for the power of this nocturnal episode lies not in the visible but rather in what cannot be seen and yet is believed to be visible. The power of the phantasm is consequently so strong that its status as *some/no-thing* appears palpably real, with a visible invisibility paralleling the impact of Love's arrow, capable of penetrating its victims with tangible force and yet leaving no perceptible mark. The absence of any wound from this weapon indicates not only desire's volatility but also the power the phantasm has over Dané, for it is there and not there, present in her emotional torment and yet, as she remains unable to realize the elusive image of Narcissus in her memory, experienced as a perpetually frustrated and unknowable absence. In the bouts of such suffering, the *some/no-thing* haunts her, marking the unfulfilled emptiness she experiences, the all-too-real yet invisible wound piercing her flesh, and the puzzling lack of an unshared love with a fantasy her alienating desire has forced upon her.[23]

The contranymic nature of *riens* defines not only the image of Narcissus's beauty carried by Dané in her thoughts, but also the nature of Narcissus himself. In fact, such a dichotomy exemplifies his existence within the lay, where he appears as "authentic" while displaying the characteristics of a statuesque *infant*, a mute non-self, a mirrored image who unknowingly implants his simulacrum in those who love him. For Narcissus, in truth, *should not* exist. He has no cognizance of his own selfhood—not having seen himself or come to any knowledge of who he is—and yet is strangely able to prevail so his story might be told, a story somehow capable of presenting a non-self as its central character.[24] Where his mother once had to speak for this *infant*, the activities now occupying his time—venery and falconry—step in and speak for the boy who has yet to utter a single word in the lay. These two forms of hunting (with hounds and birds of prey) are diversionary pastimes linked throughout medieval courtly literature to a tradition portraying love as a pursuit rife with bodily harm and rapacious violence, because this is *what hunting is*.[25] It is love— and a violent one—now defining Narcissus; for love within such a framework is never the fantasized reciprocal meeting of two like-minded individuals, but rather is always a battle where a hunter stealthily works to dominate his unsuspecting prey. This hunter is a keen marksman, capable of spotting victims with his eyesight, described as *vair* (brilliant and shining) by the lay's author, the same adjective used by numerous Old French writers to describe—not only the luminous eyes of a beloved other—but the sharpened vision of birds of prey as well.[26] For Narcissus's gaze is like a hawk's, an ocular assault from without zeroing in on its casualties. And yet, despite the fact that Love has fashioned his vision with the power of enticement, Narcissus remains ignorant of any amorous inclinations, having "[d]'amer n'a soing ne rien n'en set" [no cares for or knowledge about love].[27] Going against what might appear to be his nature as an object of adoration, he is the most perilous of hunters, an unwilling pursuer of and unavoidable trap for his human prey as he sets them alight with desire all the while remaining indifferent to their pleas for reciprocation.

Dané encounters this apathy from Narcissus when she attempts to reify her hope for unity with him and gathers enough courage to meet him as he returns home one day. The tables have been turned, and the hunter now becomes the hunted in the princess's attempts to set a trap for him. Professing her desire for the *infant*, she pleads with him, claiming that only he has the power to save her from distressing pain. For, in her daytime reveries, she has already imagined an idealized future version of herself united to him in marriage and is convinced, in her fantasies directed toward the *some/no-thing*, that she can win Narcissus over by falling at his feet, begging for mercy with the words of her undying love. Her thoughts, circling around an imagined rendezvous, now appear to concretize—this fantasy may not end up negating its own existence, she hopes, but rather may turn out to be authentic after all. Believing that her presence before the hunter can turn him to an acceptance of her, she asks him to behold her—"Esgarde, saces qui je sui!" [Look, know who I am!]—expecting such a proclamation to lead to some sort of recognition on his part.[28] The directive for Narcissus *to look at her* connotes in turn Dané's longing to have the desire she projects forth return to her—as in a mirror—a return that will acknowledge her as the object of his desire, a return she hopes will clarify that ephemeral yet violent gaze from without that hit her when Love's arrow struck. The princess's hope is for such reciprocity to cure her wound and unify *dedenz* and *dehors*, inside and outside, into a singular, comprehensible structure rendering desire no longer alien to itself. Narcissus as *glace*, this icy mirror, appears to possess the capacity to return, by his sheer existence as a reflective surface, Dané's appeals for satisfaction, as if she could see her own desire rebound back upon her in a duality of mutually shared longing. Her call is one in which she wants Narcissus to want her, a desire to be desired, to be in a union where she becomes the object of his libidinal gaze, where she can, for once and for all, be healed, be *re-membered*. Instead of an instantaneously wounded self, of a self going from nothing to a duality, she can hope in fact to attain—retroactively— that intervening step of oneness, seemingly missed and yet nonetheless intensely felt as an achievable truth driving all her actions and speech.

Narcissus's response to this demand, however, is one of immediate rejection. No matter how much Dané is willing to humiliate herself for him, the frustration she experiences in her unrealized fantasies carries over into this confrontation with the *riens*, the *some/no-thing* of her longing. Narcissus's mirroring properties appear to have failed, for he claims to be too young to love and that, given the display before him, professes that he never wants to love and suffer a fate like Dané's. In this refusal to acknowledge Dané, he denies her and all she represents, attempting to protect himself from the deadly force of love and believing, in essence, that he can control such an assault along with the tortured fantasies Love would bring. This hubris will therefore be crushed at the fountain—the location of "seeing the self"—where the connection between vision and knowledge present in Dané's appeal (a joining together of the augers' predictions from the Latin and Old French versions of the tale) is shown to be intimately bound to love's power.

2.3 SEEING THE SELF: *JE ME PLAING* ("I LAMENT MYSELF")

The confrontation Narcissus experiences with his image at the fountain serves as the event that is supposed to bring the soothsayer's prediction to fruition, the place where truth and seeing—*voir* and *veoir*—coincide with one another in the boy's destruction. For, as the lay has already made evident, Narcissus will not survive the encounter, dying once he sees *his self* upon the waters. Already on the brink of destruction since his precarious creation by Nature and Love, Narcissus has never been a coherent entity, fraught with opposing elements (hot/cold, natural/unnatural, life/death) that have always put his existence in question. Haunted by an *otherness* threatening to annihilate his fragile integrity, it is at the fountain this otherness reveals its pernicious nature. For here, the *infant* comes to realize a seemingly impossible event: his own sense of self will emerge—will have already emerged—with its unavoidably concurrent fragmentation.

This ominous discovery takes place one hot afternoon while Narcissus is out tracking a stag. Feeling parched, he approaches a stream, lowers his head to drink, and: "Dedens en la fontaine voit/L'*onbre* qui siet de l'autre part./Avis li est que *le regart*" [within the fountain he sees the *shadow* that is facing him and, it seems to him, is *looking at him*].[29] Ignorant this is his own reflection, Narcissus mistakenly believes to have encountered another person whose gaze is focused upon him. And this gaze holds the promise, he hopes, of reciprocating back to him the blossoming desire he directs toward it. Despite the popular interpretation that Narcissus falls in love with himself, the young man, as the lay makes clear, is not the same as the image, a distinction, as I examine in the introduction to this book, inherited directly from Ovid's myth which makes the identical observation. Similarly, the lay points out the irony of the situation, for not only is Narcissus oblivious to what he sees, he does not understand that Love has forced him to reiterate Dané's painful yearning. For the gaze of the image already appears to cast its watchful eyes and enrapture him, following the structure felt by the princess when the *some/no-thing* haunted her through her sleepless night. This is that powerful gaze from without that cannot fall under the purview of these lovers' agency, but rather codifies their desire—striking them from beyond their control—as an unknowable and unrestrainable force. Their longing consequently rests upon a wished-for reciprocity with their object of affection, a mutual cooperation of *self* and *other*, a yearning imposed upon the *some/no-thing* to desire them in return. Were such an exchange to occur, control over one's libidinal drive would seemingly be restored—"once again"—no longer causing unrest and uncertainty.

This is why Dané, when she confronts Narcissus, asks him not simply to *look at her*, but to *know who she is* as well. For this directive—that he know her—is a demand for him to recognize her as the object of his own erotic fascination and, through this hoped-for reciprocity, for him to recognize his own desire in and through her. Dané wants, in other words, her desire also to be his, that this Narcissus-as-mirror look as well upon her *as his own mirror* in a vision of shared longing both emanating from and returning back to themselves. For Dané, though, to recognize the completion of her yearning from Narcissus, *from the beloved*, she must impose her desire *upon the beloved* as well. Such is the reason, as Simon Gaunt explains, that desire *for the other* always translates into a desire *from the other*, into a hope that the beloved, by wanting *me* in return, will reflect back to me *my own* libidinal gaze.[30] To these ends, "my gaze," that look which will be my fulfillment, is always positioned as the gaze of the *other* within a mirrored construct. This is why the lover of troubadour song never quite wishes "the erotic surrender" of the beloved lady to him, as one might expect, but rather "simply that she look at him," for "her gaze, rather than her person, is invoked as the source of salvation."[31] The gaze then has wider implications, for it is not just linked to the construct of desire, but to the construct of selfhood as well (the two being—in truth—the same thing). When Dané, for instance, creates for herself a fantasy of future perfection and stability with the *some/no-thing*, she undergoes an *imaginary identification*, or an identification with an image in such a way that "we appear likeable to ourselves, with the image representing 'what we would like to be.'"[32] The problem with such identification, though, is that it calls into question, as it does analogously with desire, as to where this gaze might be that carries the promise of an idealized self. As with the troubadours, such a gaze, always bifurcated, *does not—cannot*—come from the "self." Dané is therefore the perfect example of this, for her vision, cast upon Narcissus, carries the lack of her unfulfilled longing; Dané, in other words, cannot project outward any gaze that would render her "what she would like to be." Completion must come from Narcissus, and this is why the imaginary identification is not really about what the "self" wants at all, but rather is an identification perilously depending "*on behalf of a certain gaze in the Other.*"[33] The eye, this mirror capable of reflecting one's innermost passions, thereby serves as the organ through which the entire drama of love occurs. As a result, longing in courtly literature often reflects this dislocated gaze, where, in the traditional paradigm, a male lover situates himself, not as a desiring subject projecting his view upon the woman of his affection, but rather someone who "initiates an imaginary scenario in which he is construed as [an] object [whose] integrity and wholeness are guaranteed by the [woman's] gaze."[34] Dané's directive that Narcissus know her is an act in support of the fantasy of her integrity, of healing her wound, of her *re-membering* that can be guaranteed by an imaginary identification—located outside of herself and in *his* gaze, by having him visually direct his desire *toward her*. In such a fantasy, *dedenz* (inside) would join to *dehors* (outside), and her yearning would be fulfilled, fulfillable, and capable of rendering her wounded selfhood complete.

Of course, Narcissus before the image hopes for the same, and, attracted to its beauty, mistakenly believes it to be reaching out to him whenever he stretches his arms toward it and attempting to communicate with him whenever he speaks. Perplexed as to why he can hear nothing from this shadow appearing to interact, Narcissus remains seduced by its false nature. Curiously though, the text does not place all the blame for this misunderstanding upon the image, for even while highlighting its duplicitous nature, it posits Narcissus as guilty of self-deceit—"*il meïsmes se deçoit*"—an ambiguous phrase meaning either "he himself [*meïsmes*] deceives himself [*se*]" or "he is deceived by himself."[35] If both readings are taken into consideration, two questions arise, for: how exactly can Narcissus be tricked by his own self, especially when the projected phantasm appears to be at fault, and if he *is* tricked by his own self, *where* is this self located? Why the confusion of what would otherwise appear to be a clear-cut distinction between a duplicitous reflection-as-image and a duped Narcissus-as-self?

The confusion present here within the text is matched by Narcissus's own speech, for he proclaims, upon realizing his error of having mistaken a shadow for another person:

> Je quidai veoir quoi que soit
> De l'unbre qui me decevoit.
> [...]
> Mais ore sai que n'en voi rien.
> Por çou m'est li maus plus engrés[.]

I thought I saw something in the shadow that was deceiving me, but now I know that I see nothing [*rien*], and for that reason my torment increases.[36]

Like Dané before him, he seems to comprehend that the emergence of his desire is wound up in the contranymic *riens* (*some/no-thing*) of the shadow and that this fantasy—finally understood as such—prolongs a yearning for an authentic fulfillment now in jeopardy. Nonetheless, such knowledge quickly shifts toward a separate discourse, for Narcissus suddenly associates this reflection, not with an externalized entity separate from his body, but rather with *his own self*:

> Le cors, le vis que je la voi,
> Ce puis je tot trouver en moi.
> J'aim moi meïsme, c'est folie!
> [...]
> Je sui ce que je tant desir:
> Jou meïsmes me fas languir!

The body, the face that I see before me, I can find them entirely in me. I love myself, this is folly! I am what I so greatly desire, I am making myself languish![37]

Implying that his self now involves an image outside his body, Narcissus bases his discovery on a move compounding misrecognition upon misrecognition, for where he first viewed the image—in the hopes of a reciprocated desire—as an *authentic other*, he now refers to it as his *authentic self*. Identical to what Ovid posits in his fable, the notion of selfhood emerges as one in which "my self" becomes spatially removed from what I consider to be "me." Because of this, Narcissus's reflection upon the fountain's waters, this storehouse of fictional self-cohesion, defines his self as something that can never coincide with his body, as something that *can never* be integral, but forever alienated from itself, split between body and image, encompassing both in a tenuous unity through separation. And such an alienating identification where the self emerges in conjunction with an image is already in the language put forth by the lay, for Narcissus *deceives* himself [*il meïsmes se deçoit*], a word whose Latin etymology (*deçoit* > *decevoir* > *decipere* > *de* + *capere*) connotes a breach with its prefix (*de-*) as well as a seizure and enchantment (*capere*).[38] The beginning of Narcissus's selfhood, in other words, marks its simultaneous separation and entrapment, coming forth because it is already infiltrated, already *wounded*, by the alluring image, this other, creating it *and* rending it asunder. From the nothingness of *some/no-thing* and the muteness of the *infant*, this birth, a move from zero to two, comes to Narcissus before he can comprehend what has *already* happened—that his selfhood emerges out of a difference denying all integrity. The hunter has now been hunted, trapped by the manifestation of his "own" desire housed within an externalized image. Where the soothsayer before used one term—*se* (himself)—to reference the *infant*'s potential subjectivity, two different words meaning "self" appear, with *meïsmes* now accompanying *se*. The self, incapable of a unified existence (as suggested in the auger's curious doubling of *se*), is linguistically split as well into a *se* (self) and a *meïsmes* (self), separate terms required to speak of its emergence, separate terms that can never be identical. For this new existence is itself and yet other than itself, an altered repetition of *se* and *meïsmes*, forever barred from coinciding with one another in a unique and singular entity.

Narcissus immediately recognizes this duality regarding his selfhood, and, after speaking of his love for the reflected "self" upon the waters, begins to refer to himself in a mixture of first-person singular and plural:

> [...] car j'aim et sou amés
> Et çou que j'ain me rainme assés
> Et n'est pas en menor esfroi:
> Si n'en poons prendre conroi.
> 'Poons?' Mes 'puis,' car je sui sous
> Et ceste amors n'est pas de dous.
> [...]
> Or n'i a el: morir m'estuet.
> Las! *je me plaing*, mais nus ne m'ot;
> Parens que j'aie n'en set mot.

I love and I am loved, because what I love loves me as well, and not with any less intensity. But we cannot find a way out of this. We cannot? No, I cannot, for I am alone and in this love, we are not two. There is no other way out of this, I must die. Alas! *I lament myself*, but nobody hears me. My family knows nothing about this.[39]

Trapped between the illusion of a reciprocal love shared by two (body and image) and the reality of an isolating image that frustrates such a fantasy, Narcissus is haunted by a yearning that beckons him toward the promise of fulfillment. This yearning, however, is what shatters—has already shattered—any notion of a coherent selfhood, and his emergence as a subject becomes the direct result of desire's assault. Such a wounding of the self emerging *as fractured* and dispossessed of its own agency is the direct result of this interplay between out- and inside, self and other, tensions that similarly tormented Dané earlier in the lay. Such tensions, the lay demonstrates, can never be resolved, neither with the princess before nor with the hunter here, as long as desire remains bound to the contranymic nature of this *some/no-thing*—lifeless and yet capable of exerting a tangible power over those it enslaves and enraptures. For in its deception, its *decipere*, the reflection dispenses to Narcissus two blows: (1) despite its allure and supposed promise of reciprocation, it cannot return anything authentic to him other than a non-existent, absent gaze; and (2) this gaze, devoid of any ability to complete his longing, mirrors back instead to him his own *desire as unfulfillable*, his own desire that always was and can only ever be *unfulfillable*, forever denying him the integrated self he craves. The image housing, defining, and controlling his longing renders unto him, as he attests, a radical loneliness alienating his self *from its very self.* Narcissus learns that he cannot be the origin of his own desire, but rather its servant, byproduct, and reflection. Seeing the shade as lacking, he can now only understand himself, *his self*, as a subject infiltrated by the image's power, reflecting its lack and defined by the incomplete and divisive nature—the disjointed *inside* and *outside*—of desire itself. This is the *iste ego sum* ("I am this") the lay inherits from the Ovidian myth, and, as such, the *some/no-thing* exposes Narcissus, not as the concrete source of an aquatic projection, but rather as the fragile byproduct of its terrorizing power. The mirrored "source" upon the waters, in turn, forms him as its own tortured and lifeless narcissistic simulacrum. He has become identical to the *some/no-thing* he so desires, the *some/no-thing* denying him satisfaction while instilling within him an estrangement from his very self.

That this *infant* is revealed to be an image should come as no surprise, for the lay has alluded to this ever since Nature and Love create him as an irresistible mirror imbuing within all lovers the same gaze of divisive longing he encounters at the fountain. As an object of universal adoration, the *some/no-thing* he becomes reveals the *some/no-thing* he has always been, capable of defining and directing the longing of anyone caught within his haptic gaze that, in turn, captures him as well. Narcissus, in other words, embodies the processes of phantasmatic love and imaginary identification embedded within the lay—there is no way to fall in love other than with an image. This is why, in a reversal of Ovid's homoeroticism, the *infant* does not see upon the water's surface a statuesque youth—gendered as masculine in the Latin myth—but rather an aquatic fairy. As Gaunt posits, the reflection of Narcissus's beauty, depicted in the lay as feminine and feminized, calls into question the nature of his masculinity and challenges the notion of a traditional gender binary.[40] For someone whose existence embodies the psychology of human desire, the inherent androgyny of his image—perceived by Dané as masculine but by Narcissus as feminine—subsequently makes sense; the simulacrum of Narcissus's beauty within the lay can stand in as *anyone's* object of affection, becoming the *some/no-thing* shaping the desire and selfhood of every human subject. As the image whose fictional reciprocity hits its victims, instilling within them a divisive longing, Narcissus is undone by the properties of his *"natural" and true self*, helplessly discovering that his subjectivity can only be formed by mirroring an absent gaze, instilled within him by Love, that undoes him in the same process. In essence, the lay becomes not so much about the connection between vision (*veoir*) and truth (*voir*), but rather the veracity brought about by the lacking gaze—the absence of vision—that the image, by its fictional nature, projects outward.

It is this absence of *veoir*, of a *vision without vision* embodied by the image, that brings about Narcissus's ultimate destruction. Proclaiming in desperation that he is alone, a reference to the radical alienation endemic to his subjectivity, the gaze he so wants to see reciprocating his own desire can never be realized. The move from nothing to two in the formation of his self continues to be haunted by the absence embodied in the image as it transforms him into a reflection of a reflection, an iteration of the *some/no-thing* cast upon the water's surface. Doubled and divided by frustrated longing, his desire has revealed itself as incapable of producing a unified presence. A singular wholeness can never emerge, and the fragile unity of elements forming him fall into mortal combat, as he is done and undone, created and destroyed, solidified and liquefied, estranged from his very self. From this tension, two things coincide with one another, for Narcissus imposes a death sentence upon himself and then makes an appeal to mourn this death, actions that play out in an interconnected drama linked to the absence of vision.

The imperative to mourn, initially appearing in the reflexive construction *je me plaing* ("I lament myself"), comes from the divisive lack Narcissus experiences from the simulacrum's inability to see and unify with him.[41] And his own language once again betrays him, as the construction he employs to posit this mourning—*je me plaing*—divides him into subject (*je*—I) and object (*me*—myself), a singular plurality incapable of self-cohesion. The *some/no-thing*, placing Narcissus within the same construct of fantasy and impossible fulfillment as Dané, is what causes him to mourn, because now any attempt at wholeness presents itself forever out of reach, a fantasy of a fantasy. The true loss, if this term can even be used, is over something that has never existed and will never exist, the dispossession of an unattainable illusion of satisfaction with a lifeless shadow. Narcissus's mourning is not simply due to the impossibility of self-integrity, but due to the reality that his subjectivity can only come forth as already destroyed, a birth that is always, and unavoidably so, a concurrent death. As a result, his weeping indexes the bizarre temporality death inhabits in the lay's narrative, for this is a temporality that does not—and cannot—adhere to a traditionally sequential chronology. Because the moment Narcissus experiences the realization that his self can never coincide with itself, can never achieve the singularity he so craves, his death becomes inevitable and—in a real sense—*has already happened*, even if the narrative must postpone this occurrence until the lay's final lines. In this manner, Narcissus's mourning follows and anticipates his death as he weeps over the eventuality of a demise that has already taken place. With this in mind, *je me plaing* ("I lament myself") acquires more urgency, especially given that the verb *plaing*, coming from the Latin *plangere*, etymologically references the beating of oneself as a sign of grief (and for this reason is related to the word "wound," *plaga* in Latin and *plaie* in French). Narcissus's mourning reveals its masochistic overtones, as he wounds himself in response to his self that emerges—has already emerged—as wounded, lacerated, rent in two due to the once-beloved simulacrum, whose horrific effects must now be destroyed. There is, in other words, no way to annihilate the image apart from annihilating the "self" it reflects.

The only attempt he can make to overcome this conflict is to try to return to the fantasy of a unified "pre-self"—a "self" that never existed before the fountain—by destroying the image directing his nightmarish existence. This is, however, not a rivalry between selves, as if Narcissus had a "self" before arriving at the fountain and is now combating some horrific "new self" that has imposed itself over the former one. In the lay, there can be no self other than the one emerging as already sundered. In fact, the soothsayer's words are clear on this—the *infant* will live to see old age if he never *sees himself,* something which does not occur until the encounter with the reflection, and before this event there is no previous occurrence of his having seen himself, of his having had a sense of what this "self" would be. Such is the nature of the estrangement Narcissus undergoes, which is not a conflict among opposing senses of self, but rather an alienation *of himself from himself,* a selfhood that emerges as unavoidably wounded by desire and without any hope for healing or satisfaction. Any attempt to shatter the reflection before him *must involve* a destruction of his self, forever divided by and yet linked to the reflection that creates him and can only ever remain an inextricable part of his irreversible reality. The harming of the self—of selfhood itself—becomes Narcissus's struggle as he works toward undoing the horrifying consequences of the *some/no-thing*'s effect on him and remedying the alienation brought on by the lacking desire of the simulacrum's vacant gaze. This is why there is no alternative to the death sentence he imposes upon himself when proclaiming "morir m'esuet" [I must die], for only in destroying the dual nothingness that he is can he try to achieve the impossible oneness he so craves.[42] The wound, in other words, cannot close, for it becomes the mark of this impossible desire that defines the self in its fatal existence, the mark resulting from this impossible desire that has struck the self so forcefully in its emergence that it can only be divided, separated in two, a gaping aperture—and unavoidably so. For the wound becomes a sort of passageway mediating the destructive properties of this divided self, the site where the tensions of alterity defining the "self," inside and outside, *je* (I) and *me* (myself), *se* (self) and *meïsmes* (self), birth and death, creation and destruction, come together to infiltrate and confuse any coherence in this porous subjectivity.

Ironically though, Narcissus's desire to do away with this wounded self born of the image only serves to reinforce the alienating power it has over him. Try as he might, the work of mourning he employs still has as its aim an intent to reverse the unattainable, to have the simulacrum finally recognize him—even with its absence of vision—as its object of desire. It seems he will accept anything to occupy the space opened by this absence, for, throughout the extended scene of his death, Narcissus desperately looks for something that can recognize him, however slight the chance. Going through various possibilities, including the fields, meadows and forests where he once chased game, the gods, his family, his hunting companions, and finally his mother, he realizes that nothing can give him the satisfaction he desires. In this extreme isolation, his request for a witness—to *see* him and grant some reciprocal acknowledgment—goes unanswered as his heart gives out, he falls unconscious, and loses the ability to speak. Narcissus's hope to see someone else is, in truth, a demand for recognition from another, for a viewer to position him as its "*viewee*" and fulfill his desire, so strong now that it drives him to his death.

What then are we to make of these destructive libidinal forces, especially when the desire of this lifeless image, this other, cannot exist for Narcissus? L. O. Fradenburg, posing a related question in her analysis of such issues in medieval courtly literature, answers it with what she calls the *logic of sacrificial desire.* Exploring the nexus between medieval literature and Lacanian psychoanalysis, Fradenburg argues that in this longing to be in a relationship with another, literary lovers are put into an impossible position where they long to be subject to the Other's (the image's) desire. In this logic of sacrifice, "the subject denies the decentered, contingent, and ultimately indifferent process through which [it] has come into being, but refiguring [its] role in that process [...] as a gift—a gift of life from the Other, and, to the extent that [its] own activity is acknowledged, a gift that gives back [its] life *to* the Other, imagined as [its] creator."[43] Despite the lacking quality of the image, of the Other, lovers like Narcissus hope that the image will desire them "in the hope that such an exchange will reward and thus perpetuate that desire."[44] The Other is viewed as the one who can grant wholeness and life, because through it the self comes into being. Narcissus consequently follows the same formula employed by the male lovers of troubadour poetry who sacrifice themselves in the hopes that the lady of their affection will finally bestow upon them her sweet gaze of recognition. The more they deny themselves though, martyring themselves to gain even a modicum of her awareness, the more they reify their divided subjectivity; in other words, the more a lover destroys himself, the more he reaffirms the true nature of his already annihilated selfhood. The self, established through its concurrent destruction, resists any undoing of its division, and any attempt to deflect the harmful effects of the image simply end up reinforcing the self's already divided status. This is why Nature and Love, when forming Narcissus, compose him of elements resembling heat and ice, for he is a concurrent life and death mask of conjoined contraries and, through his very construction, always on the verge of self-annihilation. At the fountain, he simply fulfills his preordained destiny, which is also the preordained destiny, within this narcissistic model put forth by the lay, of *any self.*

There does, however, appear to be a glimmer of hope, because prior to losing his speech, Narcissus remembers Dané, whom he rejected just one day earlier, and repents for having scorned her amorous advances. Perhaps he can finally encounter the reciprocity denied to him by the simulacrum. Dané's suffering, in other words, now meets up with his own and, seeing himself in her, as a reflection of him, her pain retroactively acquires new significance. Endeavoring to shift the gaze of the other from a lifeless shadow to a living entity, he hopes the lethal mandate inflicted upon him can somehow be reversed. Then suddenly, Dané appears, out looking for him yet again. Alone, she approaches as Narcissus opens his eyes wide, holds his arms out and tries to talk while pointing to the image in the fountain. Offering himself as the object of her desire, he presents himself as the longed-for answer to her earlier request for reciprocity. At the same time though, he has regained the muteness of his infancy, which reveals not so much a radical change from what was earlier a speaking subject to one now devoid of words, but instead points to the fact that such muteness has always haunted him, unavoidably infiltrating him from the start. Any agency he ever seemed to possess over his desire, his speech, his self was always—*has always been*—an illusion. His identity, corrupted by the image of a mute *infant* reflected upon the fountain's waters mirrors within him the emptiness of his own subjectivity, coming to him from an all-powerful silencing speech that informs him *who he is*. This is a directive he cannot escape but continues to receive while signaling to Dané the *some/ no-thing* in the fountain that has defined the radicalized emptiness of his selfhood.

The wish this somehow can all be overturned with Dané's help is shot through with the fantasy of fulfillment, as Narcissus shifts his hopes not from a lifeless image to a living person, but rather to yet another lifeless image. For in the attempts to reciprocate his desire with Dané, he unwittingly repeats, through his muteness that cannot reach anyone, the actions the shadow demonstrated earlier; he has, in truth, become a substitute for—become substituted by—the shade he reflects and was created to be. Completely impotent, he remains incapable of projecting a desiring gaze that can fulfill. Even though Dané looks at him and comprehends his actions, any reciprocity remains impossible, for she too bears the irreparable mark of lack from the *some/no-thing*. Two absent selves, fractured reflections of desire's horrific consequences, cannot come together and create a mutual oneness. It is not as if this could have been avoided had Dané arrived sooner, or had Narcissus accepted her love when she first offered it to him, for the desire dividing the self can never be repaired; Dané, in other words, will *perpetually arrive too late* to satisfy Narcissus. With each as an iteration of the *some/no-thing*, Narcissus and Dané can only highlight the absent vision now inhabiting them both, and as they die together at the tale's conclusion, Dané is merely capable of admitting that this final encounter is nothing more than a "si mal *asanblement [a-sanble-ment]*," a tragic coming together (*asanblement*) of two lifeless simulacra (*sanblants*).[45] In a quest for libidinal satisfaction, both are doomed to find in their mortifying sacrifice a continued division through mutually unfulfillable desire and endlessly impossible self-unity.

2.4   Postscript: The Impossibility of *V(e)oir*

Having now completed its testimony regarding Narcissus's demise, the narrator's voice, in an echo of its original interdiction, returns one final time at the close of this death scene to warn against the dangers of foolish love: "Or s'i gardent tuit autre amant/Qu'il ne muirent en tel sanblant!" [Now let all other lovers beware so they do not die in a similar way!].[46] As such, the lay presents itself as self-contained and self-coherent, *a narrative that fulfills itself in its own telling*. The story of Narcissus, in other words, completes the lay's warning by serving as its sole anecdote while the lay's warning gives the story of Narcissus its reason for existence—both parts forming a perfectly mirrored construct reminiscent of the mutual reciprocity that the lay praises as the only love Nature will honor. Given, though, what the text has just finished stating regarding such reflective structures, the self-assurance proclaimed in its final verses becomes suspect. The perfect mirroring it claims to embody may be subject to a similar fate as the one suffered by Narcissus—and this may have already happened. For some clarification on this, it is necessary to return to the soothsayer's prediction that the *infant* will not perish as long as he does not see himself, a prediction that his ultimate demise, much like the text's cautioning regarding foolish love, retroactively testifies to as true. In this warning, however, a tension arises, for while the lay's narrator holds up Narcissus as a universal lesson (or non-example, as it were) for all lovers in the prologue and conclusion, the soothsayer holds him up at the start of the lay as a rather singular case (as, say, opposed to others who may see themselves and survive the encounter). Warning and exemplum might therefore not mirror one another as perfectly as the lay proclaims.

Some questions unavoidably arise here. Why is Narcissus the sole character within the text proclaimed to be at risk for suffering such a fate when Dané identically parallels his? If Narcissus is a singular example of destruction through self-vision, could his fate have been avoided? Could Dané have avoided hers? What if she, in other words, had never been struck with Love and he had never seen his "self"? As the lay's prologue and narrative profess though, love cannot be avoided, and so the initial and concluding warnings regarding foolish love, and that one must bypass them at all cost, now fall flat. Narcissus and Dané cannot—could never—escape their fate. Love destroys indiscriminately and completely—and both figures serve as proof to this. The lay's narrative then directly opposes its own prologue, for it is not a choice between love *or* annihilation as the opening remarks claim, but rather a mandate to love *and* be annihilated. This is why the lay can offer no specific advice on how to achieve worthiness other than its cursory remarks on an idealized mutuality between lovers. Even at the tale's ending, where Narcissus and Dané finally come together in an attempt at reciprocity, it is a complete failure, even *as* she kisses his eyes and cheeks. And it can only be such, for the lethal power of desire always destroys as it forms, rendering any attempt at mutual satisfaction, already shot through with the lacking *veoir* (vision) of the phantasm, always impossible—and this is *irreversible*. There is, ultimately, no good advice to be offered because there is no good advice *that can be offered*.

This cannot be an isolated case affecting solely Narcissus (and Dané by proxy) but rather holds, if one reads the lay, as it were, "against itself," as a universalized truth. The soothsayer has no choice but to be blind to the veracity of his own prophecy. It would be impossible for him to proclaim, and to believe while proclaiming it, that the self learns, through recognition of itself, that it cannot be the source of its own desire, falling victim to a fatal and lacking gaze from without that separates its self from its very self. *Voir* (truth) and *veoir* (vision) cannot coincide in the prophecy, because the moment the soothsayer speaks, he can only remain incapable of witnessing to the veracity that has already blinded him. The lay's warning to lovers as well as the seer's prediction are consequently haunted by the *infant*, the muteness silencing and undoing their speech in its formation, the moment it is uttered, rendering it incapable of coinciding with its *self*, with the truth it claims to purport. The text, in other words, bears the mark of a separation from itself, of a wound mirroring, in truth, that of Narcissus's *je me plaing* ("I lament myself").

The *enfant* (infant) of the Old French *Narcissus* comes directly from its Ovidian source, as this same structure of mute speech—of *infans*—inhabits Tiresias's Latin prediction as well [*si non se noverit—if he does not know himself*]. For this prophecy, nearly identical to its counterpart in the lay, cannot speak to the fact that the self it professes—that *my self*—bears the mark of a fatal wound causing it to die in its formation. Such a statement, as Claire Nouvet argues, is impossible to speak, impossible precisely because it is always and forever marked by the mute *infans* rendering it *unsayable even as I say it*:

> Narcissus's death actually proves the truth contained in Tiresias's voice, but a truth Tiresias cannot allow himself to know. The truth speaking in Tiresias's voice is a truth no subject can understand or speak. Any story claiming to "understand" this deadly truth can only fail to do so. Any attempt to tell Narcissus's story [...] is condemned to cut itself from the knowledge of self-hood that it records, a knowledge demanding that "I" say this impossible sentence, impossible because it is liquefying: "I am dead, stillborn." The knowledge of this fatal birth is a knowledge that can only be forgotten, even when we try to remember it. "I" erase it even as "I" write it down.[47]

The Old French *Narcissus* invariably suffers, and unavoidably so, from the amnesia Nouvet outlines in its attempt to walk the impossible line of proclaiming that one must somehow love *without* suffering the inevitable lethal consequences of desire and selfhood. Undoing its own messaging through its articulation, the lay forgets—because it must—the horrific knowledge it explores. Consequently, each part of the lay, both the warning of its prologue/epilogue and the exemplum of its narrative, do mirror one another, not as two halves complementing each other through shared plenitude, but, rather like Narcissus and his image, like Narcissus and Dané, in an assembly (*asamblement*) of mutual lack. For, in warning its readers against Narcissus's fate, the lay uncontrollably proceeds to present it as the sole possibility for its audience's *always-already* (non-)existence. This is the tension at the heart of the Narcissus myth—of any version of it—and these paradoxes between telling and failing to tell, seeing and failing to see, come together to form the double bind that *voir* (truth) and *veoir* (vision) cast over the literary texts, all of which reiterate the impossible mute *infant* of the lay, that I explore throughout the remainder of this study. In a discussion of Alain de Lille's *Plaint of Nature* in Chap. 3, I explore what happens when this mute *infant* of speech causes language to fall deficient, in turn wounding language itself, and to such a point that it seems to have lost its capacity to transmit what was once a seemingly coherent and stable meaning. Narcissus's wound, his *je me plaing* ("I lament myself"), reveals itself to have the power, not simply to disrupt the desiring self, but the desiring self's use of language as well.

NOTES

1. Martine Thiry-Stassin and Madeleine Tyssens outline the connections scholars have made between the lay and Ovid's myth in their introduction to *Narcisse: conte ovidien français du XIIᵉ siècle* (Paris: Les Belles Lettres, 1976), 56. For more on the lay and troubadour poetry, see Penny Eley's introduction to *Narcise et Dané* (Liverpool: University of Liverpool, 2015), 23–27.

2. *Narcisse: Conte ovidien français du XIIᵉ siècle*, ed. Martine Thiry-Stassin and Madeleine Tyssens (Paris: Les Belles Lettres, 1976), vv. 9–15, 81. Quotations from the lay are cited by verse and page numbers. English translations are my own.

3. Ibid., vv. 33–40, 82.

4. Scholars have argued that Dané embodies Echo along with other female mythological characters. See: Helen C.R. Laurie's article "*Narcisus*" in *Medium Aevum* 35 (1966), 111–16 and Albert Gier, "L'Amour, les monologues: le *Lai de Narcisse*" in *Conjunctures: Medieval Studies in Honor of Douglas Kelly* (Amsterdam: Rodopoi, 1994), 129–37.

5. Ovid, *Ovid's Metamorphoses, Books 1–5*, ed. William S. Anderson (Norman: University of Oklahoma Press, 1997), v. 3.348, 97; *Narcisse*, v. 52, 82.

6. *Narcisse*, vv. 41–42 and 45, 82.

7. Ibid., vv. 52–53, 82.

8. As Stephen G. Nichols posits, the almost perfect similarity between *voir* and *veoir* reinforces the link between vision and truth. See: "Parler, penser, voir: le *Roman de la Rose* et l'étrange" in *Littérature* 130 (2003), n. 31, 114.

9. *Narcisse*, v. 48, 82.

10. I refer to Narcissus as an *infant* throughout this study. Although he is not developmentally an infant when he has his encounter at the fountain, he still holds the traits of his infancy, for he "recouvre et occulte une enfance, une non-parole, qui persiste et endure au sein de la parole" [covers over and hides an infancy, a non-speech, persisting and enduring at the heart of speech]. Claire Nouvet, *Enfances narcisse*, 60, my translation.

11. For this in an Ovidian context, see: Nouvet, *Enfances*, 27–28.

12. *Narcisse*, vv. 64–65 and 68–70, 83.

13. Ibid., vv. 62–63, 83.

14. Ibid., vv. 72 and 75–76, 83.
15. Ibid., vv. 98–105, 84.
16. I draw upon Frederick Ahl who reads the red blush as "the *flowing* of life, the inner *FLUMEN*." See: *Metaformations: Soundplay and Wordplay in Ovid and Other Classical Poets* (Ithaca: Cornell University Press, 1985), 245–46.
17. *Narcisse*, vv. 155–156, 86, emphasis mine.
18. Ibid., vv. 25–28, 81.
19. Ibid., vv. 231–32 and 235–39, 88–89.
20. See Agamben's discussion of the phantasmatic process in *Stanzas: Word and Phantasm in Western Culture*, trans. Ronald L. Martinez (Minneapolis: University of Minneapolis Press, 1993), 73–89.
21. *Narcisse*, v. 239, 89.
22. R. Howard Bloch discusses "remembrer," related to "membrer/menbrer" in Old French, which implies "a reassembling of that which has been scattered, a recuperation of that which has been fragmented and lost […] to heal the wound of dismemberment and loss." See: *The Anonymous Marie de France* (Chicago: University of Chicago Press, 2003), 40–41.
23. Milena Mikhaïlova-Makarius relates Dané's scene of *innamoramento* to the typical male lover of *fin'amor*, remarking that she becomes a female version of the courtly lover, undergoing the same visual adventure that proves Narcissus's undoing. See: *Amour au miroir: les fables du fantasme ou la voie lyrique du roman médiéval* (Geneva: Droz, 2016), 33–34.
24. For these ideas in an Ovidian context, see: Nouvet, *Enfances*, 13–19.
25. References to hawking and falconry serve as popular motifs for love in medieval culture. See: Michael Camille, *The Medieval Art of Love: Objects and Subjects of Desire* (New York: Harry N. Abrams, 1998), 94–119.
26. Baudouin van den Abeele documents this usage of *vair* to describe a hawk's eyes in Old French literature in *La fauconnerie*, 160–61, 299–300.
27. *Narcisse*, v. 119, 85.
28. Ibid., v. 468, 97.
29. Ibid., vv. 644–46, 103, emphasis mine.
30. Simon Gaunt, *Love and Death in Medieval French and Occitan Courtly Literature: Martyrs to Love* (Oxford: Oxford University Press, 2006), 31.
31. Ibid., 31.
32. Slavoj Žižek, *The Sublime Object of Ideology* (London: Verso, 1989), 105.
33. Ibid., 106.
34. Gaunt, *Love*, 32.
35. *Narcisse*, v. 666, 104, emphasis mine.
36. Ibid., vv. 851–52 and 854–55, 111.
37. Ibid., vv. 861–63 and 907–08, 111, 113.

38. This process of division through apprehension is identical to the "captation" (related to *capere*) that Lacan outlines in his "Mirror Stage," where he states the experience before the image involves a "captation spatiale" [spatial capture]. As Lorenzo Chiesa explains, *captation* signifies *capture* and *captivation*. See: Jacques Lacan, "Le State du miroir" in *Ecrits* (Paris: Edition du Seuil, 1966), 86; Lorenzo Chiesa, *Subjectivity and Otherness: A Philosophical Reading of Lacan* (Cambridge: MIT Press, 2007), 15.
39. *Narcisse*, vv. 911–16 and 920–22, 113, emphasis mine.
40. Gaunt, *Love*, 175.
41. *Narcisse*, vv. 921, 113.
42. Ibid., v. 920, 113.
43. L. O. Aranye Fradenburg, *Sacrifice Your Love: Psychoanalysis, Historicism, Chaucer* (Minneapolis: University of Minnesota Press, 2002), 157.
44. Ibid.
45. *Narcisse*, v. 987, 116, my emphasis.
46. Ibid., vv. 1001–02, 117.
47. Nouvet, *Enfances*, 151–52. My translation of: "La mort de Narcisse prouve effectivement la vérité contenue dans la voix de Tirésias, mais une vérité que Tirésias ne peut se permettre de connaître. La vérité qui parle dans la voix de Tirésias est une vérité qu'aucun sujet ne peut comprendre ou parler. Tout récit qui prétend 'comprendre' cette vérité mortelle ne peut que la manquer. Toute tentative de raconter l'histoire de Narcisse [...] est condamnée à se couper de la connaissance de soi qu'elle inscrit, une connaissance qui exige que 'je' prononce cette phrase impossible car liquéfiante: 'Je suis mort, mort-né.' Le savoir de cette naissance mortelle est un savoir que l'on ne peut qu'oublier alors même que l'on tente de s'en souvenir. 'Je' l'efface alors même que 'je' l'inscris."

References

Agamben, Giorgio. 1993. *Stanzas: Word and Phantasm in Western Culture*. Trans. Ronald L. Martinez. Minneapolis, MN: University of Minneapolis Press.

Ahl, Frederick. 1985. *Metaformations: Soundplay and Wordplay in Ovid and Other Classical Poets*. Ithaca: Cornell University Press.

Bloch, R. Howard. 2003. *The Anonymous Marie de France*. Chicago: University of Chicago Press.

Camille, Michael. 1998. *The Medieval Art of Love: Objects and Subjects of Desire*. New York: Harry N. Abrams.

Chiesa, Lorenzo. 2007. *Subjectivity and Otherness: A Philosophical Reading of Lacan*. Cambridge: MIT Press.

Eley, Penny. 1992. Introduction. In *Narcise et Dané*, 7–30. Liverpool: University of Liverpool.

Fradenburg, L. O. Aranye. 2002. *Sacrifice Your Love: Psychoanalysis, Historicism, Chaucer*. Minneapolis, MN: University of Minnesota Press.

Gaunt, Simon. 2006. *Love and Death in Medieval French and Occitan Courtly Literature: Martyrs to Love*. Oxford: Oxford University Press.

Gier, Albert. 1994. L'Amour, les monologues: le *Lai de Narcisse*. In *Conjunctures: Medieval Studies in Honor of Douglas Kelly*, ed. Norris Lacy and Keith Busby, 129–137. Amsterdam: Rodopoi.

Lacan, Jacques. 1966. Le Stade du miroir. In *Ecrits*, 93–100. Paris: Editions du Seuil.

Laurie, Helen C.R. 1966. Narcisus. *Medieum Aevum* 35: 111–116.

Mikhaïlova-Makarius, Milena. 2016. *Amour au miroir: les fables du fantasme ou la voie lyrique du roman médiéval*. Geneva: Librairie Droz.

Narcisse: Conte ovidien français du XIIᵉ siècle. 1976. Ed. Martine Thirty-Stassin and Madeleine Tyssens. Paris: Les Belles Lettres.

Nichols, Stephen G. 2003. Parler, penser, voir: le *Roman de la Rose* et l'étrange. *Littérature* 130: 97–114.

Nouvet, Claire. 2009. *Enfances narcisse*. Paris: Galilée.

Ovid. 1993. *The Metamorphoses of Ovid*. Trans. Allen Mandelbaum. New York: Harcourt Brace.

———. 1997. *Ovid's Metamorphoses, Books 1–5*. Ed. William S. Anderson. Norman: University of Oklahoma Press.

Thiry-Stassin, Martine and Madeleine Tyssens. 1976. Introduction. In *Narcisse: Conte ovidien français du XIIᵉ siècle*, 17–75. Paris: Les Belles Lettres.

van den Abeele, Baudouin. 1990. *La fauconnerie dans les lettres françaises du XIIᵉ au XIVᵉ siècle*. Louvain: Leuven University Press.

Žižek, Slavoj. 1989. *The Sublime Object of Ideology*. London: Verso.

PART II

Selfhood and the Open Wound

CHAPTER 3

Narcissus and Mourning: Alain de Lille's *Plaint of Nature*

As I suggest in Chap. 2, the Old French *Narcissus* invokes an *imperative to mourn* when its titular *infant*, upon realizing his selfhood emerges as stillborn, begins to lament his death. Such a directive comes from two interconnected realities cast upon him by the *riens* (*some/no-thing*), the shadowy image he beholds at the fountain, for while presenting to him a model of unity and fulfillment, its ambiguous status (as realistic and fictitious) cannot satisfy his desire and, due to this, results in a divisive hold on his subjectivity. Narcissus's cry upon this discovery—*je me plaing* ("I lament myself") is quite telling, for, because of its etymological connection in Latin to grievous self-harm (*plangere*) and the wound (*plaga*), it indicates not simply his despair but also marks his identity as a rupture separating him from his own *self*. The injuries he exerts put him in a double bind, and in order to destroy the image as he attempts to render it benign, he has to destroy the self-emerging from the image. Self-annihilation, nevertheless, reaffirms his status as already devoid of agency and simply concretizes the permanency of the image and its hold over him. There is, in other words, no hope for existence without the reflection, however fraught an existence it is. As a result, mourning comes forth here as a *process emerging from the loss*—or from the perceived loss—of a unified self nostalgically existing prior to Narcissus's encounter with the reflection. Due to this loss, his wounded self can never mirror the idealized model of oneness and fulfillment seemingly embodied by the image, and, condemned to mimic its lacking qualities, he is incapable of returning

© The Author(s) 2019
N. Ealy, *Narcissism and Selfhood in Medieval French Literature*, The New Middle Ages, https://doi.org/10.1007/978-3-030-27916-5_3

to a hypothetical "wholeness." Because of this deficit, Narcissus, coming to know himself as a simulacrum of the watery shadow—as, in truth, *an image of an image*—laments his failure to resemble the false plenitude now defining his wounded subjectivity.

Narcissus's mourning, as a structural part of this catastrophe, subsequently results from the notion of a *lost similitude* to perfected fulfillment and the pain this separation brings with it. Such a disconnect—couched within the context of narcissism as in the lay—finds itself at the heart of Alain de Lille's Latin cosmographical allegory the *Plaint of Nature* (*De planctu Naturae*) (c. 1168). In this work, the figure of Nature, standing as an intermediary between humanity and God, has fashioned all of creation as a chain of mirrors, connecting earth and heaven—at opposite ends of the chain—through a series of successive resemblances.[1] Embodying the qualities of goodness, chastity, and prudence, Nature has put humanity at the center of this creation, as it is she "quae ad exemplarem mundanae machinae similitudinem hominis exemplavi naturam, ut in ea velut in speculo ipsius mundi scripta natura compareat" [who modeled the nature of man in imitation of the model of the cosmic order, so that in his nature, as in a mirror, one might see this natural order inscribed].[2] Nonetheless, humanity in its waywardness has destroyed the resemblance to its celestial model, and this loss, evident from the opening of the *Plaint*, causes its poet-narrator to move from happiness toward mourning: "In lacrimas risus, in luctus gaudia verto,/in planctum plausus, in lacrimosa iocos,/cum sua Naturae video decreta silere" [My laughter turns to weeping, my joy to sorrow, rejoicing becomes lamentation, jests give way to tears, when I see that the decrees of Nature are silent].[3]

The poet-narrator's lament precedes that of Nature who, already an established figure within the neo-Platonic Christian tradition of the twelfth century, seeks to reestablish the lost unity linking created to creator.[4] Concurrently, however, the discourse regarding humanity's affinity to God overlaps with issues of desire and selfhood raised by Ovid's myth of Narcissus. As I demonstrate in this chapter, such is the reason why Narcissus—and his relationship to Nature—takes on primary significance here, melding himself to neo-Platonic discourse. For, in the Christian legacy Alain inherits, the human subject (like Narcissus) is *already* a resemblance, having been created in the image and likeness of the triune God.[5] The language of human subjectivity within Christianity is therefore the language *of the image*, where men and women are an *imago Dei* called to resemble their divine model, their "true self" from which they emanate. This understanding of self-as-image, however, never occurs through direct visual contact with God, but, always with the help of a mediating mirror in ways quite similar to the phantasmatic process of courtly literature. Here, this mediating force is represented by the Scriptures—the Word of God—which, acting as a reflective surface, cultivates and transforms Christian subjects into images of holiness, thereby positioning them, as a result, within the chain of mirrors that begins and ends in the divine.[6] Language then, that medium through which God reveals himself in the Scriptures, must remain incorrupt, as it alone allows for the most seamless intercession possible between the recipients of the Divine Word and their celestial source.

While the mirror of Scriptures may be the best stopgap possible between creator and created, there is the expectation the two will be united again, like lovers in an erotic relationship, once the human soul returns home to its godly origins.[7] In the meantime, the mirror, while a barrier blocking unmediated access, also concretizes this link—for there is, like with Narcissus, no existence without it. As the *Plaint* makes explicit, the separation from God is not permanent unless sin, which threatens this resemblance between humanity and divinity, enters the equation. The central problem Alain's work poses is then, in many ways, identical to the one found at the start of the *Lay of Narcissus*, for this is a dilemma concerning errant desire and foolish love, as humanity, due to ignorance, has fallen into idolatry and vice. The resulting tearful lament brings forth this *planctus* (plaint), not simply the title of the text in Latin (*De planctu Naturae*) but also an established genre of medieval poetry (*plahn* in Occitan and *plaint* in French and English), exploring the type of grief resulting from *loss*.[8] Etymologically related to the bereaved self-wounding of Narcissus's *je me plaing* (for *planctus* and *plaing* have a common root in *plangere*, which also gives "wound" in Latin—*plaga*—and French—*plaie*), Alain's *planctus* indicates a separation that is lamentable and a meditation upon the process of mourning. As such, the text reflects the notion that humanity has suffered, not simply a loss in its resemblance to God, but a loss in remembering how to participate in the divine reality that would maintain this resemblance. Such losses are the result of sin which, within the neo-Platonic tradition, is always couched in terms of deficiency and loss, where evil is evil because it is a *loss* of goodness.[9] Sin, in other words, destroys the reflected similarity humanity has to the creator because it marks the deficiency of the human soul. For, this is a fissure of the self from its self, and, due to this loss through sin—a *loss through loss*—unity with the image of God through the mediation of the chain of mirrors now becomes impossible.

In correlation to the laments found in the *Lay of Narcissus* and Alain's *Plaint of Nature*, no discussion of mourning could be complete without referencing Freud's influential essay "Mourning and Melancholia," which, like these medieval texts, similarly grounds mourning within the context of wounding and loss, viewing the phenomenon as a specific "reaction to the loss of a loved one, or to the loss of some abstraction which has taken the place of one."[10] This painful response, however, is never stagnant but rather always takes on the form of a *process* he refers to as the *work of mourning* that aims, in essence, *to close the wound* this loss has opened up within the psyche. Occurring over a few steps, the libido removes its attachment to the lost object, a tense start given that a withdrawal from something once holding such prominence can never be easy, and to the point that "opposition can be so intense that a turning away from reality takes place and a clinging to the object through the medium of a hallucinatory wishful psychosis."[11] Due to this conflict, the mourning process takes time, precisely because this lost object becomes "psychically prolonged" until the libido detaches from "each single one of the memories and expectations" it provides.[12] In the end, however, the libido emerges once again as "free and uninhibited," the wound inflicted by loss has been healed, and the work of mourning becomes a thing of the past.[13] The aim of mourning, therefore, is never simply to have the libido enter into a newly found liberty, but rather always deals with the sundering caused by loss in its aim to bring about *reconciliation* and *consolation*.[14]

I bring up Freud, not simply to demonstrate how a pre-modern understanding of mourning maps itself onto his theories (which do not emerge in a vacuum), but to point out how much the notion of an original separation or wounding (*plaga*) fraught with intrusions of hallucinations and phantasms finds itself at the heart of both. Freud's ideas regarding mourning can therefore enter, and quite easily so, into a conversation with Narcissus's *je me plaing* ("I lament myself") and Nature's plaint, all of which deal with the notion of an open wound mourning works to heal. Although such a wound within Alain's text exists metaphorically in the separation from God that humanity has experienced due to its turn toward sin and vice, the wound also assumes a physical manifestation upon Nature's body. For, as the intermediary appears before the *Plaint*'s narrator, he is struck by her garments, which picture all that is alive within creation. The place on her clothes where humans appear, nonetheless, is rent asunder: "In huius vestis parte primaria homo, sensualitatis deponens segnitiem, directa ratiocinationis aurigatione caeli penetrabat archana. In qua

parte tunica, suarum partium passa discidium, suarum iniuriarum contu-
melias demonstrabat" [On the most prominent part of this garment Man,
casting off the dulling effect of sensuality, probed into the mysteries of
heaven, born along a straight path by his rational faculty. But in this part
the tunic had been torn apart, and clearly revealed the injury it had suf-
fered].[15] Humanity, in other words, is an injury upon the world, a wound
Nature wears upon her body that causes her to mourn as it sunders her
otherwise seamless garments, her otherwise seamless *self*. As such, Nature's
planctus is not just her plaint, but her *plaga*, her *wound*, as well and, due
to this, her mourning becomes a desire to bring humanity and divinity
back into contact with one another as well as an attempt to undo the violent sundering done to her.

In Alain's meditation upon loss, sin, already marked as *deficient*, stands
as the original loss separating any resemblance between humanity and
God—evident by the tear in Nature's garment that destroys the image of
humanity and reflects its forgetting of reason and knowledge. Because of
the open wound, not only is humanity in danger, but language—that link
connecting the Christian subject through the Scriptures to the divine—is
also under threat, for if human reason can be obliterated, any comprehension of the Word of God, of *language* itself, will also fail. The aim of this
work of mourning within the *Plaint*, in a certain sense, is to uphold the
integrity of its own message, to bring together an understanding of language *back to language itself*. Attempting to move creation from sin—
from this *loss as loss*—to a place where it can close the wound brought
about by such vice, the goal of the *Plaint* is to reorient humanity toward
the divine through the mediating mirror of the Word so it can reflect its
source as an *imago Dei*. Such work must first begin with Narcissus, whose
presence in the text serves as a model for the reflective structure that not
simply causes the original wounding imposed by sin upon language but
also points to its potential healing as well.

3.1   NARCISSUS MOURNED: THE WOUNDING
OF LANGUAGE

The elevation of Narcissus to the figure who embodies the wounding
between the terrestrial and celestial worlds begins in the *Plaint* during its
opening verses where, in the midst of lamenting humanity's disregard for
reproductive sexual coupling, the poet-narrator uses him to compare the
attractiveness of men and women. Narcissus may be—along with Adonis—

the most handsome of men, but his beauty remains inferior to Helen of Troy, the most alluring woman of classical literature. Yet, despite the fact that masculine beauty will forever remain subservient to its feminine counterpart, men like Narcissus, preferring other men in a confusion of gender and sexual roles, ignore and despise her. Why, Alain's narrator mourns, would a man choose another man when so many alluring women abound?

Adonis, paired with Narcissus, proves to be a fitting choice in this exemplification of relations between women and men, for not only is he the god of beauty and desire, but he fathers several children with his beloved Aphrodite. Notwithstanding his good looks, Narcissus, on the other hand, does not consort with women at all—most famously spurning Echo's advances—and instead loves a reflection. This does not elude Alain who, despite attempts to "straighten" Narcissus by rhetorically coupling him with Helen, later employs him in the *Plaint* as the primary illustration for vice and misdirected desire. Nature, for instance, in a speech explaining the intent of her visit, enumerates various transgressive practices into which humanity has fallen by citing a few myths as exempla: Helen committed adultery, Pasiphae engaged in bestiality, Myrrha suffered incestuous longing, and Medea killed her own children. At the end of this list of *femmes fatales*, Nature posits Narcissus, condensing the drama of his tale into one telling phrase: "Narcisus etiam sui umbra alterum mentita Narcisum, umbratiliter obumbratus, seipsum credens esse se alterum de se sibi amoris incurrit periculum" [Narcissus, too, when his reflection feigned another Narcissus, was left in darkness by this shadow. Believing himself to be this other self, he brought upon himself through himself a perilous love].[16] It might seem odd that Alain even includes Narcissus here, for the women Nature mentions all break traditionally accepted taboos regarding sex and/or violence, and yet this boy and his shadow serve as the final and most striking introduction to her tirade against those who engage in all sorts of "unnatural" and non-generative intercourse. Scholars have written at great lengths about this section of the *Plaint*, and instead of entering into a discussion about the types of couplings presented here, my interest lies in the slippage between Nature's mention of Narcissus and her subsequent move to those who misuse their sexual organs, employing the "Veneris malleos in incudum transtulerunt officia" [hammers of Venus to perform the function of the anvil].[17] How can Nature make a logical move from desire for an image to non-vaginal sex between ambiguously gendered individuals? Her synopsis of Ovid's story provides, at the very least, a starting point, as Narcissus's lust for his reflection, unlike the women mentioned here, embodies the entire spectrum of non-heteronormative sex, gender identity, and desire that the *Plaint* denigrates as corrupt. There is, in other words, much for the poet-narrator to mourn when it comes to this adolescent.

Sixteen years old when thirst lures him to the fountain, Narcissus is at an age of androgynous pubescent beauty, displaying an attractive softness, with smooth hands and a tender body, that maidens and young men find alluring. His name, from the Greek for numbness according to folk etymology (νάρκη—*nárke*, as in "narcosis" and "narcotic"), further attests to this gendered ambiguity of feminized passivity as he lies spellbound before the mirrored waters reflecting his image.[18] For, ignorant that what he sees deceives him, he begins to lust after what he believes to be a flesh-and-blood "self"—a self that is simply another man like him. The homoeroticism present in Ovid's myth allows the *Plaint* to open up its mournful rant on non-generative sexual couplings that disrupt the heteronormative gender/desire binary while concurrently serving as the primary example of those who transgress the sex/gender binary (where a man is always "male" and a woman always "female"). For if a "true man" only desires women, what is Narcissus as he longs for his reflection? Lusting not with the gaze of a straight man, he looks upon this other self as a gay/bisexual man or a straight/bisexual woman would look upon another man, further contradicting his already ambiguously "natural" male gender by embodying male *and* female qualities.[19] He is, in modern parlance, an individual who is gay, intersex, and transgender—all at once—something that stretches even the contemporary imagination.[20] And his entire myth speaks to such ambiguity, for not only is this androgyne desired by both genders and yearns for what he believes to be another man, but Tiresias, who predicts the adolescent's demise, moves between the male and female genders during his lifetime. Narcissus and those surrounding him repeatedly queer the heteronormative constructs of sex, gender, and desire that Nature strives to maintain intact.

Due to such turmoil, Alain's narrator has quite hyperbolically lamented from the opening verses of the *Plaint* all those individuals who follow Narcissus by confusing Nature's design for sexual coupling:

> [...] Venus in Venerem pugnans illos facit illas,
>   cumque sui magica devirat arte viros.
> [...]
> Activi generis sexus se turpiter horret

sic in passivum degenerare genus.
Femina vir factus sexus denigrat honorem,
Ars magicae Veneris hermafroditat eum.

Venus warring against Venus, makes he's become she's, and unmans men
with her magical art. [...] The active sex is thus horrified that it falls dis-
gracefully into the passive role. Man become woman demeans the dignity of
his sex; the art of a Venus turned sorcerer renders him hermaphrodite.[21]

Identical to the mythic boy, these men, acting on their wayward lust,
transmute into an intersexual ambiguity, betraying their gender as it
changes into something *else* that denigrates the entire person—body and
soul alike. As Narcissus before the mirror, they become *hermaphrodites*
(*hermaphroditat*), the exact term Alain chooses to describe this transformation. He can posit this because such destruction finds itself within the
myth of Hermaphroditus, coming just a few tales after Narcissus in Ovid's
Metamorphoses, where the nymph Salmacis, longing to embrace this beautiful youth, entwines herself around him as he swims in a crystalline pool.
Eyes blazing with desire, she prays never to be parted from him, and the
gods, hearing her appeal, fuse her to the body of the one for whom she
longs in such a way that: "nec duo sunt sed forma duplex, nec femina dici/
nec puer ut possit, *nec utrum*que et *utrum*que videtur" [no longer two
but one—although biform: one could have called that shape a woman or
a boy: for it seemed neither and seemed both].[22] Not man nor woman and
yet somehow both, Hermaphroditus joins together within the same body
not simply two genders, but the opposition of "either" [*utrum*] and "neither" [*nec utrum > neutrum*], terms ordinarily refusing a logical coexistence. In this confusion of oppositions where a radicalized differentiation
exists from within, Hermaphroditus—and by extension all hermaphrodites like him, such as Narcissus—threaten the order and stability Nature
has instituted for the categorization and conduct of human beings.

Interestingly though, this transmutation from man to hermaphrodite
does not happen willingly—at least not completely—but rather comes as a
force from without, beyond the control of the one transformed. In fact,
Alain refers to Salmacis's victim not as a noun, but rather an active verb
(*hermaphroditat*); this is a change done to the individual, with the implication that it cannot be a natural state occurring "as is." It is true that
Hermaphroditus, whose name combines those of his father (Hermes) and

mother (Aphrodite), and Narcissus, with his feminized numbness, already display an androgyny before their transformation, but this ambiguity becomes fully realized once the first is conquered by a nymph burning with lust and the second queered by a deceptive image in a pool. Alain's narrator blames such assaults on the witchcraft of Venus, the goddess responsible for inflicting degeneration and violent divisions upon the world, who herself is fraught with the tensions of an internalized conflict, a "Venus in Venerem pugnans" [Venus warring against Venus].[23] This goddess, as the allegorical representative of desire within the *Plaint*, thereby suffers from the same disunity she bestows upon those enticed by her power. As such, Narcissus's division is one of gender *and* venereal desire, for when he looks into the mirrored pool, he realizes that erotic fulfillment comes not from within him, but rather from without, housed by the lifeless image of this "second Narcissus." Comprehending that the desire he experiences and claims as his "own" is split between an internal "self" and external image, the boy attempts to bridge this separation, trying to ensure, to the point of his own destruction, an elusive oneness with the deceptive shade. Instead of an integral wholeness though, there is—and can only be—a confused and brutal internalized externality (and simultaneous externalized internality) of his desire, neither singular nor dual but both *at the same time*, united through separation and separated through unity.

Venus's divisive joining of oppositions though is not limited to Narcissus's desire but also attacks language itself. The only way Nature can talk about desire and its consequences, for instance, is to employ speech comprised of comingled oppositions, since the goddess of love, pitting together contrary elements within the same individual (male/female, internal/external, singular/plural), also unites words hostile to one another in a violent communion, dividing their signification from within by forcing upon them a sense averse to their accepted meaning:

> Pax odio, fraudique fides, spes iuncta timori
>   est amor, et mixtus cum ratione furor;
> naufragium dulce, pondus leve, grata Caribdis,
>   incolumis langor, insatiata fames.
> [...]
> [...] nox lucida, lux tenebrosa,
>   mors vivens, moriens vita [...].

> Love is peace linked with hostility, trust with deceit, hope with fear, and madness mixed with reason. It is a blissful shipwreck, a light burden, a delightful whirlpool, a healthy weakness, an insatiable hunger, [...] a sunny night, a day of darkness, a living death, a dying life[.][24]

With such antiphrases, desire destroys words to the point where they no longer index what they should, transforming language into an entity that, like Venus, fights with itself from within itself under the sway of this alienating force, and thus hermaphroditized, becomes like Narcissus, "either" and "neither." In this attack upon language, desire, much like Love with his arrow in the *Lay of Narcissus*, pierces the term of each coupled opposition, wounding them in such a way that they are opened up, flowing into one another. Each term, as Dané when felled by Love's weapon, loses its "corporeal integrity" and, now a porous body, falls into complete destruction as it merges with its antonym. For, if desire can make concepts like "life" and "day" no longer represent what they mean but rather—confused and poisoned by their opposite—something else, if things lose the essence of *what they are*, signification itself is in danger. And Nature knows of this peril, for with desire one finds only:

> Furta doli metus ira furor fraus impetus error
>   tristities huius hospita regna tenent.
> Hic ratio rationis egere, modoque carere
>   est modus, estque fides non habuisse fidem.

> Theft, guile, fear, rage, madness, treachery, violence, folly, [and] sorrow [and situations where] it is reasonable to be devoid of reason, restraint is unrestrained, and it is honest to be wholly dishonest.[25]

Because wayward longing can infect virtues like reason, restraint, and honesty with their antithesis because evil now corrupts goodness from within and because language means something other than intended, the entire orderly structure of the cosmos is now in question. An original blueprint for signification and virtue, it would appear, has been lost—perhaps irretrievably; such loss is not only worthy of mourning, but serves as the motivation for the mourning that gives the *Plaint* its purpose for existing. For, as Alain makes explicit, grammar, logic, and rhetoric, the building blocks of language and the means through which humanity comes to understand truths as revealed in Holy Writ and the teachings of Christ—the *Word of God*—are now in jeopardy. Grammar, for one, should form the basis of this examination, as the kinship among the various parts of speech, in turn, reflects the greater harmony of the universe. Logic, distinguishing truth from falsehood, and rhetoric, a mastery of metaphors, further this education into how the divine interconnects with the cosmos. Such an investigation of these three arts is to come to understand that our ability to signify through language and reason in ways reflecting a preordained celestial order is what makes us human. This expression of intellect, known as the Trivium, leads to an understanding of intellect itself, housed within the four mathematical arts of the Quadrivium: arithmetic as numbers, music as harmony, geometry as proportion, and astronomy as rhythm in motion. Language—when capable of referencing its intended signifier— thus instructs the learner on the archetypal pattern of the cosmos reflected within each individual and prepares human intellect to participate within the unity and wonder of creation as it realizes its intrinsic dignity and origin in the divine.[26]

In *Anticlaudianus*, Alain's sequel of sorts to the *Plaint*, these Seven Liberal Arts of the Trivium and Quadrivium embody a seamless unity and coherence. Nature, appearing again, has now decided to form a newly righteous man and, because of this, commissions a journey to God to procure a soul for this perfected individual. The Liberal Arts, represented by seven maidens, are chosen to build the chariot for this cosmic voyage, as they are:

> Cautae prudentes pulcrae similesque puellae
> septem, quae vultum sub septem vultibus unum
> reddunt, quas facies genus aetas forma potestas
> una tenet, tenet una fides, tenet una voluntas[.]

> Careful, foresighted, beautiful, much alike. In their seven faces they display
> a single face, a single appearance, lineage, age, form and power unites them,
> a common integrity, a common will.[27]

Joining together a repeated singularity that remains undivided, these maidens uphold their individual distinctions while demonstrating a shared resemblance. For this resemblance not only unites them to one another, but also joins them to humanity and divinity as they provide (quite literally) the vehicle for the human soul to discover its own similitude to God and the rest of creation. As mediators between created and creator, the Liberal Arts form a chain of self-discovery in which this new individual can come to know himself as an integral member of God's works.

Narcissus however, operating under the sway of Venus, endangers this univocal coherence of the Liberal Arts, for if rhetoric fails, if the maidens no longer resemble one another, the connection between created and creator becomes unstable, ravaging the capacity for humanity to understand its similitude to the divine. And Alain makes this threat explicit in Nature's retelling of the mythic boy's tale, for here, in this dynamic between Narcissus and his reflection, the *Plaint* encapsulates an entire meditation upon the fragility of this resemblance which, as language breaks down, diverges toward an unwieldy and divisive polyvocality, to the *wounding of language* itself. For, in this condensed version of Ovid's story (which I reference here for a second time), Alain pushes language to its extreme with an irregular word order and baroque use of grammar, verbal participles, and puns resulting in a nearly untranslatable babble: "Narcisus etiam sui umbra alterum mentita Narcisum, umbratiliter obumbratus, seipsum credens esse se alterum de se sibi amoris incurrit periculum" [Narcissus, too, when his reflection feigned another Narcissus, was left in darkness by this shadow. Believing himself to be this other self, he brought upon himself through himself a perilous love].[28] Here, Narcissus appears once in the nominative (*Narcisus*), declines into the accusative (*Narcisum*), and then disappears into the ambiguously gendered and numbered pronoun *se* (him-, her-, itself, themselves). This rapid move into predicative objects strips Narcissus of his gender and singular identity to the point that he becomes a pronominal substitute for a subject undone by language itself—he and language have mutually *undone* one another, and this destruction foretells of the greater menace to come. For Narcissus does not simply threaten, as Nature has explained, the univocality of language, because grammar, the first rung of the Seven Liberal Arts, is additionally under assault. In a section of the *Plaint* that has probably garnered the most critical interest, Alain's narrator condemns the hermaphrodite as an affront to grammatical correctness. In this lament opening the text, he weeps over sexual couplings that corrupt proper syntactical structure, for, where men are ordained as the active subject and women the passive predicate, the hermaphrodite becomes identical to Narcissus—nominative lover (*Narcisus*) and accusative beloved (*Narcisum*)—by assuming:

> Praedicat et subicit, fit duplex terminus idem,
>   grammaticae leges ampliat ille nimis.
> Se negat esse virum, Naturae factus in arte
>   barbarus.

> Both predicate and subject; a single term assumes a double role, and extends
> the rules of grammar too far. He denies that he is a man, for he has become
> a barbarian in the grammar of Nature.[29]

Transformed into a subjective predicate and predicative subject, where he
is neither and both, Narcissus confuses an ordering that should reflect the
harmonious structure of the cosmos. It is even worse though, for now
rhetoric, through such antiphrasis, turns on grammar and infects it with
the vice of the hermaphrodite. The rightly separate arts blur, the Trivium
is divided against itself from within, and seamless unity degenerates into
confusion, now spawning a rhetorical grammar and a grammatical rhetoric.

Logic, that art distinguishing truth from falsehood, cannot remain
exempt from this narcissistic corruption. When Nature gives her synopsis
of Narcissus's tale, she makes sure to focus on the fundamental misrecognition he suffers. For one thing, mistaking an image for a flesh-and-blood
person is staggering in its defiance of logic, for this implies that Narcissus—
aged sixteen years in the *Metamorphoses*—has never before confronted a
mirror and is ignorant of even the most elementary properties of reflections and reflective surfaces.[30] The error though is more serious than this,
for Nature informs the *Plaint*'s narrator that the image is not simply a
shade, but a shade that *lies* (*mentita*) to this hermaphrodite ["Narcisus
etium sui umbra alterum *mentita* Narcisum"].[31] His failure to recognize
the reflection *as* reflection translates into a failure to distinguish reality
from illusion, the heart of logic itself. For where he should recognize a lie,
he sees truth and then, instead of turning away, becomes sexually attracted
to the deception before him. The irrational qualities of this reaction also
push the logic of grammar, for the false shadow (*umbra mentita*), in the
nominative, has no complementary verb in the entire sentence. Its sole
purpose, it would appear, is to bisect—and be bisected by—the accusative
alterum Narcisum, this other Narcissus, subsuming itself as its own object,
while subject and predicate alternate roles in linguistic cacophony.

Following this discussion of the adolescent and his shadow, Nature herself expounds upon a similar phenomenon in her description of non-
generative coupling where, invoking the grammatical exemplum of the
hermaphrodite as subject and predicate, she references the second language art: "Sunt qui, in Veneris logica disputantes, in conclusionibus suis
subiectionis praedicationisque legem relatione mutua sortiuntur" [Others,
disputing in the logic of Venus, render arbitrary in their conclusions the
law that governs the mutual relationship of subject and predicate].[32] Such

individuals, she explicates, cannot distinguish between their proper place in the sexual act, preferring instead its exact opposite: "Sunt qui vicem gerentes suppositi praedicari non norunt. Sunt qui solummodo praedicantes subiecti termini subiectionem legitimam non attendunt" [There are some who perform the role of the "subject," but are unable to admit predication. And some, who only predicate, have no regard for the appropriate subjection of the subject term].[33] As rhetoric infiltrated grammar, now logic follows in Narcissus's wayward example and does the same; the three language arts blend into a singular plurality/plural singularity where no one term can now distinguish itself from the others.

Nature ceaselessly mourns the result of this confusion and, laying blame at the feet of a narcissistic Venus, laments this force of desire, "sed potius se gramaticis constructionibus destruens, dialeticis conversionibus invertens, rethoricis coloribus decolorans, suam artem in figuram, figuramque in vitium transferebat" [destructive in her grammatical constructions, perverse in her dialectical conversions, using rhetorical colors only to discolor, she turn(s) art into figure, figure into vice].[34] The senseless chaos brought to the language arts, now flawed and devoid of their specificity, becomes a successive iteration of decline without resolution, for as virtue becomes vice, vice, divided from within, further decays in an endless succession of ever-increasing parasitism: "Languet fraude fides, fraus quoque fraudem/fallit fraude, dolo sic dolus instat" [Trust gives way to fraud, fraud indeed deceives fraud itself by fraud, so that guile becomes a threat to itself].[35] In this exponentially multiplying confusion, humankind, now a misdirected antiphrastic hermaphrodite unable to express or recognize any truth through language, abandons all reason and turns bestial:

> [...] absque pudore
> humanos hominis exuit usus
> non humanus homo. Degener ergo
> bruti degeneres induit actus
> et sic exhominans exhominandus.

> [W]ithout shame man, no longer human, rejects the human customs proper to a man. Now, degenerate, he assumes the degenerate behavior of a brute beast, thereby unmanning himself, and worthy to be unmanned.[36]

In such debauchery, an unrestrained narcissism—in ways sometimes challenging the imagination—has infected all humanity, intellect, and connection to the divine. If things sound desperate, it is because they are, for as narcissism destabilizes all creation, the divisiveness produced by the hermaphrodite has now infected all humanity with a narcissism that is *fallen*—and this is not simply figurative.

In some versions of his myth (such as the *Romance of the Rose*), Narcissus does not die by liquefaction as in the *Metamorphoses*, but instead plummets into the fountain and drowns, attempting to fuse to and become one with the image:

> Sor la fontaine touz adenz
> Se mist lors por boivre dedenz.
> Si vit en l'yaue clere et nete
> Son vis, son neis et sa bouchete.

> Over the fountain, he leaned forward to quench his thirst from inside it. He saw in the clear water his face, nose and little mouth.[37]

At first "over the fountain" [*sor la fontaine*], the boy appears to end up "inside it" [*dedenz*], drowning into his own image. In his desire to be one with the image, the boy, quite literally, falls into his reflection and dies, ensnared in the water. Nature similarly illustrates this descent in her version of the myth, for Narcissus drops from the nominative into the gendered and numbered ambiguity of the pronoun *se* in all the oblique cases (from *casus*, "fall"): *se* (accusative), *sibi* (dative), *sui* (genitive) and *de se* (ablative). Male, female, and neuter, a singular plurality and plural singularity, his descent into linguistic declensions is a recession into complete uncertainty marked by the shadow that divides him against his own self. Within the *Plaint*, such a fall—wrapped now in all its theological significance—appears in the opening meter as Alain references the ways in which hermaphroditic coupling destroys linguistic rules through grammatical error: "in vitium melius ista figura cadit" [this figure falls, more precisely, into defect].[38] Here, though, the now-unavoidably fractured nature of language comes in to pun the meaning of *vitium*—for while the term references linguistic defect it also signifies vice. The regression into grammatical error is a fall as well into Narcissus's pool of deceptive reflections, opaque signification and the resulting sinful nature that such acts bring. In this scenario of an extreme polyvocalized Babel, vice and grammatical error become one and the same, working in tandem to destroy the structures of the language arts, sexual coupling, and the ordered harmony of the cosmos. There is, it would seem, no return from this confusion. Nature thus takes it upon herself to serve as the force who, through the work of her mourning, strives to restructure this chaos and direct Alain's narrator—and all of humanity with him—back to his divine origin. She shall attempt to turn him from this universalized hermaphroditism and set him straight, so to speak, by reminding him of his proper place within the cosmos. Positioning herself as an intermediary force between humanity and the divine, she has, so it would seem, the potential to rectify the narcissistic error and linguistic havoc wrought on the sublunar world. If "either" and "neither" could be restored to their status as a stable binary opposition, if, in other words, the wound causing their confusion could be healed, divine virtue might no longer be mistaken for fallen vice and could, as intended, lead creation back to God.

3.2   Narcissus in Mourning: Nature as Wounded

The poet-narrator's initial lament within the *Plaint* is not simply a bemoaning of hermaphroditic narcissism, but also functions as an appeal for help—and Nature, in the form of a luminous woman, hears the call and descends from the heavens in this moment of need. She does not arrive triumphant though, but rather, the poet notices, injured and in pain, as tear-filled eyes threaten to destroy the beauty manifest in her. The *Plaint* is subsequently an exercise in mourning, and specifically in Nature's mourning, as she works to condemn the sinfulness of humanity and to provide a pathway back to the divine. Part of this work falls upon the poet, who must prepare her way so she might be capable of such tasks, and to these ends dedicates in sections of alternating verse and prose an entire third of the *Plaint* to extended praise for this divine mediator, describing her every aspect in minute detail. Her face and body, ornate headdress, clothes, and boots—elements rich in cosmic symbolism—all receive lengthy illustrations. Culminating in the seventh chapter of the text, this acclaim reaches its zenith when the poet lauds Nature as the source of all benevolent harmony on earth:

> O Dei proles genitrixque rerum,
> vinculum mundi stabilisque nexus,
> gemma terrenis, speculum caducis,
>   lucifer orbis.
> [...]
> Quae tuis mundum moderans habenis,

cuncta concordi stabilita nodo
nectis, et pacis glutino maritas
    caelica terris.

O child of god and mother of creation, linkage and firm bond to the universe, bright gem for earthly life, mirror for the fallen, daystar for the world.
[…] You who, guiding the world with your reins, impose stability in binding
agreements, and unite heavenly to earthly in the closeness of peace.[39]

Highlighting Nature in ways contrasted with Venus, the song entrenches
the disparity between the libidinal and generative forces; where Venus
brings vice and error, Nature bestows virtue, where Venus confuses
through differentiation within the heavens, Nature assigns the sun and
moon their appropriate time in a peaceful separation. The mediatrix is
accordingly established as that force bringing together earth and heaven in
a joyful union and, as such, works with the poet as co-director of the
Plaint; Nature provides the subject and model for his writing, and he mirrors her divine activity through a beautiful synthesis of well-ordered language, reflecting her celestial concord.

This symbiosis of poet and goddess, though, is not immediate, for
when the narrator first encounters Nature, he cannot recognize who she is
and, in an echo of Narcissus's fall into linguistic confusion and vice, collapses to the ground devoid of speech, "nec vivens nec mortuus inter
*utrum*que *neuter* laborabam" [neither living nor dead, but reduced to a
neutral state between the two].[40] Incarnating the position of "either"
(*utrum*) and "neither" (*neuter*), the poet embodies the hermaphrodite's
quandary as well as the living death and dying life ["mors vivens, moriens
vita"] that desire has inflicted upon humanity.[41] This misdirected longing
also brings about with it, not surprisingly, the breakdown of language. In
this state where he is neither alive nor dead—and yet somehow both—he
is far from capable of composing, say, the beautifully ordered hymn to
Nature; antiphrasis has taken over, rendering him mute and incapable of
all communication. With tearful eyes, Nature can only wait before him,
shocked and with arms outstretched, as she mourns the total impotence
and lack of recognition on the part of this human subject before her.

Nevertheless, because the narrator falls into this hermaphroditic state
of narcissism, Nature can now fulfill her role as *speculum caducis*, the "mirror for the fallen" of her hymn, and redirect the created to the creator.
Obviously, an important component of Nature's restorative process
involves her attempts to rehabilitate language itself, for, threatened by

internal division, the Trivium must be freed from its confused weaknesses and assume once again its rightful place among the other liberal arts as a mediating force in the universe. Nature consequently symbolizes this divine interconnectedness through her entire appearance, beginning with an ornate diadem she wears upon her head, a union of the Platonic soul (which joins the properties of sameness and otherness in two interlocked circles)[42] and the Aristotelian Square of Opposition (which relates contraries in dialectical thought to one another),[43] allegorically synthesizing the macrocosm of the heavens into a mirror image of the microcosmic human form.[44] In the upper part of this crown, she dons twelve sparkling gems representing the constellations of the zodiac—each corresponding to a different part of the human body which, in turn, functions as a simulacrum of the heavens' orderly movements.[45] In the lower part of the crown, seven rotating gems signify the heavenly bodies and the arts of the Trivium and Quadrivium.[46] A reflection of the entire universe, this crown combines the heavens to the human form in celestial harmony, joins language to intellect, and serves as the model of creation's unity in a seamless and mutual resemblance to itself.

While the headdress allegorizes this similitude between macrocosm and microcosm, Nature's boots, bearing depictions of nine flowers, display a corresponding synthesis of earthly beauty and artistic creation:

> Illic forma rosae picta fideliter,
> a vera facie devia paululum,
> [...]
> Concludens sociis floribus affuit
> flos illic redolens gratus Adonidis,
> Argentoque suo nobile lilium
> praeditabat agros imaque vallium.
> Illic ore thimum dispare disputans
> certabat, reliquis floribus invidens.
> Narcisi socio flore iocantia
> ridebant tacito murmure flumina.
> Vultu florigero flos aquilegius
> florum praenituit Lucifer omnium.
> Vernalisque loquens temporis otia,
> stellabat violae flosculus arbuta,
> [...]
> Hic floris speciem vivere iusserat
> quae regalis erat cartula nominis,
> scribentisque tamen nescia pollicis.

There the form of the rose, faithfully rendered and differing very little from the true flower. [...] The pleasing flower of Adonis, sweet smelling, was included in the floral company, and the noble lily bestowed its silver on the fields and deep valleys. There thyme, less fair of face, vied with the other flowers in envious dispute. Playful streams, with the flower of Narcissus as their companion, smiled with a gentle murmur. The columbine [...] shone like Lucifer. And the little violet [...] shone starlike amid the arbutus. [...] Here Nature had ordered to flourish that flower which is inscribed with a royal title [basil], though it has never known a writer's hand.[47]

The blooms prove to be quite extraordinary, as they resemble their models so much—even with the proper aromas—that spring, taken in by their lifelike quality, has "[h]iis florum tunicis prata virentibus/veris nobilitat gratia prodigi" [ennobled the meadows with these flourishing floral garments].[48] In other words, these painted images have the same nature as Narcissus's shadow, for one might confuse them for their authentic counterparts. It is no mistake, then, that the boy's flower finds itself just next to the reflective waters at the center of this literary bouquet—with four blooms before and four after as if at the nexus of mirror images. And the narcissus is the *socius flos*, the "kindred flower" of the rhyme because it unites all pictured here, sharing with them its power of deceptive similitude; it alone, above all the others mentioned in Alain's verses, most closely shares an affinity with the mythic figure to whom it is linked. For the narcissus is a flower known since antiquity to seek out shade and colder temperatures, to grow so close to water that it seems to look at its reflection, and to perish in hot weather.[49] Similarly, Narcissus, drawn to the fountain because of its cool adumbration, meets his fate, not by metamorphosis as is so typical in Ovid's magnum opus, but by vanishing completely; so overcome by the heat of his own frustrated desire, the boy—with his crimson and pale snowy complexion—liquefies into the mirrored waters before him. In this event of his dissolution, the red and white blossom with his name springs up to stand in for him—and is only capable of replacing him—because it *resembles* him so much.[50]

The logic of substitution existing between Narcissus and his flower is founded upon this logic of resemblance, for something can stand in for something else only if it holds more similarities than differences with its counterpart, imitating it to such a high degree that knowledge of one is capable *through* the other. And this knowledge of one through another, based upon resemblances and substitutions, as evident with the *infant* and his blossom, is a fundamentally narcissistic principle. It is fitting for Nature that this flower appear on her garments since she not only bears a strong resemblance to the cosmic similarities between humanity and the universe, but also as a replacement herself, standing in for God ["sui vicarum"], upon his orders, on earth.[51] She is able to do this because she participates in the invisible chain of being ["invisibilis (…) cathenis"] that joins the tangible world to its intangible source, and this link is formed by the principle of similitude—the macrocosm and microcosm resemble one another in and through Nature, who in turn resembles God in word and deed.[52] Carrying out her vicarious duties she, like her divine master, works to generate further bonds of likeness throughout creation, "in propriis incudibus rerum effigies" [stamp(ing) out the images of things] upon earth to strengthen the chain of reflections linking the sublunar and heavenly realms.[53] This resemblance, though, is limited since, as Nature explains, forging creatures in the image of their heavenly exemplar proves too mysterious for her; without divine intervention, she would easily veer off course. Overwhelmed by such work, she wishes to remain instead in her celestial palace "ubi accidentalis nox nubium aetheris indefessum diem non sepelit" [where no misfortune of cloudy darkness covers the sky's unending day], and chooses Venus to oversee her work.[54] Such a substitution does not go well, and the goddess of desire, gone rogue, destabilizes the primal order established by God, an act that has been the cause of Nature's mourning ever since. This secondary replacement remains, however, one of the most mysterious sections of Alain's *Plaint*, one which James Sheridan deems a "fatal flaw from an artistic point of view within the text" since no "sufficient reason is given" as to why Nature would choose to abandon her divine imperative and elect such an "incompetent deputy."[55] For, if Venus is such a malevolent force within the text, wreaking destruction wherever she goes, how could Nature have chosen her as her vicar?

Something definitely is amiss in Nature's story, and this seeming breakdown in its narrative logic right at the moment these substitutions occur—Nature for God and Venus for Nature—is, I posit, no accident (despite what Sheridan claims) but rests instead on the logic of resemblance. Yes, Nature does take after God in that she is able to carry out her generative duties, producing like from like, but she speaks of her relationship with the divine also in terms of dissemblance—resemblance, in other words, does not equate to identical parity:

Ego enim operans operantis Dei non valeo expresse inhaerere vestigiis, sed a longe quasi suspirans operantem respicio. Eius enim operatio simplex, mea operatio multiplex; eius opus sufficiens, meum opus deficiens; eius opus mirabile, meum opus mutabile. [...] Et respectu divinae potentiae meam potentiam impotentiam esse cognoscas, meum effectum scias esse defectum, meum vigorem vilitatem esse perpendas.

[M]y work is not capable of following closely the footsteps of the work of God, instead I sigh as I behold his work from afar. His working is simple, mine is manifold. His is complete, mine is incomplete. His is miraculous, mine is changeable. [...] Understand that in relation to divine power my power is impotence; know that my successes are failures; consider my strength to be as nothing.[56]

Stacked against God's, Nature's work proves incomplete, and she reveals herself as a deficient replacement, even later explaining that she can lead humanity so far up the chain of resemblance before needing the help of Theology—to whose knowledge she has no access—as a necessary supplement to her shortcomings. That this lack comes to define her and her capabilities seems ironic since throughout the *Plaint*, Nature also references *Venus* in terms of deficiency. Her substitute, for instance, causes words to stray from the fullness of their meaning, she deviates from the "original plan" for sexual coupling—and these losses are contextualized with allusions to Narcissus and his shadow. It is he who confuses gender, sex, and sexuality; threatens correct grammar; and fails to heed logic by falling in love with a reflection. His entire existence is defined by such deficiencies—he lacks the wholeness of heteronormative masculine sexuality, and his image lacks the ability to reciprocate that gaze of longing from its starry eyes. Venus does share many of the qualities Narcissus represents, and the frustrations of hostile peace and fearful hope she dispenses upon humanity in the form of wayward desire find their illustration in the reflection of the *alterum Narcisum*. Nowhere in the *Plaint*, however, does Alain ever present a verbal portrait of Venus's appearance, but in the poet's lengthy description of Nature, he does point out numerous traits this divine intermediary shares with Narcissus's phantasm. Like the reflection, she incarnates light, has a statuesque appearance compared to durable materials (teeth like ivory, a chin like crystal and silver), her eyes are like twin stars, and she wears a mantle that creates the illusion of colored images on water ["colorem imaginabatur aquatilem"].[57] Additionally, the hues adorning her face, evident in the "lacteo liliata colore lilio" [milky lily-whiteness] of her forehead and the "rosarum succensus murice" [color of roses] on her cheeks, blend together the snowy whiteness and crimson of the narcissine shade.[58] Even her arms and lips participate in the likeness, for similar to those of the image of the fountain, they appeal for reciprocation to the poet who stands before her. All of her countenance speaks to this lack shared with the aquatic reflection—to her lack—of the limits of nature, desire, and humanity.

With Narcissus's flower on her boot and likeness on her face, Nature and *infant* resemble one another—from head to toe—in a mutual reciprocity of lack and desire-as-lack, orienting the divine intermediary toward a resemblance, not only with God but also with Venus, that embodiment of longing who spreads deficiency throughout the world. Nature, although officially opposed to Venus, operates in a sort of symbiotic reversal to this supposed nemesis. Nature takes care, for instance, to condemn Venus for having created an incomprehensible mixture of day and night in her litany of antiphrases, the two confused so much that they become joined in a hermaphroditic disunity resulting in "nox lucida" [a sunny night] and "lux tenebrosa" [day of darkness].[59] Nature however, longing to abandon her God-given tasks and live in an endless day where there is never darkness, equally destroys the dichotomy between these two terms, for day mixed with night is no longer day, but neither is day devoid of night. Venus may have wrought unimpeded chaos, but Nature has sought a correspondingly problematic undifferentiated order in an equally impossible, radicalized homogeneity. The search for singularity without differentiation, in fact, goes against the task of her as the creator's vicar, since creation is in flux between opposed forces, never permanently stable but rather constantly in the processes of change and contradiction. Nature's own words attest to this when she describes her fashioning of the human subject, not as a singular entity but rather a creature formed through unity *and* complexity:

> Ego illa sum quae ad exemplarem mundanae machinae similitudinem hominis exemplavi naturam, ut in ea velut in speculo ipsius mundi scripta natura compareat. Sicut enim quatuor elementorum concors discordia, unica pluralitas, consonantia dissonans, consensus dissentiens, mundialis regiae structuram conciliat, sic quatuor complexionum compar disparitas, inaequalis aequalitas, difformis conformitas, diversa idemptitas, aedificium corporis humani compaginat.

> I am she who modeled the nature of man in imitation of the model of the cosmic order, so that in his nature, as in a mirror, one might see this natural order inscribed. For just as the concordant discord of the four elements, a uniform plurality, a dissonant consonance, a dissenting consensus, hold together the structure of the cosmic realm, so the compatible incompatibility of four temperaments, an unequal equality, a dissident conformity, a differing identity, holds together the edifice of the human body.[60]

The self is a fractured whole, a wounded entity from its inception, differentiated from within, born in a moment of generative incongruity—in other words a subject resembling *in speculo*—*as in a mirror*—the same incongruity within Nature and the universe. The external macrocosmic diversity of the heavens comes to be reflected within the microcosm of the human body; otherness, embodied within the unified diversity of the self is the "natural order" of things. The framework narcissism provides in its interplay of mirrored resemblances, tenuous fusion of oppositions, and internalized dichotomies accordingly renders humanity's existence possible. Creation exists due to this narcissism, and its innate alterity is always destined to appear and reappear in the complex terrain of lived experience.

Nature tries to have it both ways within the *Plaint*, proclaiming a uniformity she holds up as the sole possibility for meaning while declaring that "dissonant consonance" is the makeup of creation. And whenever she lauds unalterable singularity, she abandons the logic of the binary, forgetting that things only mean *what they are* when juxtaposed with what they are not. Ultimately, Nature proves herself just as guilty as Venus, for while this goddess takes the mediator's order and renders it chaotic, she in turn takes Venus's chaos and orders it, the two keeping one another in check through mutual support *and* mutual sabotage. Venus is the only logical choice Nature *can* make when seeking a replacement, for both figures, like twinned faces of Narcissus at the inception of his simultaneous formation and dissolution, participate in a relationship of perpetual homogeneity substituting for, and substituted with, perpetual heterogeneity. Nature, despite her best attempts, cannot escape this logic of unifying contraries because it is already an innate part of her, for she carries it right on her head in the diadem shaped as the Aristotelian Square of Opposition. Differentiation, quite literally, crowns her and the cosmic order she represents.

As such, the role of Nature merits a reassessment within the *Plaint*, for, whenever she speaks of herself in complete opposition to Venus, her nemesis comes to blur them into an antiphrastic venereal Nature and natural

Venus—a "uniform plurality" required for both their existence. Nature reveals herself as divided from within, differentiated from herself, a *Natura in Naturam pugnans*, something proving to be, as it turns out, her *natural state*. The contrast between "natural" and "unnatural" fall away, as this confusion has existed not only in Nature's most basic of duties but in her appearance as well, where in the portrait the poet-narrator ascribes to her, one can see these narcissistic principles have defined her from the start. The golden comb adorning her head, for instance, is not part of her body and yet resembles her hair to such an extent, the narrator states, that the two—natural hair and unnatural comb—remain indistinguishable from one another. Her boots similarly form a parallel illusion, joining natural and unnatural as they "[c]alcei vero, ex alutea pelle traducentes materiam, ita familiariter pedum sequebantur ideas, ut in ipsis pedibus nati ipsisque mirabiliter viderentur inscripti" [traced the form of the feet so intimately that they might have been born there, inscribed on the feet themselves in a wondrous way].[61] The fake flowers decorating them, in a heightened authentic inauthenticity, can substitute for the real thing, so much that spring itself is fooled. The narcissine image has fused with its source and the copy has outdone the original as *utrum* (either) and *neutrum* (neither) blur into an indistinguishable mixture of collapsed differentiation.

Due to this, Nature not only demonstrates throughout the text her many narcissistic traits, but also many of the hermaphroditic traits (for the two are one and the same in the *Plaint*) regarding sexual roles and practices that she condemns in others. As Mark Jordan points out, the hammer and stylus which Nature uses to forge new creations to inscribe their images are the tools the narrator first uses to describe male sexuality and their misuse a deviation from a heteronormative imperative. In other words, Nature herself reproduces "by means of the instruments of masculinity" and passes them on to Venus in her stead.[62] What Jordan suggests is quite radical, for hermaphroditism, far from a state reserved solely for a vice-ridden humanity, becomes in essence the natural state of things in the *Plaint*, as the intermediary is the first to employ ambiguously gendered acts in order to create life on earth. This is something reflected in the text's interpretation of Narcissus's myth, for alterity and difference are already there, must be there, within the natural world and at the birth of the human subject. Unique singularity proves to be impossible, and this includes heteronormative sexuality, which is already divided against itself and infiltrated with its opposite. It is no surprise, therefore, that the animals pictured on Nature's garments engage in a panoply of generative, sexual, and gendered practices: the bat embodies male and female traits, the ram is an unmarried polygamist, the beaver castrates itself, and the turtledove is celibate. Nature's project for creation, as Jordan points out, "seems to include the drunkenness of desire, hermaphroditism, polygamy, and sexual self-mutilation," in other words, the entire spectrum of sexual expression.[63] The blossoms on her shoes play a part in this as well, for, embedded in their mirrored structure, the bouquet illustrates the anomalies of grammatical gender that the poet, from the start of the *Plaint*, tries to equate to some kind of natural and logical order. The rose (*rosa*) and violet (*viola*) are feminine; the pheasant's eye (*adonium*), lily (*lilium*), and thyme (*thymum*) are neuter; the narcissus (*narcisus*) and columbine (*aquileius*) are masculine; the arbutus (*arbutus*) is feminine but with a masculine ending; and basil (*basilica*) is feminine but bears a king's name. If anything, the arbitrariness of language correlates to the arbitrariness of the natural world, and Nature, from head to foot, embodies all these ambiguities—*either* and *neither*, hermaphrodite, transgender, and linguistic anomaly—all in one.

The *Plaint* consequently reveals Nature in a perpetual tension between the extremes of sameness and differentiation, and her insistence upon the suppression of this innate struggle within creation has been at the forefront of her endeavor to direct not only sexuality but signification as well. When the poet asks her, for instance, about the merits of artistic inventiveness as a possible human parallel to divine creation, Nature reproaches him saying: "[A]n umbratilibus poetarum figmentis quae artis poeticae depinxit industria fidem adhibere conaris? [...] An ignoras quomodo poetae sine omni palliationis remedio auditoribus nudam falsitatem prostituunt [...]?" [(A)re you attempting to claim credibility for the shadowy fictions of the poets, which the efforts of the art of poetry have depicted? (... D)o you not know how poets prostitute naked falsehood to their audience with no protective garment (...)?].[64] Such experimentation is dangerous, she proclaims, because it has the potential to destroy linguistic signification through deception, leading the reader astray toward perilous untruths. These "shadowy fictions" of the poets, mirroring Narcissus's own dishonest shade, are dangerous for their inherently polyvocal nature, appearing as one thing, while signifying something else. The duplicity, however, does not wait to reveal itself at some later point, but is already there, present, the moment the linguistic shadow materializes, innately doubling itself as it affects the reader. The same happens to Narcissus as he gazes upon his own watery image, Nature states, for he is "*umbra*tiliter ob*umbra*tus," overshadowed by the shade emerging not once but *twice* in her words.[65] The action she implies is in present tense and passive voice in the original Latin, for by the time Narcissus beholds the phantom, it has already overshadowed him with this dual nature, concealing its truth from him, revealing itself as something *other* the moment it emerges.

Simultaneously though, Nature must admit that language can also reveal truths, and that at times poets can even "tamen aliquando hystoriales eventus ioculationibus fabulosis quadam eleganti sutura confoederant, ut ex diversorum conpetenti iunctura ipsius narrationis elegantior pictura resultet" [join historical events to their own playful fabulations by a sort of elegant stitching, in order that from the artful conjoining of these diverse materials a more elegant narrative pattern may emerge].[66] Literature cannot be trusted, and then it can be trusted, but there is no way to know when language, structured by its own innate alterity, is doing what, and Nature offers no rubric to help poet or reader discern the difference— because, quite frankly, she cannot. The Trivium, far from a seamless and cohesive structure where grammar, rhetoric, and logic work in unison to reflect the natural world and divine order, traffics in divisiveness, tension, and uncertainty, rendering language as something that has the capacity to hold back meaning or multiply its own signification. Nature's insistence upon linguistic univocality falls away as quickly as her insistence upon heteronormativity, something to which even the *Plaint* bearing her name testifies. In his employment of a variety of sources and literary genres, Alain has synthesized this diversity into a unique whole that undermines and multiplies its own meaning through numerous puns and word-plays— and so much, as Sheridan has argued, that the text, "one of the most difficult [he has] ever encountered," defies and resists a coherent reading.[67]

Language, like sexuality, is already divided from within, polyvocal from its inception, a trait mirroring, in Nature's own words, that of creation itself. This is exactly the same linguistic havoc Nature accuses Venus of having formed, for in an unequal equality terms blur together, lose their distinction and threaten the stability of the Trivium. It is through such antiphrases and heterogeneity that Nature is able to create the altered homogeneity she lauds as authentic and thus, in lamenting the presence of differentiation upon the world, resultantly mourns the thing creating the resemblance between humanity and the cosmos, the thing rendering her and all her work possible. All this casts Nature as an ambiguous figure within Alain's text as she begins to resemble more and more that duplicitous *umbra mentita* (deceptive shadow) reflected on her face. As such, she fulfills her role as *speculum caducis*, this mirror for the fallen that her hymn proclaims her to be, but not always quite as it intends, for as the polyvocality of language transforms her, it also transforms the poet's words. She can—yes—serve as a mirror for the fallen and help them in their path to the divine, but she can also be that reflection into which humanity falls and loses itself among the shades of desire where there are only antiphrases and frustrated longing. For, when the poet regains consciousness from his own fall before Nature, he states that it is like he "sed potius eius apparentia, velut monstruosi fantasmatis anomala apparitione percussus" [had been stricken by her appearance as if by the uncanny apparition of some monstrous phantasm].[68] There is a dark side to Nature she tries to keep hidden, a side revealing her as divisive as Venus and deficient in her ability to link humanity to divinity. Her work, however, may not be completely in vain and, as I shall explore in the concluding section to this chapter, these failures on her part can serve as the source—and indeed the model—that starts to heal the wound opened up by sin. Her work of mourning has the potential to transcend its nature.

3.3   Mourning (Un)Done: The (Im)Possibility of Closure

Toward the end of the *Plaint*, Nature's son Genius comes to denounce humanity's misplaced inclinations in an edict banishing those who pursue Venus from the communal order of the cosmos. Applauding her son's speech, Nature then departs, taking with her the "imaginariae visionis [...] speculo" [mirror of this imaginary vision] that makes up the *Plaint* and thereby ends the dream for the poet-narrator.[69] This sudden conclusion appears to offer no long-lasting solutions to the problems of hermaphroditic narcissism so central to the text's raison d'être. The sinful—yes—remain in a constant state of perpetual lack, but Nature's exit leaves any opportunity for change, even within the allegory's dream, permanently frustrated. What is the role of this mourning that seems to be cut off before accomplishing any long-lasting resolution at healing the wound sin has caused?

Some answers take shape earlier in the *Plaint* as Nature gives her own speech about desire, preemptively condemning those who fall under the sway of its seductive grip. Nonetheless, she concurrently states that she has no grudges against it per se, for as long as it remains true to its generative function, it does serve a valuable purpose. Desire, subsequently, is in constant need of temperance, requiring strict limitations upon its defining principles for, when it outstrips these boundaries, problems arise. If, as Nature puts it, desire's "scintilla in flammam evaserit" [spark expands to flame] or its "fonticulus in torrentem excreverit" [small stream grows into a torrent], wickedness and vice are always the end result.[70] In her continuous need to separate and categorize though, Nature attempts to divide the libidinal drive against itself, creating an opposition between its tempered and excessive modes, favoring the former over the latter. This dichotomy is tenuous at best, especially when the illustrations she earlier uses for God—that he is a "vita indefesse non moriens" [inexhaustible, undying vitality] and "fons semper scaturiens" [ever-flowing fountain]—are of a similar excess.[71] For desire, transgressing its restrictions, may conflate antonyms, confusing such things as the adulterer and monk—categories of behavior the divine vicar has separated—but following Venus in her exuberance need not lead to vice. The divide between adulterer and monk does not imply, even if the requisite possibility always exists, that the monk will become an adulterer; he may simply endeavor to remain a monk in opposition to the adulterer. At the same time, the adulterer could remain as such or might just raise his aspirations heavenward and adopt the habit, orienting his impulses toward holiness. And Nature's description of God as an "ever-flowing fountain" just might have something to do with this potential redirection of desire.

The symbolic link between divinity and aquatic imagery, a metaphor found numerous times in Scripture and patristic writings, follows a well-established tradition of comparing God to a well of eternal nourishment and unending life where the soul comes to partake of the waters from which it sprang.[72] Here, God bestows his love in the act of creation, an act tying him in a libidinal bond to this creation, which he desires will be forever with him. Drawn by this bond to the celestial fountain, the soul longs to find its own similitude to God which, mimicking his creation, it will consistently re-create upon earth through further acts of divine virtue. Such re-creation though requires a repeated yearning to fashion oneself anew in and through this likeness with God, an act possible with the help of Magnanimity, or that strength of the soul to take up its abode "[i]n corde vero velut in medio civitatis humanae" [in the heart, as the center of the human city] in order to pledge itself "sub Prudentiae principatu suam professa militiam" [to serve under the command of Providence] and act "prout eiusdem imperium deliberat" [in accordance with (its) commander's decisions].[73] This relationship, as Nature explains, unites two companions through the cordial love and spiritual coming-together of like-minded forces on equal terms: "Quoniam similia cum dissimilium aspernatione, similium sociali habitudine gratulantur, in te velut in speculo Naturae resultante similitudine inveniendo me alteram, tibi nodo dilectionis praecordialis astringor [...]. Quare circularis debet esse dilectio, ut tu talione dilectionis respondens nostram fortunam facias esse communem" [Since similars rejoice in sharing the condition of similars, while rejecting the dissimilar, I find in you another self, as if my likeness were reflected in the mirror of Nature; I am bound to you by a bond of heartfelt devotion (...). Thus our love should be circular, so that you, answering with reciprocal affection, would make our fortunes a common concern].[74] The connection between these partners is one of mutual reciprocity, where each member finds its fullness when with the other, all the while maintaining a singular individuality beneficial to both. This is why, as Nature states, the love is circular, for it moves between God—perpetually creating all in his likeness—and the image of this creation which he calls back, resulting in a constant procession from him and return to him. The bond between the divine and the human soul is subsequently a consistent process of concurrent oneness and differentiation, made up of the perpetual generation from the divine and the perpetual re-creation of the soul, forever carrying within itself the similitude linking it to its source. Within this theological tradition that Alain promulgates, such love is and has always been an *erotic love*, erotic because it is fraught with the tensions of self and other, of oneness and difference, of unity and separation—in other words, the contradictions of narcissistic *fin'amor*. For, as Denys Turner points out, the relationship between God and the soul has always been put in terms of erotic love within the Christian tradition because erotic love "is the language in which [such] polarities find their natural mode of expression, because it is, in fact the language *of* these polarities."[75] And God himself has conjoined these oppositions in an explosion of libidinal energy "cuiusdam reciprocae habitudinis relativis osculis foederando" [by a mutual kiss in a coexistence acceptable to both] where creation *possesses* this love while simultaneously *is possessed* by it.[76]

Subsequently, the godly and narcissistic modes of desire share an identical structure as the human soul and Ovid's *infant* come to know themselves as an image reflected in a fountain, an image that instantaneously defines *what they are*. For, when Narcissus comes to the waters seeking to quench his thirst, he discovers the oppositions of united differentiation and differentiated unity, where *self is other* and *other is self*, the same principles keeping in motion the circularity of longing between creator and created. Narcissus's situation however, unlike that of the soul, turns cata-strophic, for whereas the internalized externality and externalized inter-nality of desire becomes life-giving for creation, the same process ends in the boy's self-destruction. However, it is the image—the thing defining his desire—that short-circuits the amorous circularity and fulfillment he craves. Narcissus's problem is not a consequence of the excesses of his desire nor his discovery of a longing fraught with tension, for God and the soul have identical passions in their libidinal exchanges. As the *Plaint* states though, the problem with those like Narcissus is that they have been "umbratili credulitatis deceptus imagine" [deceived by shadowy imagin-ings of credulity].[77] The reflection Narcissus beholds, like a literary text, is caught within a complex web of meaning between knowledge and ignorance, between insight and blindness rendering it "shadowy," and not simply in the literal sense. Rather, this image exists and does not exist *at the same time*, occupying a liminal space between truth and illusion, what is and is not, a *some/no-thing*, *utrum* and *neutrum*—where it is simultane-ously both and neither. When Narcissus looks into the fountain, he does not see, as he believes, another being, but then neither is *nothing* there—because a reflection is *not exactly nothing*—and it is from this not-exactly-nothing that he reads something about the definition of his selfhood, a definition to which he conforms. This moment of conformity involves interpretation—and yet, as we know from Nature, such narcissine shades are never easy to discern, always caught somewhere between the balance of univocal- and polyvocality.

This is why Plotinus, writing about reflections almost a millennium before Alain, warns that they can bring about—exactly as we find in the *Plaint*—a literal fall into moral destruction when not read within the param-eters of such oppositional reasoning. In Plotinus's cosmology, the world, as an image of its divine source, can produce its own reflections upon water, mirrors, and other like substances. Through a false univocality blind to alter-ity, these secondary images pose a threat to mutable creation which, when it misreads them, is led away from the celestial Beauty upon which all primary resemblances are based. And Plotinus, perhaps not unsurprisingly, posits Narcissus as the principal example of such victimization:

> [He who] sees corporeal beauties [...] must no longer rush at them, but, knowing that they are only images, traces, and adumbrations of a superior principle, he will flee from them, to approach the Beauty of whom they are

merely the reflection. Whoever would let himself be misled by the pursuit of those vain shadows, mistaking them for realities, would grasp only an image as fugitive as the fluctuating form reflected by the waters, and would resemble Narcissus who, wishing to grasp that image himself, according to the fable, disappeared, carried away by the current. Likewise he who would wish to embrace corporeal beauties, and not release them, would plunge, not his body, but his soul into the gloomy abysses, so repugnant to intelligence; he would be condemned to total blindness; and on this earth, as well as in hell, he would see naught but mendacious shades.[78]

Narcissus's miscalculation of falling in love with an image that directs him away from its source leads to error and condemnation. For if he cannot recognize its multidirectional signification, that its resemblance to him should index the manifestation of God reflected in him, he fails to see that which makes him "him," that which makes him a reality of divine similitude. To perpetuate the unidirectional reading he imposes upon the shade, focusing himself not heavenward but toward something ephemeral, Plotinus suggests, is to put a lie in the place where the divine should instead find itself. Such an act, to replace God with something transitory, to see a secondary reflection where the creator should be (essentially eradicating the creator in the process), is the sin of idolatry from which, Nature laments in the *Plaint*, originate all the narcissistic vices that have infected the world. On the other hand, to have recognized himself as a reflection of God *through* his own reflection would have proven to be the source of eternal nourishment and divine acknowledgment.

Like desire, the narcissistic encounter—as the two are in truth synonymous—reveals itself to be polydirectional, serving as the blueprint for vice *and* virtue. Whereas its vicious mode misreads the image as a signified in and of itself, virtue reverses this process, treating the same image as a signifier indexing greater realities that transform something lifeless into a life-giving revelation. This epiphany though, given the duplicitous nature of the image, is fraught with complications similar to those that infect vice, emerging in a space between comprehension and mystery, visibility and invisibility, discovery and concealment. Such liminal terrains reflect the nature of God himself who, as Alain frequently states, is "spaera intelligibilis cuius centrum ubique, circumferentia nusquam" [an intelligible sphere whose center is everywhere, whose circumference nowhere].[79] God's presence—this center—is reflected *everywhere* in the image of everything proceeding from him, unveiling his invisibility, and rendering him knowable through mutual similitude to his beloved creation. At the same time, however, any such revelation exposes the unknowable nature of the divine, for the uncontainable God is *nowhere* to be found in the mutable image, his celestial mysteries forever hidden and inaccessible to the dissimilarity of human thought. To see God is to witness his invisibility, to comprehend God is to know his unknowability—and yet not to see him is to know he is present, discernable, and all-encompassing. Confronted with such narcissistic antiphrases of divine truth (visible invisibility/invisible visibility and knowable unknowability/unknowable knowability), language has no choice but to fail—and disastrously so—for, as Alain admits in his *Anticlaudianus*:

> [...] lingua [...]
> quomodo Naturae subiectus sermo stupescit
> dum temptat divina loqui, viresque loquendi
> perdit et ad veterem cupit ille recurrere sensum;
> mutescunt soni, vix balbutire valentes,
> deque novo sensu deponunt verba querelam[.]

language, being subject to Nature, is confounded when it tries to speak of things divine; it loses the power to communicate, and longs to retreat to old meanings; sound is struck dumb, scarcely capable of a stammer, and words lay aside any dispute about new meaning.[80]

Grammar, logic, and rhetoric fall silent, incapable of even approaching this realm to which human thought has no access and where antiphrastic oppositions used to form and comprehend the cosmos are "[s]ubtilibus igitur invisibilis iuncturae cathenis concordantibus universis, ad unitatem pluralitas, ad idemptitatem diversitas, ad consonantiam dissonantia, ad concordiam discordia, unione pacifica remeavit" [brought into concord by the subtle cords of an invisible chain, plurality returned to unity, diversity to identity, dissonance to consonance, discord to concord, in peaceful union].[81] In this heavenly realm univocality reigns, a oneness beyond oneness fracturing the capabilities of the language arts. This, by the way, is the realm of unadulterated purity beyond all differentiation Nature desires to inhabit, that place where "accidentalis nox nubium aetheris indefessum diem non sepelit" [no misfortune of the cloudy darkness covers the sky's unending day].[82] Within human reason, though, such univocality is unthinkable, and can only even be considered and framed within discourse, when simultaneously considering its opposite which infects it from the start. For Nature cannot speak of such unending day without mentioning cloudy darkness, she cannot speak of peaceful consonance without mentioning dissonance, else there would be no reason to bring up this requisite alterity in the first place.[83] Unadulterated oneness consequently eclipses the limits of language and, like Nature's relationship to Venus, shares an inverse similitude to the extreme polyvocality of life, both only capable of expressing themselves through the interplay of *utrum* (either) and *neutrum* (neither).

The differentiation inherent to human subjectivity and language is therefore the sole framework through which one can tenuously begin to approach this unknowable nature of transcendental celestial oneness. For if the goal of creation, aided by divine eros, is to work toward such radical univocality, Narcissus, even despite his wayward gaze and self-destruction, is not too far off the mark. Yes, he uncovers the alienation of his desire *and* his desire as alienation, but this is simply the requisite byproduct of his overarching yearning to achieve undifferentiated coherence to the object of his affection, something that is, within the theological landscape of Alain's cosmology, the ultimate goal of humanity's experience in the divine. And Narcissus's mourning, the reaction to the fateful discovery that he falls short of achieving, is the same frame of mind in which those exiled images about which Alain writes in his "Sermon on the Intelligible Sphere" find themselves, for, within their world of differentiation they, "fluitantis materiae contagio fluctuantes esse caligantes umbratili de suae caligationis fuligine conquerentes" [lament (...) that they are blinded by the murky gloom of their dark condition] where "idem diversum, individuum dividuum" [same becomes different, individual becomes divided], and yet they strive, nonetheless, to return "ad verum esse" [to true being].[84] The necessary outcome of an existence born of and defined by alterity, such lamentation, such *mourning*, can only signify, like the image causing it, a greater reality serving as the motivational drive toward the goal of unknowable oneness. The *Plaint* thereby establishes human existence as something only capable as *wounded within mourning*, and, true to her calling, Nature serves as the role model for humanity in this endeavor, even if the hope for transformational metamorphosis proves impossible. Bound by the structure of the cosmos, this mourning is born from the hermaphroditic polyvocality that moves all creation away from divine univocality. At the same time though, Nature must lament her own limitations, for attempting to envision this goal forces one to work within and against her already-wounded and already-hermaphroditic identity, within and against language, within and against existence itself. As such, mourning becomes the marker of the unavoidable reality that alterity imposes upon subjectivity and discourse even as it signals a longing for concordance, for *healing and closure*, beyond these restrictions. Consequently, Nature's *work of mourning* can never be a *working through of mourning* to where she would reach some catharsis by moving beyond the divisions desire has wrought upon the earth, for this would signal her end, as well as that of humanity. She thereby finds herself in a double bind, for if differentiation is eliminated, she threatens to destroy herself, but if differentiation is maintained—as evident with Narcissus—the same result might occur.

Nature, then, is not simply mourning that there is a loss, but is mourning a loss humanity *has forgotten*, rendering humanity not simply as lamented but as having an existence of lamentation, an existence to which it is ignorant. It is this ignorance, however, that Nature finds so threatening, for humanity, like the poet-narrator when he first sees her, does not recognize her, does not remember her. From humanity's point of view, the work of mourning has been wildly successful, for the loss of resemblance to the divine, this loss caused by sin, has been moved to the past and forgotten; humanity, in other words, has *gotten over it*, redirecting its energies now into simply a proliferation of more sin through the open wound of its existence. At the same time though, this mourning has also failed, because while humanity is now in a constant state of grieving—grieving to which it is ignorant—the mourning cannot stop. Mourning in this sense, as I point out in the introduction to this chapter, references the wound sin has imposed as well as the forgetting that there is a wound to begin with. In this tension between remembering and forgetting, of successful and failed mourning, the *Plaint* constantly tries to remind its readers of this wounding that defines humanity, the wounding that, in the resultant loss of divine similitude, divides the self from its self and renders us polyvocal and rent asunder. Consequently, the mourning will always fail in the face of this reminder, as humanity is only capable of existing within such a state of mourning. This is the place where the narcissistic *infant* enters the text, that narcissistic muteness, as I explore in Chap. 2, that voids any intention Nature may put into her voice, undoing her words as she speaks them—that our self is wounded, has been wounded, due to the phantasmatic loss defining us. And this is unsayable even as she says it. Such an *infant*, however, only becomes possible due to the fact that mourning, as Henry Staten posits, is linked to eros, to *desire*, for "as soon as desire is something felt by a mortal being for a mortal being, eros (as desire-in-general) will always be to some degree agitated by the anticipation of loss – an anticipation that operates even with regard to what is not yet possessed."[85] Narcissistic muteness and desire operate together with such force that the work of mourning, that desire to heal the wound opened by loss (as Freud posits), is constantly under threat. Desire and polyvocal speech-as-desire, in other words, are always ready to hinder any closure, precisely because "[t]he movement of desire is structured by mourning; the movement out of mourning is predicated upon the redistribution of desire."[86] As with everything else, desire divides mourning against itself, wounds its coherence, rendering it identical to Venus's antiphrastic language, and to such a point that the *Plaint* now must promulgate a mourning at war with its very self, transforming the work *of* mourning into the work *against* mourning. In other words, there can be no "successful mourning" in the same way that there can be no "successful fulfillment," as both would indicate impossibilities for terrestrial human subjectivity. Such is the reason why Nature's mantle, rent where humanity is depicted, is never sutured together over the course of the *Plaint*, as the wound of mourning, of polyvocality, of desire, finds itself at the core of what it is to be a self. The success of Nature's work is in its necessary failure, as mourning reveals itself bound by the rules of hermaphroditic division that destabilizes mutable creation all the while searching for a transcendental signifier that stabilizes univocality—and one system can only flounder in its attempt to reach the other. At the same time though, this failure to achieve the unthinkable goal of an unaltered existence is what keeps the soul moving forward in its frustrated desire. Direct access to the divine may remain impossible, but it is not as if nothing is achieved, for creation may never reach its celestial fountain, but neither is it where it was when it began this work of love.[87]

Narcissus's error in yearning for unalterable oneness—so much that he liquefies into the fountain before him—can point in fact *toward* salvation, even if the path is fraught with impossibility, for this desire is the way in which God interacts with his own self, the supreme example of erotic love upon which the relationship between creator and created is built. God demonstrates a self-sufficient love with no start or finish, he is the wellspring that never runs dry, the luminosity that is never extinguished, the "innascibilis [...] faciens" [unborn (...) maker], to use Nature's words, who "operatur ex nichilo [...] suo operatur in numine" [produces his works from nothing (...) through his own divinity].[88] These operations move out beyond even univocality itself, a celestial logic beyond earthly illogicality, where God exists in a complete and mutual coexistence of "tres personae uni et una tribus, et una uni reperiuntur aequalis" [three persons (...) equal to one, and the one to three, and the one to one], able to coincide perfectly with his own self.[89] He, as a singular yet triune deity, becomes lover and beloved of himself in a wholly reciprocal exchange fashioned by and for himself. Here, there is never any loss, only, as Alain reminds his readers in his *Anticlaudianus*, the endless creation and re-creation of more self-affection:

> qualiter ardor amor concordia forma duorum
> Spiritus est, in quo propriae Pater oscula proli
> donat et in Nato sese Pater invenit, in quo
> se videt ipse parens, dum de se nascitur ipse
> alter et in genito splendet gignentis imago.

> How the ardor, love, harmony, form of [Father and Son] is the Spirit, in whom the Father bestows the kiss of his child, the Father discovers himself in his Son, in whom the parent sees himself, since another self is born of him, and the image of the begetter shines in the begotten.[90]

Capable of recognizing himself in and before himself—where there is no need for a mirror to mediate this face-to-face encounter—God never confronts Narcissus's fateful moment of misrecognition and altered longing, for the eternally mutual gaze of himself by himself is always restorative, moving in a circular fashion of equal giving and receiving. This is why Julia Kristeva, in her discussion of neo-Platonism, can be so bold to affirm that "God is Narcissus," a phrase equal to the New Testament proclamation that "God is love."[91] For this narcissistic love is the calling given to mutable creation—even in its impossibility—as the soul, watching from afar in its realm of differentiation, longs to share in this ideal oneness of heavenly desire. Because of this, Kristeva can claim that "if the *narcissistic* illusion is for Myself a sin, my ideal is nonetheless *Narcissan*," for, in this unalterable oneness, there can be no loss, no separation, no wounding, no *je me plaing* ("I lament myself") that would ever set any process of mourning into motion.[92]

Examining mourning and its relationship to Narcissus's *je me plaing* is not possible within the construct of divine transcendence found in Alain's *Plaint*, for the reality of oneness with the image the *infant* craves can only exist in God himself. This detail (which, we might say, is simply a detail) does not stop, however, a lover from longing for unity with and satisfaction in the image, even with the strictures that terrestrial reality might place on it. In Chap. 4, I am interested in how the process of melancholy—related to and yet distinct from mourning—reacts differently to the wound desire inflicts upon the lover, undoing, quite miraculously, the sense of loss that never leaves the *Plaint*. Melancholy, as I explore, works on behalf of the wound, making union with the image appear not simply possible but also realistic and achievable.

NOTES

1. The neo-Platonic concept of the "chain of being" comes from Macrobius. See *Commentary on the Dream of Scipio* (New York: Columbia University Press, 1990), 145.
2. Alan of Lille, *De planctu Naturae (The Plaint of Nature)* in *Literary Works*, trans. and ed. Winthrop Wetherbee (Cambridge, MA: Harvard University Press, 2013), 70–71. All quotations in English and Latin from Alan's works, with chapter, verse, and page numbers cited, when appropriate, and with line breaks removed, when appropriate, come from Wetherbee's edition.
3. Ibid., vv. 1.1–3, 22–23.
4. Nature's history exceeds the scope of this present study. For her importance, see: George Economou, *The Goddess Natura in Medieval Literature* (Cambridge, MA: Harvard University Press, 1972). For neo-Platonism in the twelfth century, see: Winthrop Wetherbee, *Platonism and Poetry in the Twelfth Century: The Literary Influence of the School of Chartres* (Princeton: Princeton University Press, 1972).
5. This idea comes from Genesis 1:26: "Then God said, 'Let us make man in our image, after our likeness'" (Revised Standard Version).
6. For the mirror in medieval theology, see: Frederick Goldin, *The Mirror of Narcissus in the Courtly Love Lyric* (Ithaca: Cornell University Press, 1967), 6–15 and Fabienne Pomel, "Présentation: réflexions sur le miroir" in *Miroirs et jeux de miroirs dans la littérature médiévale*, ed. Fabienne Pomel (Rennes: Presses universitaires de Rennes, 2003), 17–26.
7. For the erotic connection between divinity and humanity, see: Denys Turner, *Eros and Allegory: Medieval Exegesis on the Song of Songs* (Kalamazoo: Cistercian Press, 1995).
8. Nicolette Zeeman, "The Theory of Passionate Song" in *Medieval Latin and Middle English Literature: Essays in Honour of Jill Mann*, ed. Christopher Cannon and Maura Nolan (Cambridge: D.S. Brewer, 2011), 237.

9. For evil within a neo-Platonic context, see: Eric D. Perl, *Theophany: The Neoplatonic Philosophy of Dionysius the Areopagite* (Albany: State University of New York Press, 2007), 53–64.

10. Sigmund Freud, "Mourning and Melancholia" in *The Standard Edition of the Complete Works of Sigmund Freud, Vol. 14*, trans. and ed. James Strachey (London: Hogarth, 1964), 243.

11. Ibid., 244.

12. Ibid., 245.

13. Ibid.

14. Nouri Gana, *Signifying Loss: Toward a Poetic of Narrative Mourning* (Lewisburg, Bucknell University Press, 2011), 24.

15. Alan, *Plaint*, 48–49, translation modified.

16. Ibid., 94–97.

17. Ibid., 96–97. Nature makes an analogy between hammers (tools that strike) and anvils (tools that are struck) to male and female genitalia. See: Mark Jordan, *The Invention of Sodomy in Christian Theology* (Chicago: University of Chicago Press, 1997), 67–91.

18. Pliny attests to this popular etymology: "[T]he narcissus [...], its name being derived from the word narce, torpor." See: *Natural History VI*, trans. and ed. W.H.S. Jones (Cambridge, MA: Loeb Classical Library, 1961), 255.

19. Even though the categories queer, gay, straight, and bisexual are contemporary, I use them because, as Jordan argues, Alain's categories of sex conform to what today are considered heterosexual, bisexual, and same-sex relations. See: *Invention*, 82–83.

20. Shadi Bartsch points out the long tradition (which includes Narcissus) of the mirror containing the power to queer those who gaze into it. See *The Mirror of the Self: Sexuality, Self-Knowledge, and the Gaze in the Early Roman Empire* (Chicago: University of Chicago Press, 2006), 30–31.

21. Alan, *Plaint*, vv. 1.5–6 and 15–18, 22–23.

22. Ovid, *Ovid's Metamorphoses, Books 1–5*, ed. William S. Anderson (Norman: University of Oklahoma, 1997), vv. 4.378–79, 116, my emphasis; Ovid, *The Metamorphoses of Ovid*, Allen Mandelbaum (New York: Harcourt Brace, 2993), 124.

23. Alan, *Plaint*, 22–23.

24. Alan, *Plaint*, vv. 9.1–4 and 9–10, 114–15.

25. Ibid., vv. 9.59–62, 118–19.

26. For the Seven Liberal Arts, see: William Harris Stahl, *Martianus Capella and the Seven Liberal Arts*, volume one (New York: Columbia University Press, 1971).

27. Alan, *Anticlaudianus*, vv. 2.325–28, 282–83.

28. Alan, *Plaint*, 94–97.

29. Ibid., vv. 1.19–22, 22–23.
30. Pausanias, the Greek geographer writing in the second century C.E., could not imagine such a mistake on Narcissus's part could ever be true. See: *Description of Greece*, trans. W.H.S. Jones (Cambridge, MA: Harvard University Press, 1961), 311.
31. Alan, *Plaint*, 94, my emphasis.
32. Ibid., 96–97.
33. Ibid.
34. Ibid., 132–33.
35. Ibid., vv. 11.15–16, 138–39.
36. Ibid., vv. 11.44–48, 140–41.
37. Guillaume de Lorris and Jean de Meun, *Le Roman de la Rose*, ed. Armand Strubel (Paris: Librairie Générale Française, 1992), vv. 1478–81, 122, my translation.
38. Alan, *Plaint*, vv. 1.24, 22, my translation.
39. Ibid., vv. 7.1–4 and 9–12, 84–87, translation modified.
40. Ibid., 66–67, my emphasis.
41. Ibid., v. 9.10, 114.
42. The soul of Plato's *Timaeus*, as two interlocked revolving circles, is a union of similitude to, and difference from, its divine source. This coincides with the movement of the diadem, which Alain describes as turning in a circular fashion, returning to its starting point by a reciprocal path. See: *Timaeus* in *The Complete Dialogues of Plato*, trans. Benjamin Jowett, ed. Edith Hamilton and Huntington Cairns (Princeton: Princeton University Press, 1961), 1166.
43. The Aristotelian Square of Opposition is a means of categorizing and synthesizing opposing propositions in quantity and quality. James Sheridan references this in his commentary on Alain's *Plaint of Nature* (Toronto: Pontifical Institute of Mediaeval Studies, 1980), n. 14, 77.
44. The concept of the macrocosm/microcosm duality is important in medieval philosophy, resting in the belief that the human body and universe reflect one another in form and function. See Winthrop Wetherbee's introduction to Bernardus Silvestris's *Cosmographia* (Princeton: Princeton University Press, 1972), 12.
45. This is a reference to the "zodiac man" or *homo signorum*, attested to in the first century C.E. by Marcus Manilius, where each sign of the zodiac corresponds to a part of the body. See: *Astronomican*, ed. A.E. Housman (London: Grant Richards, 1912), vv. 453–65, 47–48.
46. The seven heavenly bodies relate to the seven Liberal Arts: the diamond (Saturn/astronomy), agate (Jupiter/geometry), asterite (Mars/music), ruby (sun/arithmetic), sapphire (Venus/rhetoric), amethyst (Mercury/logic), and pearl (moon/grammar). Although Alain does not make this

explicit, other medieval authors, such as Alexander Neckam in *On the Nature of Things* (*De naturis rerum*), attest to this. See: *De naturis rerum*, ed. Thomas Wright (London: Longman, Roberts and Green, 1863), 283.

47. Alan, *Plaint*, vv. 3.1–2, 5–16 and 18–20, 54–55, translation modified.
48. Ibid., vv. 3.25–26, 56–57.
49. Pierre Hadot, "Le mythe de Narcisse et son interprétation par Plotin" in *Narcisses*, ed. Jean-Bertrand Pontalis (Paris: Gallimard, 2000), 128–29.
50. Even though Ovid describes the narcissus flower as *croceus*, normally translated as golden, Hermann Fränkel argues this word signifies "'reddish' [...], as can be seen from Ovid's describing the *crocus* flower as *ruber*." See: *Ovid: A Poet between Two Worlds* (Berkeley: University of California Press, 1956), 214.
51. Alan, *Plaint*, 108.
52. Ibid., 108.
53. Ibid., 108–09.
54. Ibid., 110–11.
55. Sheridan, Notes in *Plaint*, n. 44, 147.
56. Alan, *Plaint*, 78–79.
57. Ibid., 44.
58. Ibid., 28–29.
59. Alan, *Plaint*, 114–15.
60. Ibid., 70–71.
61. Ibid., 52–55.
62. Jordan, *Sodomy*, 71.
63. Ibid., 70.
64. Alan, *Plaint*, 100–01, translation modified.
65. Ibid., 94, my emphasis.
66. Ibid., 100–01.
67. Sheridan, Forward in *Plaint*, no page number.
68. Alan, *Plaint*, 82–83.
69. Ibid., 216–17.
70. Ibid., 120–21.
71. Ibid., 102–03.
72. See, for instance, Psalms 42:1–2, Psalms 63:1, John 4:10–14, Revelation 7:16–17 (RSV).
73. Alan, *Plaint*, 74–75.
74. Ibid., 194–95.
75. Turner, *Eros*, 58.
76. Alan, *Plaint*, 108–09.
77. Ibid., 204–05.
78. Plotinus, *Enneads*, trans. Stephen Mackenna (New York: Penguin, 1991), 53–54.

79. Alan, "Sermon on the Intelligible Sphere," 2–3.
80. Alan, *Anticlaudianus*, vv. 5.118–23, 370–71.
81. Alan, *Plaint*, 108–09, translation modified.
82. Ibid., 110–11.
83. Eileen Sweeney comes to similar conclusions regarding Alain's allegories in *Theology, and Poetry in Boethius, Abelard, and Alan of Lille: Words in the Absence of Things* (New York: Palgrave Macmillan, 2006), 166.
84. Alan, "Sermon," 6–9.
85. Henry Staten, *Eros in Mourning* (Baltimore: Johns Hopkins Press, 1995), xi.
86. Gana, *Signifying Loss*, 28.
87. I borrow the terms "successful" and "failed mourning" from Jacques Derrida. See: *Memoires: for Paul de Man*, trans. Cecile Lindsay (New York: Columbia University Press, 1986), 1–43.
88. Alan, *Plaint*, 78–79.
89. Alan, "Sermon," 16–17.
90. Alan, *Anticlaudianus*, vv. 5.161–65, 372–73.
91. Julia Kristeva, *Tales of Love*, trans. Leon S. Roudiez (New York, Columbia University Press, 1987), 111; I John 4:8 (RSV).
92. Ibid., 111.

REFERENCES

Alan of Lille. 2013a. *Anticlaudianus*. In *Literary Works*. Ed. and Trans. Winthrop Wetherbee, 219–517. Cambridge, MA: Harvard University Press.

———. 2013b. *The Plaint of Nature (De planctu Naturae)*. In *Literary Works*. Ed. and Trans. Winthrop Wetherbee, 21–217. Cambridge, MA: Harvard University Press.

———. 2013c. Sermon on the Intelligible Sphere. In *Literary Works*. Ed. and Trans. Winthrop Wetherbee, 1–19. Cambridge, MA: Harvard University Press.

Bartsch, Shadi. 2006. *The Mirror of the Self: Sexuality, Self-Knowledge, and the Gaze in the Early Roman Empire*. Chicago: University of Chicago Press.

Derrida, Jacques. 1986. *Mémoires: for Paul de Man*. Trans. Cecile Lindsay. New York: Columbia University Press.

Economou, George. 1972. *The Goddess Natura in Medieval Literature*. Cambridge, MA: Harvard University Press.

Fränkel, Hermann. 1956. *Ovid: A Poet Between Two Worlds*. Berkeley, CA: University of California Press.

Freud, Sigmund. 1964. Mourning and Melancholia. In *The Standard Edition of the Complete Works of Sigmund Freud, Vol. 14*. Trans. and Ed. James Strachey, 243–258. London: Hogarth.

Gana, Nouri. 2011. *Signifying Loss: Toward a Poetics of Narrative Mourning.* Lewisburg, PA: Bucknell University Press.

Goldin, Frederick. 1967. *The Mirror of Narcissus in the Courtly Love Lyric.* Ithaca, NY: Cornell University Press.

Guillaume de Lorris and Jean de Meun. 1992. *Le Roman de la Rose.* Ed. Armand Strubel. Paris: Librairie Générale Française.

Hadot, Pierre. 2000. Le mythe de Narcisse et son interprétation par Plotin. In *Narcisses,* ed. Jean-Bertrand Pontalis, 127–160. Paris: Galimard.

Jordan, Mark. 1997. *The Invention of Sodomy in Christian Theology.* Chicago: University of Chicago Press.

Kristeva, Julia. 1987. *Tales of Love.* Trans. Leon S. Roudiez. New York: Columbia University Press.

Macrobius. 1990. *Commentary on the Dream of Scipio.* Trans. William Harris Stahl. New York: Columbia University Press.

Manilius, Marcus. 1912. *Astronomicon.* Ed. A.E. Housman. London: Grant Richards.

Neckam, Alexander. 1863. *De naturis rereum.* Ed. Thomas Wright. London: Longman, Roberts and Green.

Ovid. 1993. *The Metamorphoses of Ovid.* Trans. Allen Mandelbaum. New York: Harcourt Brace.

———. 1997. *Ovid's Metamorphoses, Books 1–5.* Ed. William S. Anderson. Norman: University of Oklahoma Press.

Pausanias. 1961. *Description of Greece, Vol. 4.* Trans. W.H.S. Jones. Cambridge, MA: Harvard University Press.

Perl, Eric D. 2007. *Theophany: The Neoplatonic Philosophy of Dionysius the Areopagite.* Albany, NY: State University of New York Press.

Plato. 1961. Timaeus. In *The Complete Dialogues of Plato.* Trans. Benjamin Jowett and Ed. Edith Hamilton and Huntington Cairns, 1151–1211. Princeton, NJ: Princeton University Press.

Pliny. 1961. *Pliny: Natural History VI (Books 20–23).* Ed. and Trans. W.H.S. Jones. Cambridge, MA: Loeb Classical Library.

Plotinus. 1991. *Enneads.* Trans. Stephen Mackenna. New York: Penguin.

Pomel, Fabienne. 2003. Présentation: réflexions sur le miroir. In *Miroirs et jeux de miroirs dans la littérature médiévale.* Ed. Fabienne Pomel, 17–26. Rennes: Presses universitaires de Rennes.

Sheridan, James J. 1980. Forward and Notes. In *The Plaint of Nature,* ed. Alan of Lille and Ed. James J. Sheridan. Toronto: Pontifical Institute of Mediaeval Studies.

Stahl, William Harris, Richard Johnson, and E.L. Burge. 1971. *Martianus Capella and the Seven Liberal Arts.* Vol. 1. New York: Columbia University Press.

Staten, Henry. 1995. *Eros in Mourning.* Baltimore: Johns Hopkins Press.

Sweeney, Eileen C. 2006. *Logic, Theology, and Poetry in Boethius, Abelard, and Alan of Lille: Words in the Absence of Things.* New York: Palgrave Macmillan.

The New Oxford Annotated Bible with the Apocrypha (RSV). 1977. Ed. Herbert G. May and Bruce M. Metzger. New York: Oxford University Press.

Turner, Denys. 1995. *Eros and Allegory: Medieval Exegesis on the Song of Songs.* Kalamazoo: Cistercian Press.

Wetherbee, Winthrop. 1990. Introduction. In *The Cosmographia of Bernardus Silvestris,* 1–62. New York: Columbia University Press.

———. 1972. *Platonism and Poetry in the Twelfth Century: The Literary Influence of the School of Chartres.* Princeton, NJ: Princeton University Press.

Zeeman, Nicolette. 2011. The Theory of Passionate Song. In *Medieval Latin and Middle English Literature: Essays in Honour of Jill Mann,* ed. Christopher Cannon and Maura Nolan, 231–251. Cambridge: D. S. Brewer.

CHAPTER 4

Narcissus and Melancholy: René d'Anjou's *Book of the Love-Smitten Heart*

Before the start of the allegorical dream narrative comprising most of the *Book of the Love-Smitten Heart* (*Livre du Cœur d'Amour épris*) (c. 1457), René d'Anjou addresses a complaint to his nephew Jean de Bourbon.[1] Hopelessly in love with a woman he calls Sweet Mercy (Douce Merci), who does not appear to reciprocate the sentiment, René cannot decide whether to blame Fortune, Love, or his own destiny for the torment that has befallen his forlorn heart. Describing the genesis of this love to Jean, René explains that one day Fortune brought him to an unnamed beautiful and noble lady, Love shot an arrow from her gaze into his heart, and now destiny will not allow his memory any respite. In agony and thinking of her, he is unable to heal from this amorous wound and yet, at the same time, cannot escape the perpetual limbo between suffering and death.

The book he has begun, René declares, arises from this conflicted state of being and, in the outpouring of unresolved emotions, he hopes his addressee will read and offer some consolation to his tortured situation. In order to explain the initial encounter with Sweet Mercy, René creates for himself a literary counterpart who exists within and frames the fantastical landscape of the text, the creation of which parallels what occurs in Guillaume de Lorris's *Romance of the Rose*, from which the *Love-Smitten Heart* borrows in form and content. And such creation by an author of a literary counterpart, perhaps not unsurprisingly, has a direct link to narcissism. For, at the start of the *Rose*, the lover, a dreamt simulacrum of

Guillaume, falls in love with the image of a rosebud duplicated upon a fountain's crystalline surface, the same place where Narcissus has died:

> C'est li mireors perilleus
> Ou narcisus li orgueilleus
> Mira sa face et ses yauz vers,
> Dont il jut puis morz toz envers.

This is the perilous mirror where proud Narcissus looked at his face and shining eyes, because of which he fell backwards and died.[2]

The effect the mirror has upon Narcissus, which causes him to lie *envers* (backward) upon his death, has a correlation to the act of writing and the wounded self. For the word used to convey this movement can be separated into its Old French correlative, *en vers* (in verse), a reading supported by the visual rhyme in the preceding line. Narcissus's fall is not solely a descent into the fountain but also one *en vers*, into "poetic verse."[3] Expounding on this interpretation, Claire Nouvet links the self-reflection Narcissus experiences at the mirror to Guillaume's creation of his literary double, for the writer, just like his mythic predecessor, has created his own personified reflection *en vers*, in verse, in the literary world of the dream.[4] And such a reflection has profound ramifications for authors, as to write one's "self" into a literary work is to experience, *to have already experienced*, a separation of self from self that calls into question any believed integrity an author might claim over his or her subjectivity.

Similarly, René presents his separated selfhood—in reality his *wounded self*—within the same narcissistic paradigm. Existing *in verse*, his alter-ego of the *Love-Smitten Heart* appears to be the true literary manifestation of his tormented experiences with love. As evident in the *Romance of the Rose*, the primary tool René uses to bridge the textual and extratextual world is the first-person pronoun, the *lyric I* of troubadour poetry, which, present from the start of his complaint to Jean, serves to highlight his individualized grief. The *lyric I* casts a narcissistic shadow over the entire work, as this textual self becomes a catalyst for a quest that, the king hopes, will allow him to explore the cruel wounding that has stricken him so unexpectedly. At the mercy of Fortune and Love, this "literary René" must be a perfect simulacrum for the author, bearing his name, sharing his best qualities, and resembling him in every aspect. Since René claims that the image of the king within the work truly replicates his experiences, scholars have long commented upon the specular qualities of the text. As if in a mirror, he presents the *Love-Smitten Heart* as a reflection of his own story, its ensuing dream credible, and its sentiment true: "Et ainsi languis-sant demeure sans garir ne sans pouoir mourir, en faczon telle et estat proprement, comme par paraboles en ce livret ycy vous pourrez au vray veoir, s'il vous plaist a le lire" [Thus languishing, I remain incapable of healing or dying, a state that you will truly see described in the allegory of this small book, if it pleases you to read it].[5]

René, now sundered by Love's arrow, craves the wholeness he believes libidinal satisfaction will bring, and in so doing, assumes the language of Narcissus's *je me plaing* ("I lament myself"), lamenting that his life is now "plains et [...] plors" [plaints and tears] as he weeps over his divided self.[6] Following in the steps of Narcissus (both from Ovid and the Old French lay) who mourns his own unfulfilled desire (and his *desire as unfulfillable*), René perceives Love as a force that has destroyed a unified self that, in truth, never existed—and the more he grieves the wound dividing his self-hood, the more his selfhood is, in turn, further split by his grief. As I dis-cuss in Chap. 3, the work of mourning, having as its aim to close the wound opened up by loss, comes under threat by an ever-present desire ready to attack the human subject's vulnerability. The work *of* mourning, divided from within, unavoidably becomes the work *against* mourning, simply operating to maintain the wound's aperture and its annihilating consequences. Humanity's lacerated existence, as Nature's rent mantle in Alain's *Plaint of Nature* indicates, always remains exposed and without defense. And it is in this space opened up by mourning that I direct my discussion of René's injured self.

At first it might appear René is simply in mourning over his loss of Sweet Mercy—he has his own plaint and is wounded, languishing without healing in his amorous state. As it shall become evident throughout this chapter, he does not seek to close the wound as Nature in Alain's *Plaint* but, in a rather surprising move, works to keep it open; this drive to main-tain the aperture of desire's lacerating effects upon the body, and even to find them *advantageous*, remains a central tenet in courtly literature. This explains why the last arrow Love shoots into the dreamer of the *Romance of the Rose*, outlined in Chap. 1, carries not simply torment but also an ointment soothing the wound. Of course, the harm is understandable, for the painful arrow marks the lack of desire's reciprocity. How, though, are we to understand a weapon that pierces a lover's flesh and also *brings relief*? What might ultimately be the benefits of these open wounds?

Medieval literature finds answers to these questions in melancholy, an affliction believed to stem from an excess of black bile in the body which, within pre-modern cosmologies, came to be linked not simply to sadness, but, when it settles in the mind, to poetic and artistic production as well. Melancholy can therefore prove to be useful because it helps a lover fixate on what has been lost and, as a result, brings him *closer* to his beloved by keeping the wound of love *open*, a process simply heightened—as with René—through literary composition.[7]

Appearing to pick up on such ideas, Freud presents in his essay "Mourning and Melancholia" what can be considered a synthesis of medieval and modern thought regarding these two distinct yet interrelated phenomena. For, whereas mourning for Freud deals with loss *as* loss, where the object is *knowable* (such as, for instance, the lost connection between humanity and divinity in Alain's *Plaint*), melancholy, on the other hand, deals with loss where "one cannot see clearly what it is that has been lost," even to the point where the melancholiac cannot even "consciously perceive" what has been lost.[8] And this unconscious aspect of the condition halts desire from closing the division caused by loss, for the melancholiac cannot work toward the recovery of something, thereby—at least in theory—closing the wound, when the loss is *unknown*. This is why Freud, most importantly for this study, refers to melancholy, as we see in its medieval context, as "an open wound" [*eine offene Wunde*] that maintains the laceration's aperture, and, unlike mourning, does not attempt to close it.[9] In other words, if mourning has as its aim to close this wound caused by desire (which, as evident in my analysis of Alain's *Plaint*, will always fail to close it), melancholy—in its medieval and psychoanalytic contexts—has as its aim to keep the wound open so the loss inflicted upon the lover might be prolonged *and* undone. And the notion of an open wound that can somehow undo desire's mortifying effects holds an important place within the *Love-Smitten Heart*, where loss of the beloved Sweet Mercy is confused with an elusive narcissine image that, through melancholy, appears to render her tangible. Unity with her, in other words, becomes a seemingly attainable reality, something possible, as I explore, through a concerted and sustained aperture of the wounding effects desire has upon the self. In this work, René creates the perfect environment to explore melancholy, as the book, a physical marker separating him from his *lyric I*—of, in truth, "self" from "self"—concretizes Love's sundering effects as a perpetually open wound.

4.1 The Heart of Melancholy

At the start of the dream that begins the work, René inscribes the *lyric I* into the narrative, and, starting his tale from this particular point of view, describes the torment he feels while lying in bed one night:

> Une nuyt en ce mois passé,
> Travaillé, tourmenté, lassé,
> Forment pensifz ou lit me mis,
> Comme homme las qui a si mis
> Son cueur en la mercy d'Amours
> Que ma vie en plains et en plours
> La pluspart use en pourchassant
> Ung doulx octroy ouquel chassant
> Ja piecza si n'a peu souffire
> Plus de painë et de martire
> Qu'oncques corps d'amant si souffrit
> [...]
> Que voulez vous que je vous dye?

One night last month, worried, tormented, tired and profoundly pensive, I went to bed, as a weary man who has submitted his heart to Love's mercy, for I spend the greatest part of my life in plaints and tears hunting a sweet gift, the pursuit of which, already for a long time now, cannot suffice. No lover's body suffers more pain or martyrdom. What do you want me to tell you?[10]

Almost at the point of death, René's *lyric I* progresses into the world of dreams where, "without lying," he states, Love comes into his bedchamber and removes the heart from his body. Desire, also present in the room, receives the organ from Love and speaks about the honor to be achieved in rescuing Sweet Mercy, presently held captive by Danger, Shame, and Fear. The newly personified Heart, as the *lyric I* testifies, departs on this adventure to free his beloved. The authorial separation of "self" from "self" present in the opening scene proliferates, splitting the *lyric I* into three distinct personae (the narrator, dreamer, and *dreamt I*) who, despite René's best efforts, cannot all be the same. Instead, the monarch has created a text that refracts his image while opening, even more, the wounding of a sundered self the further one moves into the book's plot.[11] For René to claim that his textual self and he are one is to reenact the error Narcissus commits when he first believes the shadow he beholds is a real person. To see a person within a written and artistic creation where there is but a literary persona is the unavoidable misrecognition René must undergo if he is to claim the *Love-Smitten Heart* as a manifestation of his personal experiences.

This mistake, though, is not met with any hint of acknowledgment on René's part. In fact, the impetus in the *Love-Smitten Heart* is for even more separations within the *lyric I*. The illustration of the text's opening scene from the Vienna manuscript (Fig. 4.1) depicts this by showing the moment the nocturnal vision of René's textual alter-ego begins. Visited by the god of Love, the dreamer, displayed behind a curtain and bedsheets, has his hand propping up his head, the traditional manner of representing the dreaming and melancholic subject within medieval illustrations.[12] Love, portrayed as a hunter with large wings, holds the sleeper's disem-

Fig. 4.1   Love delivers René's heart to Desire. Codex Vindobonensis 2597, folio 2. Vienna: Österreischische Nationalbibliothek

bodied heart out to Desire, who accepts the offering with outstretched arms. As the central focus of the image, the heart incarnates the desire felt for Sweet Mercy:

> Car mon doloreux cueur s'i frit
> Si fort en ardant desirer
> Qu'il n'a pouoir de s'empirer
> Pour pire avoir sa maladie.

For my aching heart is so greatly consumed in ardent desire that it cannot experience anything worse that might aggravate its malady.[13]

Within these opening verses of the *Love-Smitten Heart*, desire manifests itself in two distinct locations, embodied by Desire and the heart containing the dreamer's fiery passion. This duality of representations is not only symptomatic of the sundering endemic to the narrative but also serves, as it does in the *Lay of Narcissus*, as bilocational, as *dedenz* (inside) and *dehors* (outside), where the phantasmatic image holds the promise of erotic fulfillment while denying Dané and Narcissus any role they might believe to have as an integral and singular source of their desire. The *Love-Smitten Heart*, due to this same rationale, exhibits a proliferation of authorial simulacra; each new split in the *lyric I* is yet another of René's attempts to fulfill his yearning which, within this narcissistic paradigm, is always divided between the self's lack of wholeness and the image's embodiment of desire from beyond the self. Within the logic of the dream, the desire of René's *dreamt I* is split like Narcissus's, divided between the allegorical figures of Heart, who represents the unfulfilled self, and Desire, its disembodied counterpart. The two then travel together, each one a representative of this wounding in René's selfhood.

If desire in courtly literature is to be understood, as Erin Labbie explains, as the uncontrollable libidinal drive that has no specified aim, something felt but whose object is not completely seen, it is love that attempts to impose "a contract as well as a construct" on such yearning.[14] Nonetheless, the divisive nature of desire upsets this supposedly felicitous symbiosis. Searching for fulfillment with Sweet Mercy, René finds that any such satisfaction is constantly beyond his reach. As evident in the opening illustration of the dream, Desire willingly accepts Love's directive to receive and accompany the heart, locus of René's internal pining. The mutual gaze between the two figures, mimicking the *innamoramento* that took place as the monarch first saw Sweet Mercy, is less assured. In visual terms, the artist has allegorized the longing from within (Love with the heart) gazing at the longing from without (Desire). In this rendering though, the face of Desire, depicted in profile and obscured by darkness, remains hidden from view. The character's gaze, that longed-for recognition from without, is a metaphor for the wholeness offered through the beloved lady's acknowledgment that René hopes to achieve in the extratextual world. In a reenactment of Narcissus's longing before his reflection, this concealed glance from the image is what Heart will seek during his adventures to have his desire reciprocatively validated. Meeting his own reflection in the representation of a perfected lover, he will subsequently attempt to capture this gaze at the Fountain of Fortune and the Diamond Mirror of Love.

4.2   MELANCHOLY AT THE FOUNTAIN

Beginning his adventures with Desire, Heart first comes to a lush meadow on the edge of a great forest. Here, before a beautiful pavilion, he catches sight of a jasper column displaying an engraved proclamation:

> O vous tous, cueurs gentilz et gracïeux
> Qui conquerir voulez, pour valoir mieulx,
> Du dieu d'Amours et de vo dame aussi
> Doulce gracë et eureuse mercy,
> N'ayez en vous changement de pensee
> Pour delaissier voz premieres amours.
> Soiez loyaulx sans varïer tousjours;
> Pitié pour vous ne sera ja lassee.

> O all you noble and gracious hearts who, in order to have greater worth, want to conquer the sweet grace and happy mercy of the god of Love as well as of your lady, harbor no changes to your thinking that might cause you to abandon your first passions. Remain constantly loyal without deviations; pity will never grow weary for you.[15]

This scene of reading, in the form of instruction to all lovers, mimics René's claim that he has established the text as a reflection of his own experience in love. Just as the monarch purports to witness his desire mirrored in the *lyric I* of the text, Heart sees within the words on the column a representation of his own idealized likeness. This alter-ego who is *in verse*, a steadfast lover focusing all attention upon his beloved, will eventually achieve his desired recompense.

The language conflating lover with beloved, forming a beautiful image of perfected unity, attracts Heart's attention and sparks his curiosity, for such a unity would close the wound Love's arrow has imposed on him. In his first mirror scene of the journey, Heart freezes in contemplation before these words while wondering who has carved the column's message. It is not until Lady Hope emerges from the pavilion and grasps the bridle of his horse that Heart's concentration is broken. During the ensuing conversation, where the knight admits to having been in profound thought before what he saw and read, he learns that Love left the words long ago for his vassals. Such a moment of static contemplation matched by Hope's entrance not only marks Heart's fascination with the image but also reveals the forceful hold it has over him; on a quest to capture Sweet Mercy's affection, he finds himself captured by the glorious reflection representing the love he seeks. This mirror, therefore, becomes a trap like the perilous fountain of Narcissus whose own likeness ensnares him on the spot. Paralleling the misrecognition of his mythic predecessor, Heart reads this generic representation of a lover receiving reward from a beloved as indicative of his personal reality and, as such, finds himself within the same double bind as René, seeing a textual alter-ego that he mistakes for himself and believes to hold the promise of his fulfillment.

True to her name, Lady Hope admits that the words on the stone are intended to comfort those seeking love and give them the will to conquer all adversity in their quest for erotic fulfillment. Continuously held out as an attainable "end point" to Heart's quest, such oneness through love with Sweet Mercy heightens his conformity to the beautiful image on the column. Nonetheless, Love's message also poses a challenge to his loyalty, for after giving her consolatory interpretation, Hope instructs the knight errant on the tests that Love will require as proof of fidelity. The first trial, Heart learns, is the Fountain of Fortune, which he and Desire soon encounter at nighttime upon seeing a black marble stone. Discovering a fountain at its base, they decide to quench their thirst; Heart, though, accidentally spills some water onto the marble rock, causing thunder and heavy rain to erupt. The intensity of the storm heightens his sadness and, while waiting underneath an aspen until it passes, he reveals the doubts he harbors to his companion. Desire, consoling Heart, reminds the knight of his strength and goodness, affirming that he *will* eventually have fulfillment:

Car si tu seuffres malle nuyt,
Encores auras grant deduyt.
Si pense au bien que recevras
Quant tu Doulce Mercy auras[.]

For even if you suffer a bad night, you will still have great pleasure. Think therefore about the good that you will receive when you have Sweet Mercy.[16]

These words mimic in a personalizing manner the universal message of the jasper stone, further concretizing the image Heart holds of himself. Now spurred on to action, he declares that he would rather die than appear to represent anything less than the lofty ideals of the column's inscription.

Heart's overwhelming drive to conform to the image stems from the phantasmatic circle of desire, which, as I discuss in Chap. 1, Agamben outlines as the theory of *fin'amor* based on such shades that, like Narcissus's image, contain the constant promise of erotic fulfillment. And Heart, smitten with the idealized message of the column, has experienced this process while Desire, encouraging its permanence in his companion's memory, reminds him to think about the reward he will receive. In a scene where the phantasm proves so crucial, it is no surprise that the knight, upon falling asleep, enters the world of nocturnal imagery where, in a marvelous dream, his horse brings him to a narrow bridge beneath which flows a river of blackened, troubled water. Having arrived at the middle of the bridge, Heart's oneiric double sees a threatening bull charging toward him that hits him and his horse with such brute force that they are both knocked into the river below where he, due to his heavy armor, begins to drown. Just in time, however, a lovely blonde mermaid emerges incredibly from the depths of the water, holds her arms out, pulls him up, and takes him safely to the shore.

Although critics have focused on the intertextual and prophetic nature of the dream, a reassessment of this nocturnal vision is required within the context of the melancholic love and narcissism that occur at the Fountain of Fortune. For, the commonality of Heart's dream and the fountain is their aquatic nature; the black and troubled water of the river within the nocturnal vision is strikingly comparable to that of the fountain which, Heart discovers upon waking the following morning, is "noire, hideuse et malnecte" [black, hideous and dirty].[17] Thinking he never would have drunk the water had he seen its dark color the night before, he reads the inscription on the stone from which the liquid springs, which informs him:

[...] qui bura a la fontaine,
Il en souffrera puis grant paine,
[...]
Par quoy, quant aucun tastera
De ladicte eaue et gictera
L'avance sur ce perron cy,
Tantost sera l'air tout nercy,
Car quelque beau temps que face,
Couvient qu'a coup y se desface.

Whoever will drink from the fountain will suffer great sorrow because of it.
This is why, when someone tastes this water and spills any remaining water
on the block of marble, the air will soon darken entirely and whatever nice
weather there might be will immediately be undone.[18]

The fountain, Heart learns, is the reason for not only the storm but the
heightened despair he experiences as well, its dark waters directing him to
negative thoughts that render unity in love elusive. When Desire awakens,
Heart shows him the inscription and the two, now cognizant of its warning, follow the stream produced by the fountain until it becomes a hideous
river, not unlike that of the dream, flowing past Melancholy's house. The
connection raised by the *Love-Smitten Heart* between these troubled
waters and this allegorical persona is not by chance, for melancholy and
lovesickness, considered identical ailments in the medical literature of the
Middle Ages, were believed to result in an excess of black bile—$\mu\varepsilon\lambda\alpha\gamma\chi o\lambda\acute{\iota}\alpha$
(*melancholía*) in Greek—within the body.[19] The darkened waters Heart
drinks, this humor of lovesickness, mark the Fountain of Fortune and the
ensuing storm as physical manifestations of melancholy, the violent nature
of love, and its resulting mental instability.

Even as the black bile of the fountain causes Heart to focus on the idea
that erotic fulfillment is an impossible wish, it, nevertheless, has useful
properties for him. In the young knight's dejected state, these negative
thoughts create a space where union with Sweet Mercy becomes a constant fixation. Recognizing this occurrence, the text's narrator states that
Heart changes his mind after reading the fountain's warning. Had he
known the danger of its waters the night before, he would have now still
drunk from them: "Mais de s'en garder de boire pour doubte de mal ou
de paine qu'il lui en deust advenir, il ne l'eust fait en nulle maniere, car il
lui eust esté tourné en recreandise et mauvaisitié" [But to keep himself
from drinking for fear of any evil or suffering that might befall him, he

would have not done in any way, for this would have turned him toward cowardice and wickedness].[20] The image of oneness in love, therefore, even in its effacement, remains ever present and rooted in his memory.

Melancholy, as evidenced within the *Love-Smitten Heart*, demonstrates its influence over the ambiguous nature of images, present within memory while absent in reality. As with the message of the perfected lover from the jasper column, the Fountain of Fortune offers Heart an enticing reflection ensnaring him in its appeal for erotic permanency. Not surprisingly, there is a strong impetus to make the image also present in reality, as the actions of both travelers attest; Desire first concretizes in his comforting speech that union with Sweet Mercy can be a definitive eventuality and Heart, willing to drink the black water, desires to capture the illusory promise of love's rewards. Melancholic obsession consequently has the power to collapse the inherently ambiguous nature of the image, rendering a disembodied hope "present" in the world of tangible objects. By making the unreal seem real, melancholy thereby transforms everything the phantasm lacks into a fictional untruth, eradicating its divisive nature as the problems of narcissistic misrecognition and the beloved image's elusive gaze vanish. And because melancholy has this power to transpose reality and fantasy, the lovesick affliction Heart undergoes to achieve and realize the image thus becomes for him a welcomed torture. Longing for validation from the disembodied hope and willing to do anything for the simulacrum, even to the point of death, Heart now finds himself in the same fatal situation as Narcissus, something he affirms at the beginning of his journey when he "jura ses bons dieux qu'il ne arresteroit en nesung lieu ferme jucques il eust par prouesse conquis la tresdoulce mercy de sa tresgente dame, ou senon, sans faulte mourroit en la paine" [swore to the gods above that he would not stop in any place until he had conquered the very sweet mercy of his very noble lady with his prowess, or if not, he would without doubt die trying].[21] This perpetual martyrdom Heart is willing to endure that melancholy affords him therefore not only ensures fidelity to the image of Sweet Mercy, but also serves to guarantee that fulfillment in love is something achievable with her.

We can see something, in fact, quite similar in Freud, whose own theory regarding melancholy shares much in common with the medieval concept of melancholic lovesickness, since for him the phenomenon also operates on a logic of transposition where the connotations of loss—and lack as loss—are unknown:

[A] loss [...] has indeed occurred, but one cannot see clearly what it is that has been lost, and it is all the more reasonable to suppose that the patient cannot consciously perceive what he has lost either. This, indeed, might be so even if the patient is aware of the loss which has given rise to his melancholia, but only in the sense that he knows *whom* he has lost but not *what* he has lost in him. This would suggest that melancholia is in some way related to an object-loss which is withdrawn from consciousness.[22]

This unknowable nature of the object-loss then is paramount and relates, within the framework of narcissism, to that perceived loss of wholeness that never existed—because it cannot exist. Heart, for instance, never had unity with Sweet Mercy, and the sense that he has been deprived of completion through desire is not really the loss of *something* but rather of *nothing*, and an impossible nothingness at that. This nothing, however, proves to be quite important, for, due to the transpositional logic of melancholy, an object appears as lost even when it was never possessed—its non-existence seems *as if it were real*, as if it were something that could be precariously acquired and precariously lost. In a passage appearing, quite openly, to correspond to the phantasmatic logic of narcissistic *fin'amor*, Freud speaks of the ego and the ways in which an identification such a precariously "lost object" comes to inform the self:

> The shadow of the object fell upon the ego [*Der Schatten des Objekts fiel so auf das Ich*], and the latter could henceforth be judged by a special agency as though it were an object, a forsaken object. In this way an object-loss was transformed into an ego-loss and the conflict between the ego and the loved person into a cleavage between the critical activity of the ego and the ego as altered by identification.[23]

His use of the term shadow (*Schatten*), quite interestingly, points to both the phantasmatic process of melancholy and the shadow (the *umbra*) that Narcissus beholds upon the fountain's waters. For such a shadow of the object perceived as lost, this *Schatten des Objekts*, falls uncontrollably onto the self, at once separate from and united to it, to the point that the self identifies with the shade that has come to infiltrate its being. And, due to this identification, it does not matter if Heart has never had an authentic exchange with the image, for this absent relationship behaves as if it were something that could be reified, possessed, and then potentially lost and eventually mourned. Melancholy miraculously transforms the absence of a fictional loss, a negative—in the face of all logic to the contrary—into something seemingly real. This process, as Agamben states, "opens a space for the existence of the unreal and marks out a scene in which the ego may enter into a relation with and attempt to appropriate it such as no other possession could rival and no loss possibly threaten."[24] Melancholy thereby affords Heart a way to undo the negative absence defining Sweet Mercy and, in the process, to possess the image that possesses him.

The image consequently becomes the sole reality possible in this work of melancholy, for, even if Sweet Mercy's phantasm is shot through with absence, it nonetheless achieves a realistic presence within Heart's memory and thoughts. His obsession, working to keep the wound of melancholy open (evidenced in René's divided selfhood within the *Love-Smitten Heart* or in Freud's *offene Wunde*), collapses the ambiguous nature of the likeness (absent in reality and present in memory) and renders it a truth. And because the figment seems real, unity and satisfaction are always *there*, just waiting for Heart. Melancholy, it could be said, signals that voice of the image-as-other responding from across the wound of reified loss and narcissistic alienation—and this response will always return and be made manifest in an endless repetition. In this transposition of fantasy and reality, Heart finds himself in a shared and unbreakable bond with the phantasm, rendering this relationship the strongest and most fulfilling of all possible connections.[25]

This is something most obviously denied Narcissus who, after realizing his reflection is an elusive shade, tears at his own flesh in desperation, while crying out for recognition. Narcissus's parallel destruction in the *Romance of the Rose*, as I explore in Chap. 3, ends with him inside the fountain, falling into his reflection and drowning. A similar death in the image appears inevitable for Heart's somnial double. Led to the water by his horse and blocked by the bull, to fall is the only solution. His plummet into the black waters of the dream, a simulacrum of the Fountain of Fortune's bile, mimics Narcissus's descent into the perilous mirror. In the dream, though, Heart's double is unlike his mythic predecessor in two obvious ways: he does not fall into a lifeless image nor does he drown. Instead, just when all seems lost, he lands quite incredibly into the saving arms of a lovely aquatic woman. It is as if she were destined to arrive there just for him. To be recognized by a living being who comes up from the depths of the water—is this not the stark realization of Narcissus's wish?

Heart's dream is thus a concretization of the boy's error, who does not realize, at first, that what he sees is an image, mistaking it for a real person who is *someone else*. Were the reflection alive, his hope is that it would rise up out of the pool and render his desire complete with a welcoming embrace. When Heart's somnial double therefore falls into the bile of the black river, immersed in the substance that transforms fantasy into truth, the melancholic structure of his desire allows for the mermaid to rescue him in the place where a lifeless simulacrum should signal his demise. Within the logic of the dream, the near-death experience of this oneiric "self" signals that experiencing the wounds of desire is indeed a worthwhile endeavor and Heart, in his awakened state, will continue forward in his search for recognition, at any cost, before the Castle of Pleasure on the Island of Love.

4.3 MELANCHOLY AT THE MIRROR

Approaching the Castle of Pleasure on foot, Heart, Desire, and Largesse, a new companion, see above its main gate a Diamond Mirror flanked by two statues (*ymaiges*) representing Imagination and Fantasy. The mirror, as explained in a textual accompaniment, will confront all who dare to look in it with a perilous test, potentially revealing an unfavorable image to the beholder and expose, in a most radical way, his true nature:

> S'en ce mirouër nul se mire
> Qui ne soit voir loyal amant,
> Le dieu d'Amours si lui fait dire
> Qu'il s'en repentira briefment;
> Car ceulx la auront dueil et ire
> Qui en amours font faulcement,
> Et verra l'en entierement
> Leur barat la et leurs faulx tours,
> Leur tricherie evidenment.
> Or s'en garde qui aura paours!

If anyone looks at himself in this mirror without being a truly loyal lover, the god of Love will cause it to speak in such a way that he will soon repent; for those who act falsely in love will have suffering and anger, and they will see all their dishonesty and deceit, their treachery will be obvious. Beware he who fears such a thing![26]

Crossing the castle's drawbridge, Heart, so transfixed by what he sees, feels compelled to look yet again at the statues and inscription, unable to remove his eyes from the mirror and these two *ymaiges*. The diamond, another example of the already familiar textual trap set for the victims of love in the *Love-Smitten Heart*, causes Desire to notice that his companion has been ensnared yet again in this latest incarnation of Narcissus's fountain.

Even though the mirror is a test of loyalty, it offers a seemingly consolatory message; capable of disclosing the lover's perfidy, the mirror also has the power to transform him into a faithful vassal of Love. Were he to look within and see deceit and treason, the viewer, moved by his own shame, could not help but change. Many critics purport that Heart has a positive experience before the mirror and statues, given that he remains there for quite a while. If the jasper pillar and the Fountain of Fortune are any indication, it appears the representation of an already-perfected lover here fascinates Heart as he mirrors the ideal qualities encapsulating the impetus of his quest. Nonetheless, given the emphasis upon waking and nocturnal vision throughout the *Love-Smitten Heart*, it is curious that the text does not allow access to the image Heart sees in the mirror. This silence proves even more intriguing given that the narrator has attempted to relate as truthfully as possible the events of this allegorical journey, transmitting to the best of his abilities an objective portrait of Heart's unwaveringly faithful nature and the fantastical landscape about which he moves. The Castle of Pleasure is a perfect example of such detail. With an eye toward Love's intricate dwelling, the narrator admits that, although impossible to describe in totality, he nevertheless feels compelled to comment at length on the precious materials and gemstones adorning the castle. As if of the narrative's own volition, the story demands at the very least a partial rendering before returning to the adventures at hand: "Et combien qu'il n'est langue qui peust fournir a diviser les grans richesses, merveilles et beaultez du beau chastel, touteffoiz le conte s'entremectra d'en diviser aucunes choses, non pas toutes, car il ne sauroit, mais partie" [And although no tongue could tell of the great riches, marvels and beauties of the castle, the story, nonetheless, will strive to tell of some of them, not all, for it would be unable to do so, but just a part].[27]

The importance of vision in this scene begins just before the narrator's description of the Castle of Pleasure while Heart, Desire, and Largesse are still at a distance from Love's abode. Raising their sights toward the jeweled fortress, they are immediately struck down, to the point of losing consciousness, by the sun's rays shining off its walls. The castle, as a structure capable of reflecting such overwhelming light, serves as a mirror dazzling anyone who looks in its direction. Its walls, the narrator states, are made of crystal, which not only gives them their specular luster but also a particularly optic quality. Medieval theories of vision, Kenneth Knoespel demonstrates, link crystals to the crystalline humor, the substance giving the eye its aqueous, mirrored appearance and visual capability and beneath which is the optic nerve leading to the brain.[28] As he points out, a work titled *The Ten Treatises on the Eye* (*Liber de oculis*), known in Europe from the late eleventh century, makes this connection between the crystalline humor and vision: "The eye is composed of many different parts. Vision, however, arises from only one of these parts which is called the crystalline humor. [...] It is white and shiny so that it may quietly receive a variety of colors."[29]

The Castle of Pleasure, as a crystal eye reflecting the sun's gaze upon the travelers, subsequently comes to embody the enlightenment Heart has pursued since the beginning of the dream. In his analysis of the Vienna manuscript miniatures for the *Love-Smitten Heart*, Jean Arrouye equates this quest for light, traditional symbol of purity and goodness, to Heart's search for Sweet Mercy. Beginning at night in the darkened bedchamber of René's dreaming alter-ego, the traveler has gone from discovering the secret of the fountain at daybreak to the Castle of Pleasure, where the sun is already well into the sky.[30] The hope of Sweet Mercy's recognition, until now out of reach, finally seems to appear as true in front of the palace, striking him in an array of overpowering brilliance. The light emitted from this crystal mirror, though, is anything but enlightening, rendering Heart and his companions blind and temporarily unable to continue their journey. The scene, in fact, recalls the opening complaint to Jean de Bourbon: Love first used an arrow to strike René's eye, but the god now uses the sun's rays on Heart to achieve the same end. In the illustration for the Fountain of Fortune from folio fifteen of the Vienna manuscript (Fig. 4.2), Arrouye points out that the sun is inside a dark halo, a sign, he contends, of the scene's continuing enchantment, now made permanent by the light shining everywhere.[31] The artist who, as most critics believe, worked in tandem with René, has shown the sun emitting light filtered through the same color as the fountain's marble stone and its waters. Casting melancholic rays upon Heart's adventures, the sun enshrouds all he perceives within an aura of lovesickness. His journey toward light has, consequently, also been a journey into the properties of its black humor.

Identical to melancholy in the *Love-Smitten Heart*, light also has the ability to transpose reality and fantasy. As Heart stands in rapt attention before the jasper column, Fountain of Fortune, and Diamond Mirror, the sun permits him to *see* specular likenesses upon their surface. He willingly

Fig. 4.2 Heart at the Fountain of Fortune. Codex Vindobonensis 2597, folio 15. Vienna: Österreischische Nationalbibliothek

undergoes this ensnarement because light allows for an illusory reciproca-tion of desiring gazes, promoting the hope of erotic wholeness. Nonetheless, the medium allowing him to see blinds him to the truth: the image, required for the genesis and maintenance of love, is itself intangible and lifeless. Like Narcissus's reflection, the stone does not reciprocate a gaze of unity in love because it cannot project any. Heart's own unsatisfied desirous gaze returns to him as incomplete; his wounded division of "self" and "image" will not become one. This is the blinding reality Heart can-not accept, for to do so means that he would know the goal of his entire quest with all its torturous ordeals as an impossible hope.

The literal blinding that occurs before the Castle of Pleasure foreshad-ows the symbolic blinding before the mirror above its portal. The narrator remains silent about the beautiful albeit illusory image Heart sees in the Diamond Mirror because he, in his fidelity to this reflected *other*, remains oblivious to its non-existent gaze. Such unavoidable blindness is not new within the *Love-Smitten Heart* but has existed ever since René's *lyric I* mistook Heart as the embodiment of his own needs. Evident in the opening miniature of the Vienna manuscript, the dreamer's closed eyes, in addition to marking him as the sleeping monarch, also connote this inability to see the truth when confronted with a lacking representation of desire. In order to maintain the melancholic fantasy, the artist has portrayed Desire's embrace, an iteration of Narcissus's and the mermaid's, ready to receive the heart with open arms. Love though has already removed René's heart, placing his longing outside his body, beyond his reach, and unalterably alien to him in the face of Desire whose own gaze is obscured from sight.

While the crystal Castle of Pleasure functions as an eye that blinds vision, the rock upon which Love's abode is constructed works as a mirror that gives insight. Made of emerald, this jewel, as noted in the *Prose Lapidary* (*Lapidaire en prose*), a popular fourteenth-century treatise on gemstones, is known for its connection to vision: "Esmeraude amende les ieuls et garde la veue d'ampirier. A celui qui en bonne creance l'esgarde moult est bone esmeraude a esgarder et a mirer. Noirons en ot un mireor ou il se miroit, et savoit par la force de ceste pierre ce qu'il voloit enquerre" [The emerald enriches the eyes and keeps vision from deteriorating. Whoever in good faith looks at it a lot, this is a good emerald to see and look at. Nero had a mirror of them where he would look at himself, and by the strength of this stone he knew what he sought to know].[32] This gem, the lapidary states, hinders blindness because it is a good stone "to look at" [*mirer*]. From the Latin *mirare*, meaning "to look attentively," the word implies in Old French recognition and the process of mirroring or reflecting. Referencing Nero, whom Pliny believed to have a green mirror made of emeralds in which he would watch the likenesses of fighting gladiators, the *Lapidaire* thereby makes an obvious link between the mirror, the emperor's visual reflection on it, and the knowledge he receives from this speculation.[33] Able to see his own image in the emerald, evidenced in the reflexive construction "il se miroit" [he would look at himself (reflected)], the text professes that he gains understanding about himself precisely because he sees himself *as an image*.

The deadly knowledge Narcissus attains before the mirror is this same cognizance of his "self" as a simulacrum for, realizing he is the embodiment of the image's non-existent gaze, he comes to learn that the doubling of "self" and "image" is, in truth, a horrific symbiosis of two images imitating each other in their mutual incompleteness. Heart, hoping for oneness with the image on the Island of Love, must be subjected to the same fate as his mythic predecessor. Even before he looks into the Diamond Mirror, the text highlights his self-as-image with the emergence of "ung umbre tresplaisant" [a very pleasant shadow] that blocks out the blinding light of the sun.[34] In a similar fashion, the illustration of the Fountain of Fortune mimics this emphasis upon the shadow, where the artist has depicted in careful detail the darkened silhouettes cast by the trees, Heart, Desire, and the marble stone over the black water, which, in its Ovidian context, references the *umbra* (shadow) Narcissus sees in the fountain as well as his lover's "transformation" into an image.

The shadow appears pleasing, though, and the false relief it brings indicates that Heart will not comprehend his terrible metamorphosis before the Diamond Mirror. As critics have pointed out, this gemstone, *dyamant* in Middle French, introduces a play on words into the scene before the lover ever looks within the mirror; able to distinguish between the loyal and disloyal disciple, they posit, it reveals the *dy-amant*—a combination of *dy-* (the Latin prefix signifying division) and *amant* (lover)—or dual lover (faithful/unfaithful) in its reflection.[35] I would argue, however, that it is *not* a dual lover revealed by the Diamond, but rather that the mirror radically exposes the *divided* lover, the melancholiac wounded by love, and the two are not the same. The true *dy-amant*, in other words, is split between the lifeless image in the mirror and the lacking image of the "self." The narrator has constructed the entire scene around this division, with the dual mirrors of crystal and emerald along with the shade appearing before the castle. Even the statues of Fantasy and Imagination, always referred to as "two images" [*deux ymaiges*], expose what Heart will witness in the deadly truth of the Diamond Mirror; the self is not autonomous, it is incomplete and unfulfilled, it is an imaginary fantasy reflected from another imaginary fantasy. The mirror, along with the Fountain of Fortune, thereby serves to rewound Heart's selfhood, keeping the laceration that melancholy has imposed upon him as an open and permanent fixture.

The scene, pictured on folio 103 of the Paris manuscript of the *Love-Smitten Heart* (Fig. 4.3), depicts the *dy-amant* (wounded lover) before the Diamond Mirror. In the bottom right corner of the image, the travelers are pictured from afar as they approach the Castle of Pleasure. While Desire and Largesse look ahead, Heart looks up to the statues, mirror, and inscription. The three are present again directly before the portal as the knight gazes above for a second time. His gaze, though,

Fig. 4.3 Heart at the Diamond Mirror. Ms. fr. 24399, folio 103. Paris: Bibliothèque nationale de France

obstructed by the helmet, connotes the blindness he experiences during this horrific metamorphosis. The mirror and the two renderings of Heart follow the same trajectory within the illustration to form a visual representation of him as the *dy-amant* of the scene. And yet, Desire and Largesse are not immune from the mirror's inescapably terrifying power. The diamond's invisible strength, portrayed as visible rays around the castle door, blinds them to its truth as the mirror reaches out and transforms them as well into *dy-amants*.

Cast upon immovable stones such as jasper and marble in the *Love-Smitten Heart*, the image and its effect on Heart are fixed and permanent. The diamond, strongest of the gems, most perfectly reveals the reflection's mortifying strength to demand faithfulness. The warning above the castle's portal is stern because to be an unfaithful lover would be, in essence, not to love at all. As a term, "unfaithful lover" is oxymoronic. True to its name, the diamond, from the Greek αδάμας (*adámas*), is unalterable, unbreakable, untamable, and unconquerable. One *must* love and conform in blind submission to the phantasm; fidelity to Love and fidelity to the image are synonymous. As a mirror, the diamond transmits its properties onto Heart, transforming him forevermore into an unalterable simulacrum. Nevertheless, the mirror above the portal is not the only diamond here. While Heart and his companions climb the emerald toward the castle, they encounter myriads of diamonds scattered throughout the crevasses of the hill. Stronger than the emerald, these diamonds obstruct the truth this green stone attempts to transmit. The *dy-amant* (wounded lover) is everywhere and the self-as-image is hopelessly wounded beyond repair, proliferating endlessly throughout the dream's landscape.

Nonetheless, this proliferation at the Castle of Pleasure remains paradoxical, as the imagery that erotically charges everything around Heart simultaneously negates all hope of his fulfillment. Existing because of love for the image, it is consequently this same love that destroys him, for, as the Diamond Mirror demands, an unfaithful lover is not possible, but then neither is a faithful one. When Heart tries to rescue Sweet Mercy, he simply receives a disappointing kiss before Refusal attacks, punishing him for having attempted to possess an intangible fantasy and, after a violent fight, Lady Pity finds him, fallen and mortally wounded. In order to preserve him from prying eyes, she takes him to the shade of a nearby bush where his shadowy reflection, present even here, serves as a reminder that to love an image is to exist within the realm of the phantasm, outside of which there is no satisfaction. Even in death, therefore, the shadow of love is manifest and fidelity to the image cannot be swayed. Heart's last fall on the battlefield thus echoes his previous falls in the text, where the fall into the black waters below the bridge of the dream and fall before the Castle of Pleasure in the blinding sun signal this collapse of self and image. For, even though the mermaid *appears* true as she embraces the knight, she is simply a simulacrum without a gaze in a dream. Similarly, the light rendering Heart senseless is but a representation of the sun's rays rebounding off the walls of the castle. As such, both episodes mark the unavoidable sightlessness the lover experiences before the phantasm that blinds him to his own vision.

Accordingly, the *Love-Smitten Heart* exists solely due to the melancholic transposition of seen and unseen, real and unreal, and, as a microcosm of the entire text, the manuscript illumination for the Fountain of Fortune (Fig. 4.2) perfectly demonstrates this line of reasoning where the sun, bisecting the miniature, casts its blackened rays down upon the entire landscape. On the right, Heart, blind to the fictional reality of the image, stands before the stone, reads its inscription, and believes the words to be true while Desire, asleep with closed eyes on the left, embodies the lacking gaze of the image that must be ignored in order to realize the fiction of unity in love. As a result, René's attempts through writing to solve this paradox transforms the text into an unbreakable phantasmatic cycle, where the imagery of its language serves to reinforce its already refractive and traumatizing effects. René, like Heart, must now become part of this "endless loop" in order to experience an autobiographical reality where there is but a fictional allegory. His appeal at the start of the text to "see truly" is now called into question, as one must either remain blind to reality or be witness to an actualized falsehood. For, as René claims to see his "self" in the face of this paradox, the text responds by transforming him into a simulacrum that reflects its lacking principles and then effaces him from its surface. The *lyric I* used to express his personalized desire, already itself an unoriginal iteration from troubadour poetry, is also the most anonymous of pronouns. Anyone, including the reader, can and must claim this universalizing desire. The *reading I* though cannot escape its eradicating consequences and, falling into the *lyric I* of the *Love-Smitten Heart*, unavoidably commits the same error of misrecognition as the monarch. Like Heart, the audience thereby becomes a *dy-amant* (wounded lover), hopelessly divided by love.

If we are not aware of this, however, the text itself steps in to remind us. In his description of the Castle of Pleasure, the narrator states that: "Pour ce n'estoit pas merveille, a la façon que *le conte vous a divisé*, c'il rendoit grant lueur quant le souleil luisoit sus, combien que pas ne vous a divisé la moictié de la beaulté du beau chastel" [It is not surprising, according to what *the story has told you*, it emitted a great glow when the sun shone above, though it has not told even half of the castle's beauty].[36] To read the story with ourselves in the place of the *lyric I* is to accept its hopeful message that erotic fulfillment is possible, and this "the story has told you" [*le conte vous a divisé*]. Nonetheless, this initial reading of *le conte vous a divisé* is not the entire message. The story only relates half the beauty of the castle because its other half is terrifying. The attractive nature of the story and its illustrations blinds us to their horror. Like the Diamond

Mirror, the text not only refracts images but meaning as well, for, playing on the double signification of *diviser* in Middle French ("to tell/devise" or "to divide"), *le conte vous a divisé* must also be read as "the story has *divided* you." In the *Romance of the Rose*, Narcissus is *envers*, backward, because he is dead in the face of the phantasm. The initial sundering that occurs within René's mistaken reflection *en vers* (in verse), in the world of the text, coincides with his erasure. The *reading I* meets an identically unavoidable separation before the enticing story. This *has already occurred*, and, in the mirror of the *Book of the Love-Smitten Heart*, we find ourselves inevitably falling toward our own divided self, becoming, like it, a disembodied simulacrum, a perpetually open melancholic wound, with no hope of fulfillment. As such, the self is already sundered from the start and the text simply maintains this division as it demonstrates to us our own melancholic status. In the next chapter, I move from this notion of the perpetually open wound to that of repeated wounding, something to which René's work already alludes and the ways in which trauma, as the discourse that speaks to such iteration, allows for new understandings of narcissism as it relates to knowledge of what occurs during the confrontation with a narcissine image and the ability to witness to such an event.

NOTES

1. Portions of this chapter appeared as: Nicholas Ealy, "The Poet at the Mirror: René d'Anjou and Authorial Doubling in the *Livre du Coeur d'Amour épris*" in *Fifteenth-Century Studies* 37, ed. Barbara Gusick and Matthew Heintzelman (Rochester: Camden House, 2012): 17–46. *The Book of the Love-Smitten Heart* exists in seven manuscripts, two of which will be considered for this study. The Vienna manuscript (Österreichische Nationalbibliothek, Cod. Vind. 2597) has 127 folios measuring 290 x 207 mm, dates from approximately 1460, and contains sixteen framed miniatures. The Bibliothèque nationale de France manuscript 24399 has 137 folios measuring 310 × 215 mm and contains seventy miniatures.
2. Guillaume de Lorris and Jean de Meun, *Le Roman de la Rose*, ed. Armand Strubel (Paris: Librairie Générale Française, 1992), vv. 1568–71, 126, my translation.
3. David Hult, *Self-Fulfilling Prophecies: Readership and Authority in the First "Roman de la Rose"* (Cambridge: Cambridge University Press, 1986), 297.
4. Claire Nouvet, "A Reversing Mirror: Guillaume de Lorris' *Romance of the Rose*" in *Translatio Studii: Essays by His Students in Honor of Karl D. Uitti for His Sixty-Fifth Birthday*, ed. Renate Blumenfeld-Kosinski et al. (Amsterdam: Rodopoi, 2000), 194.

5. René d'Anjou, *Le Livre du Cœur d'amour épris*, ed. Florence Bouchet (Paris: Librairie Générale Française, 2003), 86. Quotations in Middle French, with verse and page numbers cited, when appropriate, are from this edition. English translations are my own.

6. Ibid., v. 6, 88.

7. For melancholy in the Middle Ages, see: Giorgio Agamben, *Stanzas: Word and Phantasm in Western Culture*, trans. Ronald L. Martinez (Minneapolis: University of Minneapolis Press, 1993), 11–28.

8. Sigmund Freud, "Mourning and Melancholia" in *The Standard Edition of the Complete Works of Sigmund Freud, Vol. 14*, trans. and ed. James Strachey (London: Hogarth, 1964), 245.

9. Ibid., 253; "Trauer und Melancholie" in *Psychologie des Unbewußten 3*, ed. Alexander Mitscherlich (Frankfurt: S. Fischer, 1994), 206.

10. René, *Cœur*, vv. 1–11 and 16, 88.

11. Nouvet recognizes this in the *Romance of the Rose*. See: "Reversing," 190.

12. François Garnier, *Le Langage de l'image au moyen âge: signification et symbolique* (Paris: Léopard d'or, 1983), 117.

13. René, *Cœur*, vv. 12–15, 88.

14. Erin Felicia Labbie, *Lacan's Medievalism* (Minneapolis: University of Minnesota Press, 2006), 128.

15. René, *Cœur*, vv. 75–82, 100.

16. Ibid., vv. 265–68, 124.

17. Ibid., 130.

18. Ibid., vv. 317–18 and 321–26, 132.

19. See Chapsters 2, 3, 4, and 5 of Agamben's *Stanzas*, 11–28.

20. René, *Cœur*, 132, 134.

21. Ibid., 98.

22. Freud, "Mourning," 245.

23. Ibid., 249; Freud, "Trauer," 206.

24. Agamben, *Stanzas*, 20.

25. Part of this discussion of melancholy is based on my previous work: Nicholas Ealy, "'Tu es déjà rentré?': Trauma, Narcissism and Melancholy in François Ozon's *Sous le sable* (2001)" in *Studies in French Cinema* 17.3 (2017), 217–35.

26. René, *Cœur*, vv. 1853–62, 400, 402.

27. Ibid., 394.

28. Kenneth J. Knoespel, *Narcissus and the Invention of Personal History* (New York: Garland, 1985), 86.

29. Ibid., op. cit. 86.

30. Jean Arrouye, "Le Cœur et son paysage" in *Le "Cuer" au moyen âge: réalité et sénéfiance*, ed. Margaret Bertrand (Aix-en-Provence: Université de Provence, 1991), 36.

31. Ibid., 38.
32. *Le Lapidaire en prose*, ed. Léopold Pannier (Paris: F. Vieweg, 1882), 294, translation mine.
33. For Pliny's commentary on Nero, see Book 37 of his *Natural History X*, ed. and trans. D.E. Eichholz (Cambridge: Loeb Classical Library, 1962), 212–15.
34. René, *Cœur*, 398.
35. See: Gilles Polizzi, "'Sens plastique': Le Spectacle des merveilles dans le *Livre du cuer d'amour epsris*" in *De l'étranger à l'étrange ou la 'conjointure' de la merveille*, ed. Margariet Rossi and Paul Bancourt (Aix-en-Provence: Université de Provence, 1988), 395–430.
36. René, *Cœur*, 398, my emphasis.

REFERENCES

Agamben, Giorgio. 1993. *Stanzas: Word and Phantasm in Western Culture*. Trans. Ronald L. Martinez. Minneapolis, MN: University of Minneapolis Press.

Arrouye, Jean. 1991. Le Cœur et son paysage. In *Le "Cuer" au moyen âge: réalité et sénéfiance*, ed. Margaret Bertrand, 27–42. Aix-en-Provence: Université de Provence.

Ealy, Nicholas. 2012. The Poet at the Mirror: René d'Anjou and Authorial Doubling in the *Livre du Coeur d'Amour épris*. *Fifteenth-Century Studies 37*, 17–46. Rochester: Camden House.

———. 2017. "Tu es déjà rentré?": Trauma, Narcissism and Melancholy in François Ozon's *Sous le sable* (2001). *Studies in French Cinema* 17 (3): 217–235.

Freud, Sigmund. 1964. Mourning and Melancholia. In *The Standard Edition of the Complete Works of Sigmund Freud, Vol. 14*. Trans. and Ed. James Strachey, 243–258. London: Hogarth.

———. 1994. Trauer und Melancholie. In *Psychologie des Unbewußten 3*, ed. Alexander Mitscherlich, 193–212. Frankfurt: S. Fischer.

Garnier, François. 1983. *Le Langage de l'image au moyen âge: signification et symbolique*. Paris: Léopard d'or.

Guillaume de Lorris and Jean de Meun. 1992. *Le Roman de la Rose*. Ed. Armand Strubel. Paris: Librairie Générale Française.

Hult, David. 1986. *Self-Fulfilling Prophecies: Readership and Authority in the First "Roman de la Rose"*. Cambridge: Cambridge University Press.

Knoespel, Kenneth J. 1985. *Narcissus and the Invention of Personal History*. New York: Garland.

Labbie, Erin Felicia. 2006. *Lacan's Medievalism*. Minneapolis, MN: University of Minnesota Press.

Le Lapidaire en prose. 1882. In *Les lapidaires français du moyen âge des XIIᵉ, XIIIᵉ et XIVᵉ siècles*. Ed. Léopold Pannier, 286–297. Paris: F. Vieweg.

Nouvet, Claire. 2000. A Reversing Mirror: Guillaume de Lorris' *Romance of the Rose*. In *Translatio Studii: Essays by His Students in Honor of Karl D. Uitti for His Sixty-Fifth Birthday*, ed. Renate Blumenfeld-Kosinski et al., 189–205. Amsterdam: Rodopoi.

Pliny. 1962. *Pliny: Natural History X (Books 36–37)*. Ed. and Trans. D.E. Einchholz. Cambridge, MA: Loeb Classical Library.

Polizzi, Gilles. 1988. "Sens plastique": Le Spectacle des merveilles dans le *Livre du cuer d'amours espris*. In *De l'étranger à l'étrange ou la "conjointure" de la merveille*, ed. Marguerite Rossi and Paul Bancourt, 395–430. Aix-en-Provence: Université de Provence.

René d'Anjou. 2003. *Le Livre du Coeur d'Amour épris*. Ed. Florence Bouchet. Paris: Librairie Générale Française.

PART III

The Wounded Self as Witness

CHAPTER 5

Narcissus and Trauma: Chrétien de Troyes's *Story of the Grail*

At the start of one of the most enigmatic scenes from Chrétien de Troyes's unfinished *Story of the Grail* (*Conte du Graal*) (c. 1181), Perceval, the hero of the romance, arises early one summer morning and, heading out in search of adventure, notices that it has snowed during the night. With the sun rising, a flock of geese, blinded by the brightness of the snow, catches his attention as they flee a pursuing falcon overhead. The falcon, however, attacks one of the geese midair, causing it to fall to the ground where it, "navree el col,/Si sainna trois goutes de sanc/Qui espandirent sor le blanc" [wounded in the neck, bled three drops of blood that spread out onto the white snow].[1] The combination of blood and snow transfixes Perceval, reminding him so much of the crimson lips and pale cheeks of his beloved Blancheflor, that he remains there for hours until the sun melts it away. This moment of prolonged *innamoramento* before a red-and-white image, evoking the narcissistic process of love so popular in courtly literature, can only be understood, according to Michelle Freeman, as nothing other than an intentional reading of the tale of Narcissus. For Ovid, who describes Narcissus's reflection as "in niveo mixtum candore ruborem" [blood-red mixed with snow white], approaches Chrétien's description of the image Perceval beholds[2]:

> The snow and blood-red [in Chrétien's work] are continually associated with blinding light. [...] The same detail is reiterated in another image Ovid had used to describe Narcissus as he dies. Narcissus fades or withers away

like the yellow wax in a flame or as *morning frost* under the warming rays of the sun. [...] All these details are completely shared as *metaphor* by the two texts, even to the point at which the pining-away of Narcissus parallels the evaporating of the blood drops themselves under the rays of the sun.[3]

The similarities Freeman uncovers between the fable and Chrétien's romance find their basis in the specular confrontation endemic to both texts involving a mistaken identification with a red-and-white image; Narcissus believes to see a flesh-and-blood adolescent who desires him, whereas Perceval's affection for Blancheflor increases when he perceives her face upon the frozen ground. Each character, in other words, identifies with a chimera, takes it to be *something else* other than what it is and, in the process, undergoes—to use the Lacanian term—a *méconnaissance* (*mis-recognition* in English).[4] For Narcissus and Chrétien's hero fail to see their own positioning before the image, and, in their misrecognition, find themselves in its place, a place from which they receive a deceptive sense of unity. Perceval, staring at the bright snow that has already blinded the geese, identifies with a likeness of his beloved that holds a false promise of reciprocity and, as with all narcissine encounters, sees something before him that is, in truth, not there. This experience reinforces for him the wounded nature of his selfhood, as he is forever separated from—and yet nonetheless longing for—libidinal satisfaction. Such misrecognition is something to which Perceval is blind, for he cannot see in the moment of its occurrence the injury that the image imposes upon him. Caught with this "double character of vision," he experiences what it is *to behold an image*, which, as Michael Newman posits in his discussion of the Narcissus myth, always involves a type of seeing that "wants to see and not to see," a type of seeing that transforms what is perceived into "a screen revealing and concealing a non-visible alterity—account[ing] for the possibility that vision here is ready to tip into trauma."[5]

I find compelling this link between trauma and the invisible alterity housed within the narcissine image, as it suggests that the blindness—the misrecognition—infiltrating the onlooker's vision is, at its core, traumatic, and not simply because Narcissus suffers a catastrophic fate at the end of his story. There is something more complex here in the collapse of vision and blindness, where vision, infiltrated by blindness, undergoes a sunder-ing before the image, an infiltration identical to the wounding alterity shaping Narcissus's selfhood. To become enraptured with a narcissine image, Newman suggests, is *to be traumatized* by the blinding misrecognition it imposes upon the viewer. But, of what does this trauma consist? How does it operate in conjunction with misrecognition? And how, ultimately, does it bring a greater understanding of Perceval's encounters with narcissine imagery throughout his adventures? To answer these questions, I turn to the origins of the term "trauma," which, coming from two related words in Greek, τραῦμα (*trauma*) and τιτρπσχω (*titrpscho*), meaning "wound" and "piercing," respectively, has been used to indicate, even in the classical period, "an injury where the skin is broken as a consequence of external violence, and the effects of such an injury upon the organism as a whole."[6] The etymology and definition of trauma prove key for the *Story of the Grail* in that every narcissine encounter Perceval experiences is an image—as in the blood-on-snow scene—put in conjunction *with a wound* resulting from a bodily piercing. To describe such lacerations, as in the attack upon the goose, these scenes almost always employ a form of the Old French term *navrer*, a verb referencing a specific type of injury that results from piercing or cutting a body—in short, the act, etymologically speaking, of trauma itself. As such, the *Grail* holds *navrer*-as-trauma as a repeated element that brings misrecognition to the center of its narrative and, in so doing, explores the blinding effects that the narcissine image has upon Perceval's desires and selfhood.

In conjunction with trauma's physical wounding though, the phenomenon, as evident from the mental distress Narcissus experiences, involves what contemporary thought considers to be psychological effects as well. And such a recognition of trauma's physical and psychological aspects has not escaped scholars studying the Middle Ages, for, while Wendy J. Turner and Christina Lee do concede that "[t]he physical trauma of a body is more in line with what the term 'trauma' meant in the premodern world: a wound," they nonetheless posit that: "In the Middle Ages, traumatic events, as defined today, were in abundance. There is evidence of trauma experienced by many parts of the population [...]. The evidence of individual psychological trauma and social trauma in poetry and literature, of mental and physical trauma in court records, of blunt and sharp force trauma on medieval skeletons is varied and rich."[7] In a similar vein, Freud, when speaking of traumatic neuroses in *Beyond the Pleasure Principle*, likewise joins trauma to a discussion of wounding in literature, seeking to understand how the two discourses inform one another. Before arriving at this literary intervention, however, he explores trauma's physical origins, understanding that the phenomenon stems from "accidents involving a risk to life" while presenting a variety of symptoms that appear comparable to other psychological disorders:

> The symptomatic picture presented by traumatic neurosis approaches that of hysteria in the wealth of its similar motor symptoms, but surpasses it as a rule in its strongly marked signs of subjective ailment (in which it resembles hypochondria or melancholia) as well as in the evidence it gives of a far more comprehensive general enfeeblement and disturbance of the mental capacities.[8]

Trauma, consequently, has come to imply physical wounding and, as Freud observes, *mental disturbance* resulting from a "psychological impact" that "retains the sense of a wound caused by an exterior agent."[9] Such an effect, I would argue, analogously finds itself in René's experience with Love's arrow in the *Love-Smitten Heart* (Chap. 4), where this weapon, a marker of the image's wounding gaze—the "exterior agent"—seems to pierce through his flesh, signaling that "his" desire is never integral but rather always divided, strangely operating inside and outside of his bodily confines. Within this context, trauma can be read, at least initially, as that wounding, which operates within the breakdown of oppositions (like *vision* and *blindness* or *within* and *without*), disturbing them in a manner that creates "a piercing or breach of a border that puts inside and outside into a strange communication" and opens "passageways between systems that were once discrete, making unforeseen connections that distress or confound."[10] That trauma has the power to collapse oppositions, however, makes it sound close to melancholy, the marker *par excellence* of narcissistic lovesickness that similarly collapses oppositions. When René's Heart, for example, is struck down by the sun's melancholic rays reflected off Love's castle, he is blinded to the reality of the image he beholds and ensnared in an illusory relationship with a lifeless entity. However, as I point out in the previous chapter, this event *recalls and repeats* the occurrence of Love's arrow hitting René's eye. As such, one cannot grasp the first blinding without examining it retrospectively through the collapse of vision and blindness caused by the sun's rays that, in turn, shroud all of Heart's adventures within the cloak of melancholic transpositions.

Dominick LaCapra, referencing this theoretical link between trauma and melancholy, speaks of trauma using the language of melancholy, likening it—not to a phenomenon that happens once—but rather to a type of *iterated melancholy* where "one is haunted or possessed by the past and performatively caught up in the compulsive repetition of traumatic scenes—scenes in which the past returns and the future is blocked or fatal-istically caught up in a melancholic feedback loop."[11] For LaCapra, trauma does not simply collapse oppositions, but, due to the repeated nature of its "melancholic feedback loop," involves a temporal aspect as well, where a haunting from the past remains ever present, creating "aporias and double binds" that "might be seen as marking a trauma that has not been worked through."[12] If, following LaCapra, trauma is to be cast as a type of iterative melancholy, the wounds of subjectivity, like I explore in Chap. 4, are main-tained through melancholy as *repetitively open*. As Roger Luckhurst argues, however, such repetition "has become a cultural shorthand for the conse-quences of traumatic events: individuals, collectives and nations risk trap-ping themselves in cycles of uncomprehending repetition unless the traumatic event is translated from repetition to the healthy analytic process of 'working through.'"[13] And it is this tension between repeating and working through trauma—if this is even possible—that finds itself at the heart of Perceval's adventures in Chrétien's *Grail*, for it is he who experi-ences wounds (*navrer*) on numerous occasions in the form of a narcissine image. One place to begin exploring the theoretical implications of such repetitively open woundings and the ways in which they may resist resolu-tion is to turn to Cathy Caruth's work on trauma where she, like LaCapra, links the phenomenon to an iterative structure.

Starting with a reading of Freud's *Beyond the Pleasure Principle*, Caruth explores how certain catastrophes from the past have a tendency to linger in the present, haunting those who have experienced them to quite a degree that a duplication of suffering appears "not to be initiated by the individual's own acts but rather appear as the possession of some people by a sort of fate, a series of painful events to which they are subjected, and which seem to be entirely outside their wish or control."[14] To discuss such horrors, she explains how Freud interestingly turns to literature—specifi-cally to two episodes from Tasso's sixteenth-century epic *Jerusalem Delivered*—to give what he calls "the most moving poetic picture of such a [traumatic] fate."[15] In this text, Tancred, the work's hero, unknowingly slays his beloved Clorinda in a duel while she is disguised. Traveling later through an enchanted forest, he strikes a tree housing her soul and unex-pectedly hears her voice come through the slashed bark—telling him that he has unwittingly harmed her yet once again. What Caruth finds so tell-ing about Freud's use of this tale to explore trauma is not so much the duplication of an unpleasant experience, but instead the way in which the wound carries a message emerging, not in the initial injury, but rather *in its repetition*. For it is in this iteration that the "enigma of the otherness [...] cries out from the wound, a voice that witnesses a truth that Tancred himself cannot fully know."[16] And, more often than not, such traumatic repetitions, she points out, come under the guise of *imagery*, as "intrusive hallucinations, dreams, [or] thoughts" continuously hark back to the event that sparked them, an event "not assimilated or experienced fully at the time, but only belatedly, in its repeated possession of the one who experiences it."[17] Building from Caruth, I want to demonstrate in this chapter that it is around an image that wounds—in a moment of narcissistic misrecognition—that narcissism and trauma, as a type of continuous melancholy akin to what is evident in the *Love-Smitten Heart*, might begin to speak a similar language. With this in mind, I would argue that the phantasmatic process with its emphasis upon imagery, so central to the scenes of narcissine wounding in the *Grail*, is the space in which trauma and narcissism meet, to the point where one must begin to speak in terms of a *traumatic narcissism* and *narcissistic trauma*. As such, I focus in this chapter on the aspect of trauma that deals specifically with the image and the ways in which it, by finding itself at the heart of the repetitive experience, complicates notions of the specular ordeal that comes to define, within a narcissistic framework, knowledge of self.

This appeal to understand traumatic narcissism and narcissistic trauma through repetitive wounding begins to make sense, for, in the blindness— the misrecognition—inherent to any confrontation with a narcissine image, there is *always* a *failure to see, to comprehend* in the instant of desire's wounding. Like Tancred, Narcissus in the lay (Chap. 2), seduced by the image while ignorant of the violent laceration it inflicts upon him at the fountain, remains strangely "absent" to what happens, an absence that he tries to regain in the "melancholic feedback loop" of *je me plaing* ("I lament myself"), the moment of iterative wounding that only works to reinforce his already-sundered self. Narcissus's failure to see, in truth a failure of being "present" to his "own" sundering, renders narcissistic trauma/traumatic narcissism as an event, it would appear, that *has no witnesses*. It is for this reason that Caruth, while not addressing narcissism, can speak of trauma in the language of a "missed event," because it is here where past and present collapse, where chronology is *wounded*. The traumatic event, in other words, always comes *too soon*, without warning, unlocatable in the moment of its arrival. At the same time, it also comes *too late*, for only in retrospect does it reveal the impact of its puzzling nature.[18]

To view a narcissine image and to undergo the misrecognition it automatically exerts is to experience such a crisis of witnessing, for this is to be at the crossroads of knowing that *something has happened* but not knowing *precisely what has happened*. Read through the lens of trauma, Ovid's tale constitutes an attempt to explain how human subjectivity always emerges as a "missed event," as something bringing forth the self as *unknowably traumatized*. For, due to the blindness at the heart of this encounter, Narcissus's self emerges as divided ever before he can grasp the catastrophe that has just happened to him. To experience having a sense of self, of a desiring self—to be conscious of one's humanity, in other words—is to have undergone the traumatic wounding of misrecognition, of alterity. In an identical manner, Perceval in Chrétien's *Grail* fails to witness to the same deadly prophecy of self-knowledge imparted to Narcissus, where he cannot grasp the trauma—the *navrer*—endemic to each of his encounters with a narcissine image. And, as Caruth argues, in this place where oppositions collapse, a "complex relationship between knowing and not knowing" emerges at the heart of the traumatic repetitions that not only obfuscates understanding, but begins to speak in a language that similarly operates at the juncture of knowing and not knowing, a polyvocal language that is the same as literature itself.[19] It is here, in this context of an iterative wound that speaks but does not easily reveal its own language, that I begin my analysis of Chrétien's last-known romance.

5.1 The Wound and Knowledge (*Navrez* and *Nel Savez*)

The tension between knowing and not knowing, so central to trauma, is what establishes the *Story of the Grail* from its opening scenes. For this romance, understood by many critics to be a type of *Bildungsroman* tracing the maturation and educative process of its central character, begins with a naive Perceval ignorant of his family's legacy and even his own name. The progressing narrative deals in large part with the struggles he experiences with his ever-emerging identity and, most importantly, with the problems of navigating a world where his selfhood is questioned through a series of encounters with narcissine imagery. Such ignorance about himself, however, stems in large part from his mother, who has aimed—and for good reason—to shield her son from the violence and humiliation the institution of knighthood has brought upon the family, working instead to impart to her son an identity grounded in religious principles. While out hunting early in the romance though, Perceval *does* encounter a group of knights—the first he has ever seen—and returns home so awestruck that his mother decides to tell him how chivalry is the cause of their familial shame. His father, she relates, was one of the most glorious knights in an edenic land where the family had previously lived, but came to experience hardship when his body was harmed: "Vostre peres, si nel savez,/Fu parmi la jambe *navrez*/Si que il mehaigna del cors" [Your father, you do not know this, was *wounded* between the thighs, so his body was infirm].[20] Such an injury had immediate consequences, for the father fell into poverty and the family had to move to the Waste Forest where Perceval and his mother still reside. Additionally, Perceval had two brothers who, on the counsel of their father, went to different courts seeking knighthood, were dubbed the same day. and, while returning home, died in combat (with birds even pecking out the eyes of the oldest sibling's corpse). These losses resulting from the father's wound are what in turn spark the mother's mourning that will not allow for any closure since her husband's death. It would appear that the blindness of the father, who continued to uphold the corrupt values of a profession that brought him harm and shame to his family, comes to be reflected—and tragically so—in the demise of his oldest sons, a blindness that Perceval, in turn, is fated to carry through misrecognition in his own encounters with narcissine imagery.

Consequently, the injuries inflicted upon the men of Perceval's family speak to the horrors of chivalry, for, even as it transforms itself into an enterprise that is *wounding* and *wounded* in the *Grail*, still seems to be something that can bestow power and stability upon those who practice it. This is the reason why Perceval refuses to listen to his mother's advice regarding his family's history, insisting he does *not understand* her speech all the while proclaiming his intent to seek out the king who will make him a knight. And such a failure on his part to comprehend his mother links to the father's wound, evident in her own instruction where she, through rhyme, joins the injury of her deceased husband, his *parmi la jambe navrez* (wound between the legs), to her son's ignorance—*nel savez* (you do not know). By conflating her husband's wound with her son's lack of understanding, she therefore places the image of this piercing at the center of Perceval's legacy. Of what, though, does such a legacy consist?

To answer this question, I find it important to examine the implications of the specific site of where this wound occurs on the father's body, for the space between the legs is where the penis and testicles are located. Not surprisingly, *Grail* scholars have tended to interpret such wounding as a euphemism for sterility and castration. Such castration, however, does not simply represent the physical damage to or loss of the father's penis and the symbolic implications it brings (the loss of masculinity, authority, and paternal prowess), but also signifies that the father's body is forever divided, irrevocably split and separated from the organ that—within patriarchal discourse—makes the male body *what it is*. In addition, the penis also designates the father's libido, the potency of his sexual longing, and, with its removal, the sundering of his desire that renders any wholeness it might seem to provide as permanently frustrated. From the paternal wound, then, emerges an entire discourse on the impossibility of bodily integrity and the lack inherent to desire—a discourse, in other words, on the injury narcissistic trauma inflicts upon the self, the very cry of Narcissus's *je me plaing* ("I lament myself"). The father, as a pierced body, as a *traumatized self* in the etymological sense of the term, subsequently stands as an intergenerational appeal regarding a certain knowledge of selfhood as *divided through trauma*. Although preceding Perceval's adventures, this is *the* trauma highlighting the ignorance that follows him throughout his adventures, positing him as a figure who carries what Caruth would refer to as an "impossible history" of traumatic legacy, a legacy transforming him into "a symptom of history [he] cannot entirely possess" but nonetheless calling out to be understood through the melancholic feedback loop of narcissine imagery in the text.[21]

Such an "impossible history" is made evident in the episode preceding Perceval's conversation with his mother where he, while out hunting, perceives what he believes to be a diabolical force making its way through the Waste Forest. Recalling his mother's words to make the sign of the cross during times of danger, he decides to ignore her advice and instead readies his javelins to strike down the enemy. What emerges though are not demons but, to his amazement, a group of questing knights whom he mistakes for angels and God incarnate:

> Et quant il les vit en apert,
> Que du bois furent descovert,
> Et vit les haubers fremïans
> Et les elmes clers et luisans,
> Et vit le blanc et le vermeil
> Reluire contre le soleil,
> [...]

> Si li fu molt bel et molt gent,
> Et dist: "Ha! sire Diex, merchi!
> Ce sont angle que je voi chi.
> [...]
> Chi voi je Damedieu, ce quit,
> Car un si bel en i esgart
> Que li autre, se Diex me gart,
> N'ont mie de biauté la disme.
> [...]
> Et je aorerai cestui
> Et toz les angles aprés lui."

And when he saw them coming out of the woods and into the open space, he saw the gleaming hauberks and the bright and shining helmets, and saw the white and the red armor shining in the sun, he found all this beautiful and noble and said: "Lord God, give thanks! These are angels I see here. Here I see the Lord God, for he is more beautiful than the others I behold who, God save me, do not have a tenth of his beauty. I will adore this one and all the angels with him."[22]

Spellbound by the brilliant red-and-white armor and weaponry, colors recalling the beauty of Narcissus's reflection, Perceval undergoes here the "blinding vision"—the misrecognition—inherent to any narcissine encounter, the same blinding vision embodied by his father and brothers regarding knighthood. For, in this moment where he is captivated and captured by such a duplicitously appealing image, the misrecognition he experiences shields him from the truth of what he witnesses and, in an idolatrous move, he not only mistakes the bellicose knights for divine creatures, but sees himself *in their place*, united to them in his overwhelming longing to be *just as they are*:

> Ainc mais chevalier ne conui,
> [...] ne nul n'en vi
> N'onques mais parler n'en oï,
> Mais vos estes plus biax que Diex.
> Cor fuisse je ore autretiex,
> Ausi luisanz et ausi fais.

I have never met any knights, I have never seen any or ever heard about them. But you, you are more beautiful than God. If only I could be the same, so bright and well-fashioned.[23]

Standing in for the dazzling courtly lady, who—as in Chrétien's other romances—typically embodies the reflective properties of the narcissine image, the knights become Perceval's first object of desire in the *Grail*. For, in his haste to imitate them, he believes this "other" before him to be his destined "self," confusing the knights with a reflection of himself, with a living mirror of his own idealized self before him. And of course, as evidenced in Ovid's myth, the desire to conform to an image marks the self, not as a source, but as a *byproduct of the image*, thereby destroying any sense of an integral subject. Nonetheless, the sunlight and references to God in the scene, seeming to appeal to a source, point to Perceval's desire for unified wholeness, for an autogenerative and self-coinciding source radiating beauty, power, and strength. However, as in the adventures of René's Heart at the Castle of Love (Chap. 4), the light here is not a source—it is *not the sun*—but a reflection, an iteration of the sun's luminescence; the medium allowing for vision blinds Perceval to the truth of his own vision and the nature of his own self. And this is something escaping his comprehension, something he *fails to know* (*nel savez*), arriving in an ungraspable moment that remains, for him, unlocatable, as his vision, desire and self are irrevocably pierced through with the absent gaze of the narcissine simulacrum. In the trauma of misrecognition where he mistakes knighthood for divinity, he cannot understand, even when his mother later tells him, that knighthood can represent anything other than the potency he believes to witness here. The self emerging as nothing more than a destroyed repercussion thus bears the mark of this blinding misrecognition that wounds it at its source, at this "source" of trauma itself. Each iteration of the narcissine image in the *Grail* will pose Perceval with this same problem, reinforcing the wounding—the *navrer*—of the self, reflecting this wounding *onto him*, a wounding to which he remains blind in the instant of its occurrence. Far from benign, the reflective surface encapsulating the knights sparks his desire in a *fictional direction*, as he believes the chivalric body, appearing as beautiful and well-formed, is a model of stability, of *unwounded wholeness*.

In a stark divergence from Chrétien's previous romances, which together form a corpus dedicated to exploring the role of the knight as hero within the Arthurian realm, the *Grail*, whose ethos Perceval's mother embodies through her instruction, continuously maligns chivalry in favor of charity and religious fidelity. For, although the Arthurian world still serves as the canvas for Perceval's adventures, this romance marks a turning away from the problems that plagued the knights of

Chrétien's previous tales who are able to rescue the court from inner turmoil. Quite the opposite is true here, where chivalry, marred by a fundamental blindness to the realities of its own divisiveness upon the self and caught up in a misrecognition of its own traumatic effects, remains incapable of resolving tensions within the narrative. Instead, the text denounces chivalry as a crime barring Perceval from any truths regarding the nature of his subjectivity.

Knighthood consequently has the same divisive effect upon Perceval as it does upon his father, and his ensnarement before the image of chivalry narratively prefigures—while chronologically repeating—the father's wound through the legs. For, in this scene of *innamoramento*, of selfhood itself, Perceval is drawn to possess the image he sees and mirror it by becoming a knight, a pursuit that will haunt him during the remainder of the romance. In the *Grail*, desire for knighthood as a source of unity and stability thereby becomes a contagion, resulting in a series of wounded bodies that is passed on through Perceval—as if from father to son—during his adventures. Because of this, the longing sparked within him carries forward the legacy of the castrated sundering of the father's chivalric body, really the truth of the *self as divided*, a truth he does not know even in its repetition. For this reason, Perceval's inheritance—in fact his history itself—remains an iterated wound causing him to mirror the lacerated body of his father and, through his quest for chivalric greatness, ensures its continuation. In this symbolic reinscription of trauma's *navrez* (wounding) and *nel savez* (not-knowing), where the failure to know the history of a wound comes to the fore, Perceval, trapped by the stabilizing force of the deceptively beautiful narcissine image, unknowingly repeats a paternal ignorance that possesses him—has already possessed him—speaking through him and beyond his control.

It is for this reason that, once Perceval takes the initiative to leave and become a knight, wounded bodies within the *Grail* begin to proliferate, with his mother as the first casualty—fainting, as if dead—while her son, ignoring her, rides off into the forest. Inflicting once again upon his mother the sundering of her family, and then not to come to her aid as he pursues chivalry, marks Perceval as a naively malevolent force within the text, carrying with him not simply his traumatic inheritance, but now the stain of

> original sin in the fullest sense of the term, in a theological sense, for in the immediate wake of this demonic temptation, rupture and revolt, traits eminently satanic, manifest themselves in the child and his relation to his

mother, in the creature and its relation to the Creator. For such is the infamous sin of Perceval: a hostile and monstrous separation from the mother, who is left for dead.[24]

With this rejection of the mother now linked to the evils of chivalry, Perceval, the sole person left in his family who might resolve the chaos infesting the Waste Forest, seems to be the least prepared to do so. And because of his blindness before the image, it appears he will simply continue to be incapable of seeing what is before him. For, as Jean-Charles Huchet argues in his discussion of Perceval's encounter with the knights, "the image [in this scene] misleads; it captures the senses so that the senses continue to fail. Knighthood imposes itself on Perceval in a burst of light where white and red come together so we can better follow the trajectory of his sinfulness."[25] All he can accomplish, it would appear, is to inflict wounds repeatedly—within contexts of red-and-white narcissine imagery—while believing he is advancing knightly ideals. In his first adventure, for instance, he finds a maiden alone in a red tent and, despite her protests, takes her ring and steals a kiss from her. Her lover, believing she has now been unfaithful, consequently tortures her—and to the point that her skin is scarred, cracked, and burned. Perceval then kills the Red Knight by shooting him through the eye with a javelin, a blow that—while mimicking the trajectory of Love's arrow upon the desiring body—instantly kills his rival. Donning his blinded opponent's armor, spoils of the match, Perceval continues in his adventures now as the Red Knight, believing himself to be a paragon of chivalric prowess all the while failing to see how this attack carries with it the implications of pierced and divided selfhood, the implications of traumatic *navrez* (wounding), harking back to the sundering of his father's wounded body and his own encounter with the knights in the Waste Forest.

5.2 Blancheflor's Mirror: Agape and the Courtly Lady

The repetition of wounding in a chivalric context encounters its more traditionally amorous counterpart at the Castle of Beaurepaire where Perceval, now the Red Knight, meets Blancheflor (White Flower), a maiden who, like Alain's figure of Nature, bears a striking similarity to Ovid's narcissine reflection (see Chap. 3). For, like it, she has long golden hair, bright and shining eyes, and a countenance resembling carved stone or ivory that establishes her, similar to the luminescent knights in the

Waste Forest, as an image of seeming transcendence, beauty, and stability. Her embodiment of red and white ("avenoit en son vis/Li vermeus sor le blanc assis" [the vermilion seated on her white face befitted her]), now a regular combination of colors in the *Grail*, additionally gives her the capacity to strike Perceval with the violence of *innamoramento*, from without and beyond his control, in a way that repeats the traumatic wounding of self transmitted by the narcissine image.[26] With Perceval as the Red Knight and Blancheflor as the White Flower though, the text appears to have one color defining each character while simultaneously combining both colors together on the maiden's face. And this confusion continues into the night when, agitated and unable to sleep, the White Flower dons a red dress as her guest, the Red Knight, reposes on white sheets. Bathed in sweat, she walks to his bedchamber and, finding him already asleep, begins to lament over his body, wetting him so much that he awakens, surprised to find his face drenched in her tears.

The confluence of red and white, for one thing, serves to highlight the absence of any singularity Perceval believes to possess, the absence of singularity that emerged in the Waste Forest in his confrontation with the knights who themselves embody these combined hues. For the whiteness infiltrating the Red Knight, the whiteness coming from and already mixed with Blancheflor's redness, repeats the wounding of disintegrated selfhood, the self that is always pierced by alterity in its emergence, destroyed—liquefied like Narcissus—in its birth. It is no surprise, as the couple becomes mirror images of one another in their mixed coloring, that Blancheflor, due to her sweat and tears, literalizes the liquefying effect she has upon Perceval's subjectivity, for he awakens to find that he *is* already wet, with any sense of an individualized selfhood *already dissolved*.

Blancheflor, though, is not simply a watery form, but also is a watery form in mourning, coming to Perceval to explain her distress due to the continued violence she suffers at the hands of a neighboring knight's bellicose nature. For, as Blancheflor explains to her guest, her castle has been under siege by Aguingueron, a warrior who has captured and killed most of her men. Now, with few left to defend her, she fears he will defeat her castle and that Clamadeu of the Isles, for whom Aguingueron works, will take her captive. In order to provide her comfort, Perceval invites Blancheflor into his bed where the two, like reflections of one another, remain all night, with mouths and arms together in such a way that they resemble the structure established by Narcissus and his watery image as he longs to hold and kiss it:

Li uns lez l'autre, bouche a bouche,
Juisqu'al main que li jors aproche.
Tant li fist la nuit de solas
Que bouche et boche, bras a bras,
Dormirent tant qu'il ajorna.

They lay one against the other, mouth to mouth, until morning came. She took so much comfort from this all night that, mouth to mouth, arm to arm, they slept until dawn.[27]

Perceval's awakening into a liquefying narcissism, furthered by the chastely erotic night he spends with Blancheflor, is, however, also shot through with the diabolical forces of knighthood, a world in which the maiden is firmly ensconced. For, as the niece of Gornemont de Gohort, the seasoned knight Perceval visits before arriving at Beaurepaire and from whom he receives his instruction in chivalry, she fully comprehends the perils of arms and masculine prowess. At the same time, though, as the traditional courtly lady, she acts as the knight's love interest who, as a radiant incarnation of the narcissine image, mirrors her goodness onto the hero for his edification. And this is because, as Frederick Goldin explains, the courtly lady typically: "bestows honor; as a mirror reflects the beauty of physical things, she reflects moral perfection. She reflects honor upon us, and thus enables us to recognize the honor that is perfect in her. By her gifts we are led back to her. She is a mirror, and the light by which we see whatever is reflected in that mirror."[28] It is for this reason that Blancheflor incarnates a beauty that is specifically divine in nature, for, as the text twice emphasizes, it is God himself, and not the more common figure of Nature, who has fashioned her. And, because Perceval encounters the narcissine image Blancheflor embodies, this scene evokes, as with his encounter of the knights in the Waste Forest, a second traumatic misrecognition of what he beholds. In this search for another divine origin, his false sense of integrity strengthens; he has already gotten his armor and achieved his lady. He is now, as far as appearances go, a "complete knight."

At this nexus between knighthood and godliness, Blancheflor has the power to serve as a destabilizing force for Perceval, and not simply because her tears point to the liquefying effect undermining the seemingly perfected body of his chivalry. The more Perceval resembles Blancheflor—in his coloring, in the way he sleeps as she does—the more his erotic longing puts him in an intersubjective position, becoming a self defined through love for another. It is here the discourse of *fin'amor* in the *Grail* aligns itself with another mode of intersubjective love outlined in its prologue, for this is where Chrétien orients his readers to charity—that love based on agape—as the central theme of his romance:

> Diex est caritez, et qui vit
> En carité selonc l'escrit,
> Sainz Pols le dist et je le lui,
> Il maint en Dieu, et Diex en lui.

God is charity, and he who lives in charity, according to the Holy Scriptures, Saint Paul says this, and I have read it there, lives in God and God in him.[29]

Charity, lauded as co-equivalent to God, is established not simply as a model for love, but also as the definition of selfhood that—exactly like narcissistic *fin'amor*—breaks down oppositions between self and other, sameness and difference. As a mutual exchange of selfless giving between two parties, charity does not allow for a sense of selfhood that is untouched or not already infiltrated by an intersubjective alterity. For, whoever practices such love will forever be united, not simply to others, but to God as well, sharing with him a bond that coexists equally in both. As evident in the prologue to the *Grail*, this love requires a certain understanding that the other—the image of the other—will always dissolve the self, where any sense of individuality becomes willingly lost and wounded as the self opens up to the possibility of the other's needs. In the iteration of narcissistic imagery, each encounter Perceval has with compositions of red and white (with the knights in the Waste Forest, here with Blancheflor) presents itself as another test calling out for such understanding and, due to this, unites the theological and mythical discourses intertwined throughout the romance. And this is because the lacerated self and its traumatic repetition, as evidenced with Perceval's father, his brothers and his own self, is necessary to understanding chivalry in the *Grail*. For, as L.O. Fradenburg argues, the wounding inherent to knighthood comes to be linked, not simply to its violent overtones of physical injuries, but also to its potentially transcendental imperative to help those in need. These demonstrations of agapeic love stem from a desire, she posits, to save the notion of "selfhood" through an understanding of its unavoidable intersubjectivity:

> Heightening the fascination of un/certainty, the courtly warrior takes himself [...] so as to transform, correct, and purify [himself] and find salvation. In chivalric ordinances and romances, this "subjectification" works clearly on the level of the group as well as the individual subject. The nobleman is

to re-create himself as a rescuer and defender. [...] To sacrifice to the other on whom one's desire is founded is readily assimilated to helping oneself.[30]

In this construction of the self through coming to the aid of others, agape simultaneously works toward annihilating the self further—creating it through its own destruction: "Charity [...] obscures and exploits the interdependence of sameness and difference in the subject. If the '*I is an other*,' there is no pure self, no pure selflessness, no purely selfless love, and no pure love of self."[31] Blancheflor's role in the *Grail*, as the embodiment of a narcissistic and agapeic imperative, because they have the same structural effect upon selfhood, serves to highlight not simply the connection between the two, but also establishes the course for the remainder of Perceval's encounters with wounded bodies. The next day, for instance, he defeats Clamadeu and Aguingueron, wounding the latter through his shield ("parmi l'escu *navrez*"), acts done on behalf of Blancheflor so she might, through his agapeic intervention, be protected from harm.[32]

At the same time, he sends both troublemakers to Arthur's court as a way of confirming his dominance over them and, in so doing, aggrandizes his status—and his supposed integrity—as a knight. In Perceval's confrontation with images of the wounded and divided body, in Blancheflor's narcissistic countenance, in his own mirrored experience with the maiden, and in his attack on Aguingueron, there is a repeated ethical appeal—through the romance's emphasis on agapeic love—for a certain type of *proper witnessing* to occur before the image. It is rather a consistent failure to witness, due to misrecognition, that Perceval undergoes each time, a failure exemplified by his adherence to a false ideal of chivalry's power, beauty, and integrity. His wounding, his *navrer*, of Aguingueron in this episode is fraught with tension because, although harming another to help his lady, it also reinscribes the wounding of the chivalric body to which Perceval remains woefully blind. Such an encounter with injured knights at Beaurepaire, however, prepares the way for his central test at the Grail Castle, where he has an imperative of witnessing to the Fisher King's wounds in order to restore this monarch's realm to prosperity.

5.3   Perceval and the Grail: The Failure of Witnessing

Perceval's adventures at the Grail Castle provide his first confrontation with an injured body he did not wound himself but which, nonetheless, highlights the recurrent trauma haunting him. At the start of the scene, he arrives at the Fisher King's castle and is led into a great room where he sees his host supporting himself by the elbow and resting in bed. The monarch, greeting his young guest, informs him that he does not find it easy to rise from his reclining position, something he mentions once again before leaving for bed: "'Jou n'ai nul pooir de mon cors,/Si covenra que on m'en port'" [I no longer have strength in my body, I will have to be carried from here].[33] Beginning and ending the scene with mentions of his wounded body, the Fisher King marks his entire encounter with Perceval at the Grail Castle with a figure of chivalry—in stark contrast to the knights in the Waste Forest—that is frail and sickly. And yet, despite the fact that the king must recline the entire time he spends with Perceval, the knight remains silent, never acknowledging his host's weakness.

Perceval's reluctance to speak turns more curious when, while seated next to the Fisher King, a procession begins with a squire who, coming forth into the great room, carries a white lance with a bleeding tip. The presence of such a seemingly miraculous piece of weaponry does *cause* Perceval to wonder about it, but he never expresses himself openly. More people follow, carrying burning candles, a Grail outshining all the lights in the room, a silver carving platter—and then the Grail appears again, this time uncovered. Mimicking elements of his encounter with the knights in the Waste Forest (the same colors, the dazzling light), Perceval, unlike this earlier scene where he was eager to talk, continues to remain silent, deciding instead to inquire about everything the following morning. Upon awakening the next day, though, he finds the castle deserted and, searching for an explanation, encounters a maiden (who is, of course, his cousin as well) who tells him the Fisher King is infirm because he suffers from a wound:

> [...] il fu en une bataille
> *Navrez* et mehaigniez sanz faille,
> Si que puis aidier ne se pot,
> Qu'il fu ferus d'un gavelot
> Parmi les quisses ambesdeus,
> S'en est encor si angoisseus[.]

He was, during a battle, *wounded* and truly mutilated, to such an extent that he cannot support himself on his own. It was a javelin that wounded him between the thighs. He is still in anguish because of this.[34]

The *navrer* (wounding) from which the Fisher King suffers, however, is not a unique wound. Having been struck through the thighs, he shares an injury identical to that of Perceval's father and, like him, is linked to the sterility of knighthood, the symbolic loss of patriarchal authority and the impossibility of corporeal integrity—linked to the wound, in other words, that echoes the cry of Narcissus's *je me plaing* ("I lament myself"). Perceval's silence in the face of such wounding, though, is curious *and* expected. Curious because he has already been loquacious, beginning with his encounter with the knights in the Waste Forest where, betraying his naiveté and foolishness, his *first question* about their weaponry concerns their lance. However, when faced this time with another lance—and one that bleeds!—he remembers the words of Gornemont de Gohort, Blancheflor's uncle who instructed him in proper chivalric behavior, telling him to refrain from talkativeness. This advice has tragic consequences, for had Perceval asked about the lance and grail, he learns from his cousin, his question would have restored the Fisher King to health and his lands to prosperity. Knighthood, in other words, fraught with problems dividing it against itself, has proven to work on behalf of its own destruction. Unlike his confrontations with the Red Knight, Aguingueron or Clamadeu, Perceval does not need to raise a single weapon in order to wound as his silence of misrecognition and ignorance maintains the trauma of knighthood. An image of impenetrable knightly prowess has come to possess Perceval—even more so now given his defeat of Aguingueron and Clamadeu—and the narcissine imagery at the Grail Castle blinds him in his desire for such unbroken wholeness. To question would be to call attention to the injured chivalric body, and, in his failure to ask, he attempts to protect himself from a *navrer*, from a wounded knighthood, that has already occurred. For him to recognize the infirm body next to him in the Grail Castle would be to go against the shining image of integrity he believes to have experienced in the Waste Forest and, because of this, "he does not want to know about pain [...] because he is fascinated by a certain vision of the chivalric body as unwoundable, omnipotent. His fascination with the glory of knighthood seems to be based on criminal ignorance and denial of pain, wounding, and impotence."[35] In short, he refuses to ask because he refuses to know, condemning himself to repeat the *nel savez*, the *not knowing*, of the injured paternal/knightly body. In this mute refusal of his own identity, he consequently opens a space for the divided body of knighthood to *continue to speak* of its own wounding, to continue the iteration of traumatic narcissism.

The adventure at the Grail Castle represents a dual failure for Perceval, as he remains incapable of seeing knighthood as anything but a representative of wholeness and that the self is already wounded, having undergone the narcissistic division necessary for its existence, the narcissistic division causing it to emerge already infiltrated by alterity. He, in short, fails to see the Fisher King's pierced body as a reflection of his own wounded self. This is a rejection of charity, for to have asked about the bleeding lance, most obviously a weapon that *has already caused injury*, bearing the mark of having pierced and altered flesh, would have been to draw attention to the Fisher King's infirmity, to accept the implications of wounding and to know that knighthood itself is, in its inception, in his family's legacy, in the call to agapeic love, a fundamentally wounded principle. The bleeding lance during the Grail procession subsequently constructs the image of chivalric power while corrupting it as well, exposing the incomprehensible violence of the traumatic moment that rendered Perceval's division in the first place.

The internal divisions silencing Perceval, though, do not just affect his own voice, but also his mother's. When Gornemont instructs the young knight in chivalry, he not only warns him not to speak too much, but also not to tell others that his mother was his primary teacher and, above all else, not to repeat any of the advice she gave him. Perceval's silence is intimately bound to the silencing of the mother for, as his cousin tells him the morning after the Grail procession, his misfortunes have come from the sin he committed *against his mother*, who did indeed die from grief when he left her. This is his original sin, his "pechié" (*sin*—the exact word the maiden uses), as knighthood itself has caused him to erase the maternal voice of instruction in charity, the voice, in other words, of the divided self.[36] To deny his mother's speech is to deny the voice of the other speaking through him. Gornemont, it turns out, has reinforced within Perceval an image of chivalry unadulterated by alterity, an image of independent wholeness. For, just as Perceval fails to acknowledge the Fisher King's suffering in his blindness to a false sense of chivalric integrity, he fails to see that the Grail procession presents "the image of an error, of a crime materialized" while the bleeding lance preceding it "suggests a murder."[37] As such, the violence he committed against his mother goes unacknowledged, as does her suffering in his haste to leave her and become a knight. And his denial of his mother's suffering—of her mourning—takes on ever-increasing urgency, for now, the scene of drops of blood falling from the lance like tears becomes the third scene, after his mother's and Blancheflor's weeping, that contains references to mourning. At each confrontation where an image of mourning reflects itself onto his subjectivity, there exists an imperative for Perceval to recognize his lack of understanding, and yet, this is an imperative, given the misrecognition he repeatedly undergoes, to which he fails to witness. The *Grail* therefore joins trauma not simply to an iterated melancholy, but additionally to a repeated mourning, for in each narcissistic encounter where the wound of Perceval's not knowing, his *nel savez*, remains open, there is also an appeal to acknowledge—and to mourn—the wounded self. But he is not yet ready, for another repetition is also at work here:

> Perceval's criminal indifference towards his mother is punished by a repeated indifference, this time towards the Fisher King. Chrétien's text depicts the operation of a surprising law: the criminal who does not want to know his crime will be forced to repeat it. But with a difference: the second time around he is forced to know himself as a criminal although he still does not know that the crime of which he is accused is in fact the repetition of a previous and unacknowledged crime.[38]

Forced to repeat the sin of having caused the death of his mother, the knowledge of which continues to escape him, this original fault now joins itself to the iterated narcissine images that still traverse Perceval's journey. The remainder of his adventures grapple with the question on this guilt stemming from *not knowing* (*nel savez*) as the mother's words return to him, define who he is, and inform the wounding (*navrer*) he encounters. How might traumatic narcissism, which has thus far caused what seem to be irreparable catastrophes in the *Grail*, contain the seeds of its own salvific narrative as well? Answers begin to emerge in the blood-on-snow scene and Perceval's encounter with his maternal uncle on Good Friday.

5.4   BLOOD ON SNOW: THE GAZE OF THE OTHER

The blood-on-snow scene, with which I begin the present chapter, is perhaps the narcissine encounter within the romance most faithful to its Ovidian source, all the while setting up a distinct *narrative of blood* in Perceval's adventures that, beginning with the lance in the Grail Castle, continues through the meeting with his uncle. At the same time, the episode combines his experience at Beaurepaire with the consequences of his failure to speak at the Grail Castle, providing another appeal for him to contemplate his divided subjectivity and agapeic responsibilities couched within the eroticism of Blancheflor's narcissine image. It is at the start of the scene that the text reinstates the melancholic feedback loop of trauma, calling for knowledge of self through wounding—through *navrer*—with the goose attacked by the falcon:

> La jante fu navree el col,
> Si sainna trois goutes de sanc
> Qui espandirent sor le blanc,
> Si sambla natural color.
> [...]
> Quant Perchevax vit defoulee
> Le noif sur coi la jante jut,
> Et le sanc qui entor parut,
> Si s'apoia desor sa lance
> Por esgarder cele samblance;
> Que li sanz et la nois ensamble
> La fresche color li resamble
> Qui ert en la face s'amie[.]

The goose was wounded in the neck and bled three drops of blood that spilled out onto the white snow, which seemed like natural coloring. When Perceval saw the crushed snow where the goose had lain, and the blood that appeared around, he leaned against his lance to look at the semblance, for the blood and snow together resembled the fresh color upon his beloved's face.[39]

Given that Perceval perceives the blood and snow to be an image of his beloved, this is a scene of *innamoramento*, for the combination of colors stupefies him to the point that the knights who subsequently find him believe him to be *asleep*. And this is because the image, like all narcissine shades, captures as it spellbinds and he, as he looks, does not know he is looking at an image. Narcissus and Perceval thereby suffer from the same *not knowing*, the same *nel savez*, regarding imagery, and this has been the knight's dilemma from the start. For, as each narcissine image up to this point (the knights in the Waste Forest, Blancheflor, the bleeding lance/Fisher King) has been put in conjunction with a literal wounding, a *navrer*, Perceval, in his fascination with the beauty of each red-and-white iteration, has failed to see their violent implications. This is the trap Eros lays for him as, instead of the wound bound to each image that reveals its injurious dangers, he perceives a seductive wholeness.

It is in this seductive wholeness that *navrer* (wounding) has the power, not simply to signify the result of physical blows, but can also describe the pain brought on by erotic maladies, the trap set by Love through reflected images. For instance, in *Cligès*, Chrétien's second romance, the knight Alexander employs the same word—couched within the language of an amorous wound—while he laments the yearning that Love has inflicted on him for Sordamour:

—Ja n'i pert il ne cop ne *plaie*,
Et si *te pleinz*? Donc as tu tort.
—Naie, qu'il m'a *navré* a mort,
Que jusqu'au cuer m'a son dart tret,
N'encor ne l'a a lui retret.
—Coment le t'a donc tret el cors
Quant la plaie n'en pert defors?
Ce me diras, savoir le vueil.
Par ou le t'a il trait?—Par l'ueil.
—Par l'ueil? Si ne le t'a crevé?
—En l'ueil ne m'a il riens grevé,
Mes el cuer me grieve forment.
[...]
Li eulz n'a soing de rien entendre
Ne rien n'i puet fere a nul fuer,
Mes c'est li miroers au cuer,
Et par ce miroer trespasse,
Si qu'il ne le blece ne quasse,
Li sens dont li cuers est espris.

"No mark or *wound* appears there, and *you complain*? Are you not mistaken?"

"No, because he has so grievously *wounded* me that he shot his arrow right into my heart and he has not yet pulled it out."

"How did he pierce your body when no wound is visible from the outside? Tell me, I want to know. Where did he strike you?"

"Through the eye."

"Through the eye? And he did not puncture it?"

"My eye does not hurt at all, but it is rather the heart where the wound is serious. The eye does not worry itself with such things, for it is incapable of knowing such things; but it is the mirror of the heart, and it is through this mirror that passes, without damaging or shattering it, the emotion that sets the heart aflame."[40]

Addressing himself in the second person, a marker of the estrangement from himself that Love has caused, Alexander's *te pleinz* ("you complain") recalls Narcissus's *je me plaing* ("I lament myself") (both expressions come from the same verb), as he becomes a self divided and pierced to death—*navré a mort*—by the scar troubling him. For the knight, in pain over his unrequited desire, realizes that something has happened to him during the call and response he has with himself. And it is this other-as-self in the second person, this self emerging as wounded, who answers, witnessing to the bewildering interplay of mirrors and images that Love *has already employed* to strike him down. In other words, Alexander's *navrer* outlines, not simply the captivating effects Love has on him, but also the temporal structure of traumatic wounding, in the unknowable nature of the desire it produces, in its divisive effect on vision and human subjectivity. In short, the moment of falling in love, of narcissistic *innamoramento*, emerges as nothing less than a *traumatic event.*

With its own *navrer* (wounding), Perceval's *innamoramento* over Blancheflor's image reveals a traumatic structure similar to the one affecting Alexander, and, like him, the hero of the *Grail* experiences the violence of desire piercing him in an identical manner. For, amid the mystery of the scene, one must not forget the red-and-white image is the result of a shedding of blood, of a *wound*, as the falcon attacks the goose. The falcon, a symbol popular within courtly literature, proves important, as it implies the predatory nature of love signifying, not simply the lover's pursuit of a beloved, but also the desire from without, from *dehors* (to use the language of the *Lay of Narcissus*), that in turn rapaciously pursues him.[41] This is the desire that hunts Perceval as it, couched within the image of Blancheflor, is naturally a repetition of the same longing sparking his *innamoramento* of knighthood, as both scenes contain the same symbols (the sun, the colors, the shining beloved object) of narcissistic wounding. The blood on snow, in other words, joins the violence of Perceval's erotic pursuits to the misguided nature of his chivalric obsessions.

Read in this manner, the severity of the falcon's attack mirrors Perceval's wayward desire for the heraldic life, a direct link to the narrative of blood found throughout the *Grail*—blood that signifies injury, the result of trauma's impact upon the body, and the loss of life and corporeal integrity. His error with the Fisher King is consequently echoed in the goose's injury, for the blood from its neck "also bears an unmistakable similarity to that other drop of blood on the white lance, reminding the reader, if not Perceval, of the image of blood to which Perceval failed to respond and the tragic consequences of that failure."[42] Blancheflor's likeness connects directly to the Grail Castle episode, for while it, as a representation of the traditional courtly lady, can offer transcendence, paving the way for an understanding of aga-peic love, it also chastises. For, the narcissine image on the snow assumes a secondary function that, in its capacity to echo Blancheflor's portrait, serves as an idealized model by which Perceval is evaluated. The non-existent gaze emanating from her simulacrum reflects back to him his own lack and sterility that he has assumed by conforming to the original narcissine image of chivalry in the Waste Forest. And in the mirroring process occurring as Perceval gazes upon the blood-and-snow composition, the image of the courtly woman in any such situation

demands a comparison between a reflection and the thing reflected, between [the] object as it is itself and the perfect form it strives to attain. When the known and living lady becomes the mirror of the world, experience is resolved from a wild torrent of impressions into a stable and orderly pattern. She becomes the standard by which all things are judged, the ideal light by which they are known. She informs what she reflects.[43]

Such judgment is crucial, for the blood from the goose's wound linked to the blood dripping from the lance transforms the red of Blancheflor's simulacrum into a mirror ultimately condemning Perceval. It is here in the absent gaze of this other, that his sin comes to light and, as he contemplates the image on the snow, is marked with the red stain of his own guilt:

Si pense tant que il s'oblie,
Qu'autresi estoit en son vis
Li vermels sor le blanc assis
Com ces trois goutes de sanc furent,
Qui sor le blance noif parurent.
En l'esgarder que il faisoit,
Li ert avis, tant li plaisoit,
Qu'il veïst la color novele
De la face s'amie bele.
Perchevax sor les goutes muse,
Tote la matinee i use[.]

He reflected so much on the image that he forgot himself, for the three drops of blood that appeared on the white snow seemed like the touch of red on the white of her [his] face. He took so much pleasure from gazing upon the image that it seemed to him that what he was seeing was the fresh coloring of his beautiful beloved's face. Perceval mused on the drops of blood the entire morning.[44]

Due to the ambiguous nature of the possessive adjective "son" (*his* or *her*), the verses above can refer to Blancheflor's *and* Perceval's complexion. This ambiguity renders them, in fact, quite faithful to their Ovidian source, where, after describing the redness in Narcissus's reflection, the narrator of the text speaks to the *infant*, telling him that "ista repercussae, quam cernis, imaginis umbra est" [the face that you discern is but a shadow, your reflected form].[45] Kenneth J. Knoespel, picking up on the mirroring properties of the image, points out that in these lines, "Narcissus [...] perceives the shadow of a rebounding image" precisely because the term "*repercussa* suggests the presence of an active ray repelled by the water and sent back to the eye."[46] The image, in other words, reflects itself, and specifically its redness, onto its onlooker—and this is a *repercussion*—a "restriking" that hits Narcissus with the color denoting his shame of having fallen in love, hits him with the mark of blood, the blush, that comes to the surface of his skin. Much like his predecessor, Perceval is similarly stricken, assuming the same coloration before him, the reflection of blood signaling his own failures and shortcomings. Identical to Narcissus, he, in short, becomes a reflection of the image. And, such a repercussion is never benign, for

> [t]he reflection's blow that produces the subject also guarantees that it will be irrevocably torn apart by an interior fissure, condemning it to a difference to itself [une différence à soi] that nothing will ever be able to close. The subject originates in a repercussion and as a repercussion. [...] The red blood coloring Narcissus's marble body serves as an obscure memento. It recalls the loss that wounded the narcissistic body.[47]

The reddish reflection upon Perceval's face is the imprint of blood that marks the wounding of his subjectivity, of a subjectivity emerging as wounded. In other words, he wears the mark of this injury and trauma upon his face, the injury denoting both his sundered self and the judgment from which he cannot escape. Such a wounding, though, is indeed a "missed event" (to use Caruth's term), for Narcissus fails to see this repercussion has the traumatic implications it does—that his subjectivity has emerged from nothing into a duality, with no intervening step of wholeness ever having existed. Likewise, Perceval is completely overtaken—and unknowingly so—by the power of the likeness, capturing him in such a way that it joins together the *navrez* (wounding) and *nel savez* (not knowing) of his mother's speech. This link between not knowing and the wound is key, for, as trauma theory has always insisted, the interaction between the two centers upon an image, which comes as a "response, sometimes delayed, to an overwhelming event or events, which takes the form of repeated, intrusive hallucinations, dreams, thoughts or behaviors stemming from the event."[48] Identical to the constant red-and-white compositions that have haunted Perceval's adventures, the way in which trauma manifests itself comes to be quite close, if not identical, to the phantasmatic imagery that has shaped what the West has understood to be the root of memory and dreams as well as the process, as evident in the Narcissus myth, of falling in love.[49] It is precisely then around the image that narcissism and trauma begin to speak the same language. For, as Perceval falls in love, as he has fallen in love throughout his adventures, he suffers continuously from *fol amour* (foolish love) in his desire to claim the image as if it were real. What he has failed to understand is that, in fact, *the reverse* has always been true, for, instead of appropriating the image, it has in turn wounded and appropriated him. And this narcissistic mode of foolish love approaches the definition of trauma, which, according to Caruth, occurs when an "event is not assimilated or experienced fully at the time, but only belatedly, in its repeated possession of the one who experiences it. To be traumatized is precisely to be possessed by an image."[50] In such a possession, the phantasm takes over as the self becomes marked by memories, dreams, and flashbacks that it cannot control, phantasms coming to it, as if from without, calling for an understanding of an ungraspable event. In this manner, the traumatized self, possessed by the image—by the image that wounds—becomes identical to Narcissus, as the self becomes defined by the image, *an image of an image*.

All this gains in significance considering that Perceval is the Red Knight, the simulacrum of the knight whom he killed and whose armor he wears. For the redness, in addition to signaling Perceval's wounding, harks back to the blinding wound he inflicted upon the original Red Knight who is equal to Lucifer himself, getting his coloring from the "brilliant beauty, as well as his excessive pride" from "this characteristic that is strictly demonic."[51] Perceval, inhabited by the narcissine reflection, as well as by the reflection of the knight he murdered, undergoes an annihilation of his selfhood through the power of the image before him, losing any hope he might have had for an impermeable ideal of chivalric wholeness. This is the liquefaction of his self, symbolically referenced by the literal liquefaction of the image of blood-on-snow, which melts and evaporates before him under the warm rays of the sun. The entire structure upon which he has constructed his selfhood has proven to be permeable, unstable, and impermanent.

All may not be lost, for while blood is one of the most traditional symbols for guilt, atonement can come with purity. And this is no more evident than in Psalms and Isaiah—two biblical texts with verses glossed by medieval commentators in connection with each other—which link culpability to redness or blood and redemption to the pureness of snow: "Come now, let us reason together, says the Lord: though your sins are like scarlet, they shall be as white as snow; though they are red like crimson, they shall become like wool"; "Purge me with hyssop, and I shall be clean; wash me, and I shall be whiter than snow. [...] Deliver me from bloodguiltiness, O God, thou God of my salvation."[52] As a complex image, the maiden's simulacrum not only mirrors back to Perceval his culpability through the redness of the blood, but also his potential transformation in the whiteness of pure snow. The religious connotations cannot be overlooked, for, if he is to set himself free from the sins of bloodguiltiness and see himself as a divided subject, attempting to repair the traumatic woundings that consistently pursue him, he will have to confront the image of Christ on Good Friday, that image already alluded to in the bleeding lance (as it is a lance that pierces Christ's side). For only in the context of this final narcissine encounter can Perceval have any hope for forgiveness and transcendence.

5.5   BLOOD AND THE CROSS (SEINGNIER): THE TRAUMA OF SALVATION

Up to this point, Perceval has been unsuccessful, despite numerous encounters with wounded bodies, to see his selfhood as split, a division necessary, not simply because this is the only state selfhood can assume within the narcissistic framework of the *Grail*, but because such recognition would destroy the false image of chivalric wholeness he has attempted to possess. In this manner, he has missed the opportunity presented to him to know himself, like Narcissus, *as other*, as infiltrated by the love of and for the other in the agapeic imperative of the text. Consequently, each iteration of the narcissine image (the soldiers in the Waste Forest, Blancheflor's appeal for charity, the Grail procession with the bleeding lance, and the blood-on-snow episode) has been an appeal for the young knight to understand the sundering his subjectivity has already invariably undergone and a missed encounter with this knowledge in his failure to witness to the woundings that have pursued him throughout his adventures. It is in his last scene of the romance, the scene with his uncle on Good Friday, where all the previous encounters with narcissine imagery coalesce, where he is finally capable of linking his divided nature to the Christian instruction imparted to him by his mother.

Prior to this encounter, Perceval has spent five years searching for the meaning of the Grail and bleeding lance in an attempt to atone for his silence with the Fisher King. Along the way, he has forgotten his mother's advice regarding religious principles and remained incapable of grasping the judgment cast upon him by Blancheflor's blood-and-snow resemblance. While journeying through a deserted region, however, Perceval— carrying a lance—encounters three knights and ten maidens who are shocked to find this stranger armed. While closely paralleling his meeting with the knights in the Waste Forest, the scene stands in stark opposition to that episode, for whereas those knights deceived with a seemingly brilliant perfection, this group, walking barefoot in simple white robes, signals a turn toward penitence and redemption. One of the knights addresses Perceval, asking him whether he believes in Christ, because, if he did, he would not be here carrying weaponry on Good Friday. Shocked that Perceval knows nothing about the significance of this day, he continues his instruction, explaining that Christ, the only person free from sin, was crucified for the sins of all. Born of the Virgin, he assumed our humanity while retaining his divinity, and, through his death, raised up all those who had been lost. Those who do not believe these deeds of Christ, the knight continues, "[j]a en la face nel verra" [will never see him face to face] and that:

> Tot cil qui en lui ont creance
> Doivent estre hui en peneance;
> Hui ne deüst hom qui Dieu croie
> Armes porter ne champ ne voie.

All those who have faith in him must do penance today. Today no man who believes in God should wear weapons on roads or in fields.[53]

With these words, the knight outlines the salvation history of Christianity's understanding of how God works redemptively through time, a history to which Perceval's mother alludes in her teaching, a history where the principles of narcissism find themselves to be instrumental. For Christ, whose death is remembered on this day, is the unique human figure within this history who brings a discourse of salvific imagery with him; through him, Christianity becomes "une religion de l'image"—a religion *of the image*.[54] As divine and human, Christ *is* the perfected and ideal resemblance of both, "not only the image of God for humanity, but, resembling humanity, Christ assures the indispensable mediation of salvation [...] between us and God, bringing God to us and us to Him."[55] Due to this resemblance, he is capable, as the knight tells Perceval, of vindicating humanity's sinful nature; Christ, in other words, as an image of divinity and humanity, is the sole figure capable of restoring the image of divinity *in* humanity. What is more though, he accomplishes this because he is a narcissine image, a likeness akin to the blinding shade Narcissus sees upon the fountain's waters and the brilliant simulacrum Perceval repeatedly encounters throughout his adventures. For Christ's body, like the narcissine image, radiates light; his face "is like a sun" in which "the divine image and divine resemblance shine, through which passes a salvific force."[56] Additionally, he is also a figure of *red and white*, embodying the white purity of his divinity and the redness—the flesh and blood—of his humanity.[57] As such, the figure of Christ establishes a final *narcissine encounter* for Perceval, something to which the penitent knight alludes when he states that those who do not believe in the Son of God will never see him "face to face." This phrase, which echoes the words of the Apostle Paul from I Corinthians 13:12— "For now we see in a mirror dimly, but then face to face"—reinforces the notion that the Christian subject, only capable of mediating the spiritual through a reflective surface, the exact structure of the narcissistic encounter, must know the self as divided, defined as a repercussion by the indirect vision of the image's divine brilliance. Christ's passion, the supreme act of charity through which he restoratively sacrifices his self for others, becomes the sole deed allowing for humanity's direct encounter with God. In this sense, Christ-as-image comes to embody all the qualities that Perceval desires, and fails to receive, from the knights in the Waste Forest at the start of the romance—the longing for a source that transcends divisions of the self and where the mediating properties of ephemeral imagery are no longer needed, the longing, in other words, to know the self as whole and stable, as no longer wounded. And this is the hope of which the repentant knight and Paul speak, a potential existence of fulfillment *without the image* that, however, must first begin with the divisiveness *of the image*. Instead of undertaking the process of knowing the self as sundered though, Perceval has solely reflected on the false sense of integrity housed within the image. It is significant that this group of knights and maidens is disturbed to see Perceval as the deluded chivalric image he has become, an image standing in stark contrast to their humility. On this day, then, Perceval comes to experience transcendence to a new life through proper meditation upon the most supreme act of charity in Christian theology: the trauma of Christ's crucifixion.

It is one of the women in the group, by telling Perceval that they have just confessed to a hermit living nearby—an act necessary for those who desire to please God, she insists—that sets him on his course of action. For these words cause Perceval to cry for the first time in the romance, a mourning he continues as he moves through the forest in search of the hermitage. Mourning, as I discuss in Chap. 3, marks a realization that the self is divided by an irreparable wound along with a desire to heal the sundering it opens up. The group of pilgrims, representing through their words and deeds an image of humility and charity, redirect the line of thinking that Perceval has maintained since the start of his adventures. Here, mourning that he is not the knight he believes himself to be, shatters the beautiful image of chivalry he first beheld in the Waste Forest and he sees himself *as he is seen*. And it is such a realization, which Žižek terms a *symbolic identification*, an "identification with the very place from which we are being observed, from where we look at ourselves," that puts Perceval on this path of mourning where he can finally recognize his wound.[58] With this gaze of the other cast upon him, he undergoes the start of a radical transformation resulting in a new type of knowledge of self similar to Narcissus's moments of *iste ego sum* ("I am this" from Ovid's myth) and *je me plaing* ("I lament myself" from the *Lay of Narcissus*), a knowledge exposing the deception of the image to which he has conformed and its lethal consequences.

It is for this reason that, when arriving at the chapel, Perceval, afraid he has sinned, asks for absolution. After the hermit there inquires as to why Perceval has spent so much time away from the religious life, he replies that it is because he failed to ask about the bleeding lance and never learned whom the Grail serves. Revealing himself to be his maternal uncle, the hermit informs him that it is because of his mother, who prayed that God watch over him, that he has remained safe. Additionally, the hermit tells his nephew that another maternal uncle—the father of the Fisher King—is served and sustained by one host from the grail. Whereas Perceval believed his sinfulness was linked to his failure at the Grail Castle, he learns his failure is a result of not having helped his mother, this first wounded body he encountered, a result of not acting in a charitable way toward the woman who gave him life.

Whereas these previous wounds, however, repeated Perceval's blind ignorance, he will encounter a wound that instead brings enlightenment regarding his past crimes. And that such knowledge comes to Perceval on Good Friday—on this day commemorating Christ's death—is rich with significance as it joins Ovid's myth of Narcissus to the salvation history of Christianity. Whereas Narcissus discovers his wounded selfhood in the mirror of Nemesis's fountain, Perceval discovers here a type of salvific wounding within Christ who is not simply a narcissine image but also, in another parallel of Ovid's myth, a fountain as well. For the symbolism of Christ's bleeding wounds *as fountains*, as a *fons vitae*, is "found very frequently in devotional literature" of the Middle Ages, with the "vulnus lateris [side wound] in particular [...] often represented as a fountain from which there flows a saving and life-giving 'stream.'"[59] And Good Friday is the day that commemorates when Christ becomes this fountain upon being pierced in the side, allowing for the miraculous flow of blood and water from this wound to occur:

> Since it was the day of Preparation, in order to prevent the bodies from remaining on the cross on the sabbath [...], the Jews asked Pilate that their legs might be broken, so that they might be taken away. [...] [B]ut when they came to Jesus and saw that he was already dead, they did not break his legs. But one of the soldiers pierced his side with a spear, and at once there came out blood and water. He who saw it has borne witness—his testimony is true, and he knows that he tells the truth—that you also may believe. For these things took place that the scripture might be fulfilled, "Not a bone of him shall be broken." And again another scripture says, "They shall look on him whom they have pierced."[60]

Before exploring the significance of this event within John's gospel and its implications for the *Grail*, I find it important to examine the scriptural significance of this fountain, for John links the piercing that causes the blood and water to come forth from Christ's body to the fulfillment of the Old Testament prophet Zechariah ("They shall look on him whom they have pierced"). The reference, as scholars have argued, establishes the lens through which to interpret the piercing of this corpse, which, within its wider context, puts John's account in line with a larger narrative of the salvation history the penitent knight imparts to Perceval:

> And I will pour out upon the house of David and the inhabitants of Jerusalem a spirit of compassion and supplication, so that, when they look on him whom they have pierced, they shall mourn for him, as one mourns for an only child, and weep bitterly over him, as one weeps over a first-born. [...] On that day there shall be a fountain opened for the house of David and the inhabitants of Jerusalem to cleanse them from sin and uncleanness.[61]

Within the context of Zechariah's prophecy, John's account transforms the flow of blood and water into a cleansing fountain that gushes forth from the corpse of a dead man, as Christ's body becomes a wellspring of salvation for the sinner. The Christian subject who becomes fully repentant, uniting himself to God, comes to mirror this miracle by becoming a fountain in return, since, as Christ-as-fountain states earlier in John's Gospel: "If any one thirst, let him come to me and drink. He who believes in me, as the scripture has said, 'Out of his heart shall flow rivers of living water.'"[62] And this water, within a Johannine context, refers to "the Spirit which those who believed in Jesus were to receive [...]. In this flow of water from the side of Jesus (from within him), John sees the fulfillment of Jesus' own prophecy [that his Spirit will be poured out upon humanity], taking place in the hour of Jesus' glorification."[63] The fact that Christ makes the ultimate sacrifice by dying upon the cross for the sake of humanity's salvation is the supreme act of charity, for from his wounding, from the wound confirming his body as lifeless, miraculously comes life itself.

What is the meaning of the flow of blood and water from Christ's side, though, and how can it help in an understanding of this scene involving Perceval? According to John in his first epistle, Christ hands over his spirit through the flow of water and blood from his body, thereby assuring the Christian subject that he can render unto him or her the wellspring of faith: "This is he that came by water and blood, Jesus Christ, not with the water only but with the water and the blood. And the Spirit is the witness, because the Spirit is the truth. There are three witnesses, the Spirit, the water, and the blood; and these three agree."[64] The fountain springing from Christ's wound is therefore cause for reflection, as the lance that pierces his flesh is reminiscent of the wounding that sunders Perceval's father and the Fisher King, for this wound opens up the body, dividing it in a way that once again marks the self as a separated entity. Consequently, one cannot forget that Christ is not simply an image of God and humanity, but also *a body* as well, a body that can be pierced, wounded, *traumatized* (in its etymological and theoretical senses). For here, in this figure of Christ, the Word of God and the Son of Man, the oppositions of body and image *fuse together* and *become one*, a union of body and image that, as such, fulfills Narcissus's (and Perceval's) ultimate desire. The narcissistic division of the self between human subject and mirror image thereby becomes in Christ, not a narrative of separation, but rather one of unity and stability, a narrative undoing the mythological narcissism of Perceval's previous adventures. Here, in Christic trauma, the wound—the *navrer*—can *be healed.* The mourning and melancholy that have pursued Perceval throughout his adventures are consequently upended—and all this is possible through Christ and his passion. His death and resurrection, in other words, establish the hope (the reality even) for everlasting closure of the narcissistic sundering. On Good Friday, therefore, Perceval confronts Christ as a wounded body, a traumatized narcissine image, that paradoxically also represents a bastion of wholeness, for this is a "resurrection from death [that] was a victory for all humankind over fragmentation, separation, mutability, and decay."[65]

Christ's trauma sets up the framework for Perceval to assume the same definition of unified selfhood. And the fountain of Christ's body, in the narcissine image that it incarnates and reflects, is an appeal—exactly as the one Narcissus experiences—to know the self in the other, in this supreme act of agapeic self-sacrifice *for the other.* The specular relationship established here calls for the knight to receive his identity, his self, from Christ, and, in imitation of him, to be possessed by the traumatized narcissine image that he represents here. In this manner, Perceval can have a relationship with the Son of God as he becomes a mirrored surface, an *imago Christi*, in a mutual reciprocation of symbiotic resemblance. The Christian subject consequently assumes, through repercussion, the colors of the perfected lover, always, according to the Song of Songs, "radiant and ruddy"—*white and red*—like Christ, like Narcissus, like the narcissine image.[66] Whereas the other narcissine imagery to which Perceval conforms represent a misdirected attempt at wholeness and an "origin," Christ is able to fulfill this desire for a teleology. By both dividing the self and uniting it to its divine source through his own sundering and erasure, Christ emerges as a new self, annihilated and resurrected through God. And this is all possible solely through resemblance, through *narcissism*, for, due to Christ's passion, humanity is remade in his image, in the image of God, in a manner where we become "'co-similar,' like God's own sons. The son of man is he who carries the celestial image, the image of Christ. This metamorphosis, by Christ and in Christ, is fulfilled 'towards' God, bringing with it a kind of death, disappearance or burial and a reappearing or resurrection to the fullness of life."[67]

The message of Christ's salvific trauma, however, is not new to the *Grail*, but has been present from the start, when Perceval's mother attempts to impart to her son that he should seek out churches, the place:

> Si i sacrefion le cors
> Jhesucrist, le prophete sainte
> [...]
> Traïs fu et jugiez a tort,
> Et soffri angoisse de mort
> Por les homes et por les fames,
> Qu'en infer aloient les ames
> Quant eles partoient des cors,
> Et il les en regeta fors.

> Where they sacrifice the body of Jesus Christ, the holy prophet. He was betrayed and unjustly condemned, he suffered the anguish of death for the men and women whose souls went to hell when they left their bodies, and he lifted them up from there.[68]

Le Rider, commenting on the mother's statement, remarks that "the Christians in [Chrétien's] time experienced the mass as a sacrifice" and that, during the twelfth century, it embodied "a continuation of the Passion" where the piercing of Christ's body was remembered in the Eucharistic celebration.[69] Communion—as the body and blood of Christ—subsequently becomes an iteration of Christ's traumatic wounding, in short, *trauma as repetition*, continuously reenacted each time the mass is held. Partaking of the Eucharist, as Perceval does on Easter Sunday, is to accept, and repeatedly so, Christ's wounds and the salvific blood flowing from them. For this is to allow Christ's flesh and blood into one's body, to accept his agapeic love, to permit his existence to abide within the self, transforming it into a resemblance of unity with the divine. In this manner, the *sacrifice* (to use the word employed by Perceval's mother) that Christ undergoes in the commemoration of the Eucharist presents a sacrificial logic without any pretense. For, as I explain in Chap. 2, in the traditional narcissistic relationship between self and other, a lover sacrifices himself for the beloved as a way of denying the other's lack. In Christ though, there is no lack, and he can traumatically sacrifice himself again and again at each mass where the Christian subject, as the beloved, will always be there, ready to receive him.

It cannot go unnoticed, nonetheless, that Christ's suffering, his trauma repeated in each Eucharistic celebration, happened upon the cross. For, if Christianity is a religion of the image, it is also a "*religio crucis*"—a *religion of the cross*.[70] And, like the Eucharist, the cross first makes its appearance in the *Grail* in relation to the advice Perceval receives from his mother, when he, rejecting her directive, refuses to make the sign of the cross to protect himself from any potential evil at the start of the romance:

> Voir se dist ma mere, ma dame,
> Qui me dist que deable sont
> Les plus laides choses del mont;
> Et si dist por moi enseingnier
> Que por aus se doit on seingnier,
> Mais cest ensaing desdaignerai,
> Que ja voir ne m'en seignerai[.]

> My mother told the truth when she told me that devils are the most frightening thing in the world. She also said, to teach me, that it is necessary to cross oneself because of them. But I will scorn this sign, and never will I cross myself.[71]

It is this denial of his religious and maternal roots, starkly opposed to the deceptive ethos of chivalry, that becomes Perceval's first action in the romance, marking him with misunderstanding. The act of crossing oneself, so harshly rebuffed by the young boy, would be to accept the affliction given to Christ; it would be, in other words, to bear witness to the trauma Christ underwent, the piercing and sundering of his divine body, and a reminder to the young man that he is himself joined to Christ in an unavoidable narcissistic relationship of resemblance and selflessness. It is, in other words, a physical manifestation upon the body of the wounded self—a type of traumatic repetition with the constant hope of closure through everlasting life.

Nonetheless, Chrétien skillfully introduces the sacrifice of Christ simultaneously through its rejection when he places the verb *seingnier* in Perceval's mouth. Though it means in this context "to cross (oneself)" (*signer* in Modern French), the word in Old French also means "to bleed" (*saigner* in Modern French). In order for Perceval to rectify this grave separation from the Cross, Chrétien inscribes early on, by use of this word, the answer to the young knight's quest as one which will be an exploration—even if he does not know it, even in its negation—of the sacred meaning of blood and wounds within a theological context. For a rejection of the cross is a rejection of the traumatic narcissism necessary for the agapeic imperative the *Grail* establishes for Perceval as a Christian subject, a rejection of the wounding Christ undergoes and a reluctance to assume that wounding as one's own, to accept the self as wounded. The refusal to cross himself, in other words, is coupled with the refusal *to bleed*—for this is not simply a denial of the mother, but also a refusal to wound himself (like Narcissus does), a refusal to *see himself as wounded*, in short, a refusal of the agapeic love that should unite him to Christ through others, through the *other*. To accept the message of the cross, of the wounded self, of blood sacrifice, of charity, all invokes an erasure of the self, the emergence of the *selfless self*. Related to "percer" (to pierce), Perceval's own name, of which he remains ignorant until immediately after leaving the Grail Castle, even bears the mark of Christ's piercings, of the pierced, wounded, and traumatized self. To reject the cross is to reject his identity. Conversely, to accept the cross and Christ's suffering is to enter its mystery of blood and water, charity, and self-erasure. And because Christ is present in the cross, in the *image of the cross*, in the *act of crossing oneself*, the repetition of his wounding is, in a true sense, also always present, and an iterative eternalizing present at that. For removing "the image of the wounded Christ from its traditional narrative and temporal setting" creates a situation where

> time and space are collapsed and the beholder is free to interact with the scene in a non-linear, non-narrative fashion and to tailor the scene according to his or her own needs and desires. [...] In other words, Christ was neither far away in time and place, nor fixed within a particular moment of an historical event, but present before the beholder in his or her own time and his or her own place.[72]

Perceval subsequently comes to experience such mysteries, not only by listening to the words of the knights and penitent women, but also through intimate contact with the sacramental ritual of confession, where he worships the cross and mourns his sins ["aoura/La crois et ses pechiez plora"] with his uncle.[73]

The blood of the cross and blood of the Eucharist—as *seingnier* ("to bleed" and "to cross") joins both together through Christ's wounds—evoke once again the trauma that has haunted Perceval since the start of the romance. The bleeding lance, that object of his sin, in addition to recalling the knights in the Waste Forest, also—and naturally so—recalls the lance of Christ's passion, the passion about which Perceval's mother attempts to tell him before he leaves her for dead. For this lance, as a marker of the wounded body, along with the Grail containing a host, transforms the procession in the Grail Castle into another iteration of Christ's wounding in the Eucharist. As such, this sacrament plays on the duality of the opening and closing of Christ's wounds, of his *trauma*:

> The conviction of the theologians that the scars of the crucified [...] persist in heaven is a conviction that the saving event of the cross is both a real death and a triumph over the bodily dissolution that is what death really means. If the scars were simply erased, it would be as if the death, the separation, the *pretium*, were never paid. But those scars must be healed—or at least flowing with living blood—in order to signal that what that death achieves is life. The scars, like the blood but in a simpler sense, both assert and cancel death.[74]

Christ's wounds are able to achieve a transcendental closure in a way that the pierced bodies of Perceval's father and the Fisher King, as representatives of knighthood's sterility, could never accomplish.

The sacrifice of the Christic body subsequently comes to be repeated through the cross and Eucharist in a way that, miraculously, undoes their unknowability. The unity of humanity to the divine, sealing the wound of separation, transforms Perceval's experience here into a type of *trauma without trauma*. In distinction to every other narcissine encounter within the *Grail*, the image of a wounded Christ on the cross does away with the misrecognition so central to the traumatic event. For, where the witnessing to the truth of what is occurring is typically denied the onlooker, rendering trauma an event that has no witnesses, here there is a direct imperative *to witness*, and to do so for the sake of one's salvation. As such, trauma and witnessing, for the first time in the text, come together through the events of this day in a way where there is no aporia. And, as evident in the Gospel's account of Thomas, trauma and witnessing come together specifically *in the wound*:

Christ returned to display his resurrected wounds specifically to Thomas, for it was necessary that his doubt—representative of the universal and potential doubt throughout the ages—transform into the uncontested faith of the community. Thus the wounds and their display were explicitly connected to a scene of doubt that transformed through contact with the traces of violence. In other words, Christ's wounds were sites in which knowledge was produced.[75]

The mystery of Christ's passion, therefore, cannot exist within *not know-ing*, within *nel savez*; its message of charity and transcendence must be *known and practiced*. John in his gospel, for instance, does not simply state that the flow of water and blood from Christ's body is a miracle, but is one invoking an ethical imperative *to witness* through vision *and* action: "He who saw [the blood and water] has borne witness—his testimony is true, and he knows he tells the truth—that you also may believe."[76] There is a call to testify and carry out the message gained through the significance of this miracle, as witnessing the blood and water from Christ's wound and the witness of the Christian subject are, in truth, two facets of the same reality.[77] This is a witnessing that must transcend literal vision toward "the world of spirit," for what John speaks about is the lived witnessing of "a revelation that is important for all the Christians whom he symbolizes."[78] The revelation is to follow the humility of Christ on the cross, carrying out his agapeic imperative by mirroring him through *acts of charity*. Perceval is invited to be a witness to the humility of Christ on this cross and to fulfill this calling. *Seingnier*, in this sense, becomes a lived practice. Up to this moment Perceval has fallen in this respect, for while seeing his mother's death and the Grail procession, he failed to witness to them. As such, there can now be no denial of the wounded body, no denial of the trauma inflicted upon Christ through his agapeic love, of the trauma inflicted upon Perceval in his transformation into an *imago Christi*. It is precisely his failure to act that has stained him with bloodguiltiness, and only in adherence to the mystery of Christ's crucified body—his traumatized body—can this be overcome.

Through the transcendence experienced in this divine body, the melancholic feedback loop of trauma can be redirected toward the hope for closure. Yes, the repetition will continue to exist, but now the *Grail* points toward what Caruth would call the futurity of trauma, for this is a "futurity that lies [...] at the heart of all trauma—as deferral and future repetition, as an attempted return that instead departs."[79] With such a forward-looking point of view, the hermit instructs Perceval how he, newly formed in the image of Christ's salvific wounds, should behave: by going to church every morning, believing God, acting humbly before clergy, honoring those who do good, and helping those in need. All this, his uncle states, will be "almosne [...] enterine," acts of perfect charity.[80] Accepting the instruction as penance, Perceval is invited to remain in the hermitage until Easter when he, by receiving communion, can serve as witness to the redemptive powers of the resurrection. In this manner, he will always return—and unavoidably so—to the traumatized self, to the self divided through a continuous narcissistic encounter with Christ and through acts of charity and testimony, to the self consistently possessed by the image of the other. And this is necessary, because the repetition of Christ's wounding through the cross, the Eucharist, and acts of charity, in short, the repetition of Christ's trauma in the life of the Christian subject, relates precisely to the salvation history as outlined by the penitent knight. In this manner, Christianity is not simply the religion of the image and of the cross, but, I would posit, the religion of *seingnier*, the religion of the wound, the *religion of trauma*—and a lived trauma at that. It is not simply, therefore, the human self who emerges as traumatized in the narcissistic matrix, but the Christian self as well, called to experience life as a continuous repetition of Christ's wounds. Such a salvific experience requires, though, a temporal structure, like the trauma forming it, based on repetition, on "flashbacks" to events that hold significance today, on wounds that continue to speak and bear witness to a certain truth that the Christian subject is asked to understand. For

> Salvation requires history; it demands narrative and event; without the contingency of time, there could be no release from time, no resurrection of the dead at the end of time. [...] To unfold from the repetition of remembrance the singularity of the historical event, and to situate the audience with respect for the event so that they can become conscious of its contingency: "if this had not happened...." Without this consciousness, there can be no fear of time, no fear of the consequences of sin, and thus no fear of God.[81]

In this manner, Christic narcissism allows for trauma to break free from the ignorance that would otherwise obfuscate it. For this is now, with Perceval, a consciously repeated wounding, a wounding that finally dissolves the connection between *nel savez* (not knowing) and *navrez* (wounding) in favor of *savez* (knowledge) and *navrez* (wounding), a repetition fixing him within the historical context of commemoration and pointing to a futurity that will have as its end point this "release from time" where no traumatic iteration will be necessary. And this is the hoped-for face-to-face confrontation with the divine, where there is no temporality, misrecognition or wounding—simply an endless present of wholeness. This attempt, however, to transcend narcissistic wounding through testimony, possible within the Christian framework of the *Grail*, encounters problems when testimony, existing within a framework of linguistic polyvocality, comes to wound the loving self. It is here, in an exploration of such a tension, that I will now turn in an analysis of Guillaume de Machaut's *Fountain of Love*.

NOTES

1. Chrétien de Troyes, *Le Roman de Perceval ou le conte du Graal*, ed. William Roach (Geneva: Librairie Droz, 1959), vv. 4186–88, 123. Quotations in Old French, with verse and page numbers cited, come this edition. English translations are mine.
2. Ovid, *Ovid's Metamorphoses, Books 1–5*, ed. William S. Anderson (Norman: University of Oklahoma Press, 1997), v. 3.423, 98, my translation.
3. Michelle Freeman, "Problems in Romance Composition: Ovid, Chrétien de Troyes, and the *Romance of the Rose*" in *Romance Philology* 30 (1976), 162. In addition, Rupert T. Pickens has written about various scenes within the *Grail* that treat similar notions of mirroring. See: *Perceval and Gawain in Dark Mirrors: Reflection and Reflexivity in Chrétien de Troyes's "Conte du Graal"* (Jefferson, NC: McFarland and Company, 2014).
4. Lacan uses this term in his "Mirror Stage." *Méconnaissance*, as Lorenzo Chiesa posits, occurs as the onlooker, viewing his or her image in the mirror, does not recognize the image as such, the "other as other." Because of this, such misrecognition (*méconnaissance*) is always dual, for "the ego not only as it were, 'finds itself' at the place of the other [...] but also provides the subject with a deceptive impression of unity." This is the same process evident in Ovid's myth when Narcissus sees his image. See: Jacques Lacan, "Le Stade du miroir" in *Ecrits* (Paris: Editions du Seuil, 1966); Lorenzo Chiesa, *Subjectivity and Otherness: A Philosophical Reading of Lacan* (Cambridge: MIT Press, 2007), 16.
5. Michael Newman, "The Trace of Trauma: Blindness, Testimony and the Gaze in Blanchot and Derrida" in *Maurice Blanchot: The Obligation of Writing*, ed. Carolyn Bailey Gill (London: Routledge, 1996), 157.
6. Jean LaPlanche and Jean-Bertrand Pontalis, *The Language of Psycho-Analysis*, trans. Donald Nicholason-Smith (New York: W. W. Norton, 1973), 465.

7. Wendy J. Turner and Christina Lee, "Conceptualizing Trauma for the Middle Ages" in *Trauma in Medieval Society*, ed. Wendy J. Turner and Christina Lee (Leiden: Brill, 2018), 8.

8. Sigmund Freud, *"Beyond the Pleasure Principle"* in *The Standard Edition of the Complete Works of Sigmund Freud, Vol. 18*, trans. and ed. James Strachey (London: Hogarth, 1955), 12.

9. Roger Luckhurst, *The Trauma Question* (London: Routledge, 2008), 3.

10. Ibid.

11. Dominick LaCapra, *Writing History, Writing Trauma* (Baltimore: Johns Hopkins University Press, 2001), 21.

12. Ibid.

13. Luckhurst, *Trauma*, 9.

14. Cathy Caruth, *Unclaimed Experience: Trauma, Narrative, and History* (Baltimore: Johns Hopkins University Press, 2016), 1.

15. Freud, *Beyond*, 22.

16. Caruth, *Unclaimed*, 2–3.

17. Cathy Caruth, "Trauma and Experience: Introduction" in *Trauma: Explorations in Memory*, ed. Cathy Caruth (Baltimore: Johns Hopkins University Press, 1995), 4.

18. Caruth, *Unclaimed*, 61–62.

19. Ibid., 3. Peggy McCracken has written about this notion of repetition in Chrétien's romances, claiming they prioritize notions of time that do not follow a traditionally sequential chronology. See: "Forgetting to Conclude" in *Thinking Through Chrétien de Troyes*, by Zrinka Stahuljak et al. (Rochester, NY: D.S. Brewer, 2011), 139-62.

20. Chrétien, *Graal*, vv. 435–37, 13, my emphasis.

21. Caruth, "Experience," 5.

22. Chrétien, *Graal*, vv. 127–34, 136–38, 146–49, and 153–54, 5.

23. Ibid., vv. 176–81, 6.

24. Jacques Ribard, *Du philtre au graal: pour une interprétation théologique du Roman de Tristan et du Conte du graal* (Paris: Honoré Champion, 1989), 67. My translation of: "péché originel […] au plein sens du terme, au sens théologique, car dans le sillage immédiat de cette diabolique tentation va se manifester la rupture, la révolte—trait éminemment satanique—de l'enfant vis-à-vis de sa mère, de la créature vis-à-vis de son Créateur. Car tel est bien le fameux péché de Perceval: ingrate et monstrueuse séparation d'avec la mère, laissée pour morte."

25. Jean-Charles Huchet, "Le Nom et l'image: de Chrétien de Troyes à Robert de Boron" in *The Legacy of Chrétien de Troyes, Vol 2*, ed. Norris Lacy (Amsterdam: Rodopoi, 1988), 14. My translation of: "'l'image' […] égare; elle capture les sens pour que les sens continuent à faire défaut. La chevalerie s'impose à Perceval dans un éclat de lumière où le blanc et le vermeil se marient pour mieux tracer la voie de son péché."

26. Chrétien, *Graal*, vv. 1823–24, 54.
27. Ibid., vv. 2065–69, 61.
28. Frederick Goldin, *The Mirror of Narcissus in the Courtly Love Lyric* (Ithaca: Cornell University Press, 1967), 76–77.
29. Chrétien, *Graal*, vv. 47–50, 2.
30. L. O. Aranye Fradenburg, *Sacrifice Your Love: Psychoanalysis, Historicism, Chaucer* (Minneapolis: University of Minnesota Press, 2002), 29.
31. Ibid., 31.
32. Chrétien, *Graal*, v. 2221, 65, my emphasis.
33. Ibid., vv. 3342–43, 98.
34. Ibid., vv. 3509–14, 102–3, my emphasis.
35. Ann McCullough, "Criminal Naivety: Blind Resistance and the Pain of Knowing in Chrétien de Troyes's *Conte du Graal*" in *The Modern Language Review* 101.1 (2006), 54.
36. Chrétien, *Graal*, v. 3593, 105.
37. Paule Le Rider, *Le Chevalier dans le* Conte du Graal *de Chrétien de Troyes* (Paris: Société d'édition d'enseignement supérieur, 1978), 69. My translation from: "Le cortège qui apparaît au cours du repas offert à Perceval par le Roi Pêcheur serait [...] l'image concrétisée d'une faute, d'un crime. La lance sanglante qui le précède suggère un meurtre."
38. McCullough, "Criminal," 61.
39. Chrétien, *Graal*, vv. 4186–89 and 4194–201, 123.
40. Chrétien, *Cligés* in *Romans*, ed. Charles Méla (Paris: Livre de Poche, 1994), vv. 686–97 and 706–11, 311, emphasis and translation mine.
41. For falcons and love, see: Michael Camille, *The Medieval Art of Love: Objects and Subjects of Desire* (New York: Harry N. Abrams, 1998), 96–106.
42. Susan Potters, "Blood Imagery in Chrétien's *Perceval*" in *Philological Quarterly* 56.3 (1977), 304.
43. Goldin, *Mirror*, 78.
44. Chrétien, *Graal*, vv. 4202–12, 123–24.
45. Ovid, *Ovid's Metamorphoses*, v. 3.434, 99; Ovid, *Metamorphoses*, 94.
46. Kenneth J. Knoespel, *Narcissus and the Invention of Personal History* (New York: Garland, 1985), 11.
47. Nouvet, *Enfances narcisse* (Paris: Galilé, 2009), 130–31. My translation of: "La frappe de la réflexion qui produit le sujet garantit également qu'il sera irrémédiablement déchiré par une fissure intérieure qui le condamne à une différence à soi que rien jamais ne pourra refermer. Le sujet s'origine dans une répercussion et comme répercussion. [...] Le rouge sang qui colore le corps marmoréen de Narcisse fait office d'obscur mémento. Il rappelle la perte qui a blessé le corps narcissique."
48. Caruth, "Experience," 4.

49. See: Giorgio Agamben, *Stanzas: Word and Phantasm in Western Culture*, trans. Ronald L. Martinez (Minnesota: University of Minnesota Press, 1993), 73–89.

50. Caruth, "Experience," 4–5.

51. Ribard, *Philtre*, 51. My translation of: "l'éclatante beauté, en même temps que l'orgueil démesuré, cette caractéristique proprement démoniaque."

52. Isaiah 1:18; Psalm 51:7, 14 (Revised Standard Version). Susan Potters points out this connection between Chrétien's text and the biblical verses. See: "Blood Imagery," 305.

53. Chrétien, *Graal*, vv. 6282 and 6297–300, 185.

54. Huchet, "Le Nom," 2.

55. Robert Javelet, *Image et ressemblance au douzième siècle: de saint Anselme à Alain de Lille*, vol. 1 (Paris: Letouzey et Ané, 1967), 301. My translation of: "Non seulement image de Dieu pour les hommes, mais semblable aux hommes, le Christ assure l'indispensable médiation du salut. Il fallait un médiateur entre nous et Dieu, qui nous approche de Dieu et approche Dieu de nous." For a discussion of Christ as a mediating image, see chapter 8 of Javelet, *Image*, 298–367.

56. Javelet, *Image*, 302. My translation of: "La face du Christ est comme un soleil; en elle éclate l'image et ressemblance divines; par elle passe la force qui sauve."

57. Ibid., 303.

58. Slavoj Žižek, *The Sublime Object of Ideology* (London: Verso, 1989), 105.

59. Douglas Gray, "The Five Wounds of Our Lord" in *Notes and Queries* 10.3 (1963), 129.

60. John 19:31–37 (RSV).

61. Zechariah 12:10, 13:1 (RSV).

62. John 7:37–38 (RSV).

63. Raymond E. Brown, "Comment" in *The Anchor Bible: The Gospel According to John (xiii–xxi)*, ed. Raymond E. Brown (Garden City, NY: Doubleday, 1966), 949–50.

64. I John 5:6–8 (RSV).

65. Caroline Walker Bynum, *Wonderful Blood: Theology and Practice in Late Medieval Northern Germany and Beyond* (Philadelphia: University of Pennsylvania Press, 2007), 144.

66. Song of Songs 5:10 (RSV).

67. Javelet, *Image*, 308. My translation of: "'consemblables', comme les propres fils de Dieu. Le fils de l'homme est celui qui porte l'image du céleste, l'image du Christ. Cette métamorphose, par le Christ et dans le Christ, se réalise 'vers' Dieu: elle comporte une sorte de mort, de disparition ou ensevelissement et de réapparition ou résurrection dans la pleine vie."

68. Chrétien, *Graal*, vv. 580–81 and 583–88, 17–18.

69. Le Rider, *Le Chevalier*, 71–72. My translation of: "Les chrétiens du temps de notre auteur vivaient la messe comme un sacrifice. [...] La messe [...] était sentie au XIIᵉ siècle comme un recommencement de la Passion."

70. Richard Viladesau, *The Beauty of the Cross: The Passion of Christ in Theology and the Arts, from the Catacombs to the Eve of the Renaissance* (Oxford: Oxford University Press, 2006), 7.

71. Chrétien, *Graal*, vv. 114–20, 4.

72. Vibeke Olson, "Penetrating the Void: Picturing the Wound in Christ's Side as a Performative Space" in *Wounds and Wound Repair in Medieval Culture*, ed. Larissa Tracy and Kelly DeVries (Leiden: Brill, 2016), 320.

73. Chrétien, *Graal*, vv. 6495–96, 191.

74. Walker Bynum, *Wonderful*, 145.

75. Allie Terry-Fritch, "Proof in Pierced Flesh: Caravaggio's Doubting Thomas and the Beholder of Wounds in Early Modern Italy" in *Beholding Violence in Medieval and Early Modern Europe*, ed. Allie Terry-Fritch and Erin Felicia Labbie (New York: Routledge, 2012), 28.

76. John 19:35 (RSV).

77. Brown, "Comment," 952.

78. Ibid., 949.

79. Cathy Caruth, *Literature in the Ashes of History* (Baltimore: Johns Hopkins University Press, 2013), 81.

80. Chrétien, *Graal*, v. 6468, 190.

81. Rachel Fulton, *From Judgment to Passion: Devotion to Christ and the Virgin Mary, 800–1200* (New York: Columbia University Press, 2002), 20–21.

References

Agamben, Giorgio. 1993. *Stanzas: Word and Phantasm in Western Culture*. Trans. Ronald L. Martinez. Minneapolis, MN: University of Minneapolis Press.

Brown, Raymond E. 1966. Comment. In *The Anchor Bible: The Gospel According to John (xiii–xxi)*, ed. Raymond E. Brown, 944–960. Garden City, NY: Doubleday.

Camille, Michael. 1998. *The Medieval Art of Love: Objects and Subjects of Desire*. New York: Harry N. Abrams.

Caruth, Cathy. 1995. Trauma and Experience: Introduction. In *Trauma: Explorations in Memory*, ed. Cathy Caruth, 3–12. Baltimore: Johns Hopkins University Press.

———. 2013. *Literature in the Ashes of History*. Baltimore: Johns Hopkins University Press.

———. 2016. *Unclaimed Experience: Trauma, Narrative, and History*. Baltimore: Johns Hopkins University Press.

Chiesa, Lorenzo. 2007. *Subjectivity and Otherness: A Philosophical Reading of Lacan.* Cambridge: MIT Press.

Chrétien de Troyes. 1959. *Le Roman de Perceval ou le conte du Graal.* Ed. William Roach. Geneva: Librairie Droz.

———. 1994. *Cligés.* In *Romans,* ed. Charles Méla, 285–494. Paris: Livre de Poche.

Fradenburg, L.O. Aranye. 2002. *Sacrifice Your Love: Psychoanalysis, Historicism, Chaucer.* Minneapolis, MN: University of Minnesota Press.

Freeman, Michelle. 1976. Problems in Romance Composition: Ovid, Chrétien de Troyes, and the *Romance of the Rose. Romance Philology* 30: 158–168.

Freud, Sigmund. 1955. *Beyond the Pleasure Principle.* In *The Standard Edition of the Complete Works of Sigmund Freud.* Trans. and Ed. James Strachey, vol. 18, 7–64. London: Hogarth.

Fulton, Rachel. 2002. *From Judgment to Passion: Devotion to Christ and the Virgin Mary, 800–1200.* New York: Columbia University Press.

Goldin, Frederick. 1967. *The Mirror of Narcissus in the Courtly Love Lyric.* Ithaca, NY: Cornell University Press.

Gray, Douglas. 1963. The Five Wounds of Our Lord. *Notes and Queries* 10 (3): 82–89.

Huchet, Jean-Charles. 1988. Le Nom et l'image: de Chrétien de Troyes à Robert de Boron. In *The Legacy of Chrétien de Troyes,* ed. Norris Lacy, vol. 2, 1–16. Amsterdam: Rodopoi.

Javelet, Robert. 1967. *Image et ressemblance au douzième siècle: de saint Anselme à Alain de Lille, Vol. 1.* Paris: Letouzey et Ané.

Knoespel, Kenneth J. 1985. *Narcissus and the Invention of Personal History.* New York: Garland.

Lacan, Jacques. 1966. Le Stade du miroir. In *Ecrits,* 93–100. Paris: Editions du Seuil.

LaCapra, Dominick. 2001. *Writing History, Writing Trauma.* Baltimore: Johns Hopkins University Press.

LaPlanche, Jean, and Jean-Bertrand Pontalis. 1973. *The Language of Psycho-Analysis.* Trans. Donald Nicholason-Smith. New York: W. W. Norton.

Le Rider, Paule. 1978. *Le Chevalier dans le Conte du Graal de Chrétien de Troyes.* Paris: Société d'édition d'enseignement supérieur.

Luckhurst, Roger. 2008. *The Trauma Question.* London: Routledge.

McCullough, Ann. 2006. Criminal Naivety: Blind Resistance and the Pain of Knowing in Chrétien de Troyes's *Conte du Graal. The Modern Language Review* 101 (1): 48–61.

McCracken, Peggy. 2011. Forgetting to Conclude. In *Thinking Through Chrétien de Troyes,* ed. Zrinka Stahuljak et al., 139–162. Rochester, NY: D.S. Brewer.

Newman, Michael. 1996. The Trace of Trauma: Blindness, Testimony and the Gaze in Blanchot and Derrida. In *Maurice Blanchot: The Obligation of Writing,* ed. Carolyn Bailey Gill, 153–173. London: Routledge.

Nouvet, Claire. 2009. *Enfances narcisse.* Paris: Galilée.

Ovid. 1993. *The Metamorphoses of Ovid*. Trans. Allen Mandelbaum. New York: Harcourt Brace.

———. 1997. *Ovid's Metamorphoses, Books 1–5*. Ed. William S. Anderson. Norman: University of Oklahoma Press.

Pickens, Rupert T. 2014. *Perceval and Gawain in Dark Mirrors: Reflection and Reflexivity in Chrétien de Troyes's "Conte du Graal."* Jefferson, NC: McFarland and Company.

Potters, Susan. 1977. Blood Imagery in Chrétien's *Perceval. Philological Quarterly* 56 (3): 301–309.

Ribard, Jacques. 1989. *Du philtre au graal: pour une interprétation théologique du Roman de Tristan et du Conte du graal*. Paris: Honoré Champion.

Terry-Fritch, Allie. 2012. Proof in Pierced Flesh: Caravaggio's Doubting Thomas and the Beholder of Wounds in Early Modern Italy. In *Beholding Violence in Medieval and Early Modern Europe*, ed. Allie Terry-Fritch and Erin Felicia Labbie, 15–38. New York: Routledge.

The New Oxford Annotated Bible with the Apocrypha (RSV). 1977. Ed. Herbert G. May and Bruce M. Metzger. New York: Oxford University Press.

Turner, Wendy J., and Christina Lee. 2018. Conceptualizing Trauma for the Middle Ages. In *Trauma in Medieval Society*, ed. Wendy J. Turner and Christina Lee, 3–12. Leiden: Brill.

Vibeke, Olsen. 2016. Penetrating the Void: Picturing the Wound in Christ's Side as a Performative Space. In *Wounds and Wound Repair in Medieval Culture*, ed. Larissa Tracy and Kelly DeVries, 313–339. Leiden: Brill.

Viladesau, Richard. 2006. *The Beauty of the Cross: The Passion of Christ in Theology and the Arts from the Catacombs to the Eve of the Renaissance*. Oxford: Oxford University Press.

Walker Bynum, Caroline. 2007. *Wonderful Blood: Theology and Practice in Late Medieval Northern Germany and Beyond*. Philadelphia, PA: University of Pennsylvania Press.

Žižek, Slavoj. 1989. *The Sublime Object of Ideology*. London: Verso.

CHAPTER 6

Narcissus and Testimony: Guillaume de Machaut's *Fountain of Love*

Like mourning and melancholy, trauma and testimony share a bond in their relationship to the wound. The testimony of Chrétien's *Story of the Grail*, for instance, emerges from the confrontation with the commemoration of Christ's wounding on Good Friday, a wounding carrying with it, according to the Gospel of John, a demand to testify where the onlooker must witness to the trauma taking place before him. It is this notion of testimony as a demand coming from the wound that *compels its own witnessing* where I want to begin an exploration of testimony within Guillaume de Machaut's *Fountain of Love (La Fontaine amoureuse)* (c. 1360). For the *Fountain* is a text produced specifically as a testimonial act, a response to the injuries desire has grievously inflicted—and continues to inflict—upon a lover. Unlike with Perceval though, who carries out his witnessing through an agapeic imperative of Christian charity, testimony in the *Fountain* is constructed on the word, on the *imperative to speak* that is most closely bound up with desire, as the lover of the text must testify—and seemingly beyond his control—to the power desire has over him.

The impetus to testify about one's desire in the *Fountain* emerges in its prologue, where the poet-narrator professes his longing to "tesmongnier et dire," to *testify and tell*, regarding the events he relates herein.[1] This connection between testimony and speech goes right to the core of the text's mission, for, as its full title attests—the *Dit de la fontaine amoureuse* (*Tale of the Fountain of Love*)—this is a work that *speaks*. For the *dit*, a genre of poetry whose name comes from the verb *dire* (to tell), employed

© The Author(s) 2019

N. Ealy, *Narcissism and Selfhood in Medieval French Literature*, The New Middle Ages, https://doi.org/10.1007/978-3-030-27916-5_6

in the text in conjunction with *tesmongnier* (to testify), is typically a narrative poem intended to be *spoken*. And the *Dit de la fontaine amoureuse*, like all of Machaut's *dits*, explores *fin'amor*, *telling of love* as accurately as possible, and testifying to the wounding effects of desire.

Why speech though? What is it about the traumatic narcissism that desire inflicts upon the lover that compels him to speak about his wounds? For the lover of Machaut's *Fountain* is hardly an isolated case, as medieval texts are replete with those who feel compelled to profess the lacerations desire inflicts upon them. One such example is the twelfth-century troubadour Giraut de Borneil, who, when singing about his beloved, proclaims:

> Tostemps vuelh que·m deslonge
>   So que·l querraj.
> Mas per lo bon respieg qu'ieu n'aj
>   Deg ieu chantar,
> E si·n cuges plus gazanhar,
> Trop meliurera·ls motz e·ls sos [...]
> Chantar li dei!

> I wish her always to withhold from me any favor I might seek from her. But because of the fair hope she gives me I ought to sing, and if I expected to gain more thereby, I would do much to improve the words and the sweet notes. [...] I must sing to her![2]

Giraut's need to tell others everything stems from a longing to understand the desire that has befallen him and reflects his hope that the wounds of his desire might close (such is the impetus of many a troubadour song!). And he, it would appear, has no choice in the matter. For, as Howard Bloch posits, poets, beginning in the High Middle Ages, understand that they, in the act of creating their art through speech, bear a "responsibility not to remain silent but to share possession of knowledge" to the benefit of others, especially if such knowledge deals with matters of the heart.[3] And this responsibility to tell everyone about one's longing, related to the urgent need to understand one's passion, is found right at the heart of the *Fountain*, evident in the significance of its use of the verb *tesmongnier* (to testify), which primarily implies bringing something forth (like love) into knowledge.[4] *Tesmongnier*, in other words, is an attempt to uncover something that is not immediately evident, to move it from ignorance to comprehension, and to traverse—most importantly for this present study—the traumatic effects of narcissism's wounds. Testimony, therefore, addresses the fundamental unknowability of the traumatic wound and attempts to heal it, and quite radically so, through the *dit*, through speech itself.

In addition to bringing something forth into knowledge though, *tesmongnier* carries a second meaning involving an attempt to provide material proof through speech—for this is, naturally, the duty of the witness. There is, in other words, a simultaneous attempt to approach the *tangible*, the *real*, the *truth*, through testimony. In Machaut's *Fountain*, testimony emerges at the nexus of desire and wounding, through the trauma caused by desire, and, if this present study has demonstrated anything, it is that nothing involving trauma or desire can be clear-cut. Take Narcissus in the Old French lay, for instance, who, in the moment of his *je me plaing* ("I lament myself"), testifies to his demise as desire unalterably wounds him. The more he intends to understand his trauma, the more it simply serves to entrench the divisiveness of his selfhood. The result of his testimony, it would seem, is severed from its intent, and if *je me plaing* is read as a testimonial cry—and I believe it can be—any attempt to heal the wound through speech serves to further the injurious effects desire has upon him. It might appear there is no way to testify to the wounding effects of narcissism when the properties of narcissism work against such testimony. This is because testimony, in a certain sense, is always shot through with its own undoing. For, as Shoshana Felman points out, to testify is always "to *vow to tell*, to *promise* and *produce* one's own speech as material evidence for truth."[5] With this in mind, testimony—as something containing not simply the seeds of its own undoing, but, simultaneously, the hope of its fulfillment—always exists in a state of potentiality. It is, quite precisely, a "speech act," speech that has as its aim an intended outcome that may never arrive. Such is the case in Machaut's *Fountain*, for the testimony professed by the lover—a complicated persona to whom I refer as the *testimonial I* of the text—always exists in a state of hope that it *will reach* its intended audience, even if there are no guarantees of such a thing ever happening. How, then, can this *testimonial I* speak his desire? How can he testify to "his" desire, especially if it, the result of a traumatic wounding, remains something he is still "working through," a "working through" that may not (cannot?) end? How, in other words, to perform the seemingly impossible task of testimony?

6.1   VISION AND SPEECH (*MIRE* AND *DIRE*): THE ECHO OF TESTIMONY

An attempt to address these questions begins with the construction of the *testimonial I* in the *Fountain of Love*, which first starts as a *writing I*, assumed by the poet-narrator who, in the first person, asserts the voice of his authority over the work he is creating. He is not, however, simply the writer of this text, for, as he purports, he will also assume the roles of its primary lover (composing it in honor of his lady), literary critic (directing his readers how to interpret what he composes), clerk (writing for a specific patron), and storyteller (as he leads his audience throughout his adventures). Before launching into the narrative component of the *Fountain* though, he curiously proclaims that he has hidden his name in an anagram—within a few lines near the start of the text—along with detailed instructions to his readers on where and how to find it[6]:

> Or te dirai que tu feras:
> Jusqu'a quarante compteras
> Ces vers ci, et quarante et un,
> [...]
> Nos noms entiers y trouveras,
> Mais trois lettres en osteras
> Droit en la fin dou ver quarante.

> I will tell you therefore what you will do: you will count the verses above until forty and forty-one and you will find our complete names there, but you will remove three letters from them just at the end of verse forty.[7]

Already known for this type of cryptic signature in his other writings, Machaut-as-author though does not stand alone here. Stating that he has intermingled in the anagram his name with that of his patron, Jean de Berry, the poet-narrator suggests that the *Fountain* will not center solely upon his literary alter-ego, but will be a work where another authority—and potentially another voice—comes to join his in its creation. And so, maybe it is not surprising when the poet-narrator, while lying in bed one night in a melancholic state, hears through the open window of his room moaning and wailing. Thinking this is the sound of a ghost, the fright he experiences soon dissipates as he realizes that what he hears is not malevolent, but rather the lament of a knightly prince who, like him, has lost himself in amorous dejection. Separated from his lady, the knight professes that he will compose for her an impromptu plaint detailing all his tortured love—for his hope is that she hears it, finds it pleasing, and, in turn, understands his pain. The poet-narrator, overhearing all this, is thrilled to discover the noises originate from a kindred soul, and is even happier when he learns this unseen neighbor brings literary inspiration. As the knight begins to profess his tale, the poet-narrator shifts away from any story that might have reflected his own experiences and, taking up his writing utensils, composes until daybreak, in fifty poems, this intruding voice's lament:

> Si que je pris mon escriptoire
> Qui est entaillie d'ivoire
> Et tous mes outils pour escrire
> La complainte qu'il voloit dire.
> Si commença piteusement
> Et je l'escri joieusement.
> Douce dame, vueilliez oïr la vois
> De ma clamour, qu'en soupirant m'en vois,
> Tristes, dolens, dolereus et destrois,
>   Ne dou retour
> Ne say dire ne les ans ne les mois.

As such, I took my writing desk, which is chiseled from ivory, and all my tools in order to write the complaint that he wanted to say. He began sorrowfully and I wrote joyously: Sweet lady, please hear the voice of my plaint, because sighing I leave sad, suffering, sorrowful, and distressed, and I cannot tell the month or the year of my return.[8]

Beginning with the anagram intertwining the author with Jean de Berry, Machaut's patron, and most likely the prince of the *Fountain*, the text continues to blur their roles in the composition of this lyric cycle, as one character writes (*escrire*), while another tells (*dire*) of the desire haunting him. As this joint venture begins, any ownership the poet-narrator might have had over the direction of "his" work slips away from his grasp, his voice and meticulously-crafted persona becoming confused with the lament of the dejected knight. One might argue, nonetheless, that the author has not really made much of a sacrifice; giving up his voice for another is the duty that comes to him through his chosen profession. For, the medieval clerk, typically bereft of any amorous self-expression, normally writes on behalf of a chivalric patron who, through the visual processes afforded him in phantasmatic melancholy, displays his prowess on the battlefield of love. Knights, in other words, traditionally *see* and *love*, while clerks, relying on their auditory and verbal faculties, are conversely tasked with hearing about their patrons' love and writing it down.[9]

The *Fountain of Love*, however, while firmly planted within this tradition of knightly lovers and clerkly poets, subverts it as well—something occurring even before the nocturnal lament ever begins. For the narrator, prior to realizing that the voice he hears emanates from another lover, begins to blur the roles of knight and clerk during a defense of his faintheartedness, explaining that he, unlike his chivalric counterpart, is not prone to combating unexplained forces. As proof of this, he contrasts his profession to a warrior's, explaining how he has already had to fight his natural inclinations toward cowardice while campaigning in an unfamiliar land with his lord, and admitting he stayed by this fighter's side in order to be protected from harm. The poet-narrator, as a result, recounts a tale of the survival afforded him, even despite his "natural" clerkly tendencies, precisely due to his symbiotic relationship with a knight. For this friendship to work, the knight must remain bold in his endeavors while the clerk contents himself by employing his verbal skills aimed at composing works that explore chivalric desire:

> Qui se vuet mirer, si se mire,
> Car je vueil tesmongnier et dire
> Que chevaliers acouardis
> Et clers qui vuet estre hardis
> Ne valent plein mon pong de paille
> En fait d'armes ou en bataille,
> Car chascuns fait contre droiture[.]

Whoever wants to look at himself, may he look at himself [*qui se vuet mirer, si se mire*], because I want to testify and say [*tesmongnier et dire*] that a knight who is cowardly and a clerk who wants to be brave are not worth a handfull of straw in feats of weaponry or in battle, for each acts against what is right.[10]

In this exploration of clerkliness and knighthood, the poet-narrator espouses the oppositional nature of these professions within a context of vision and speech, evident in the rhymed couplet *mire* (looking) and *dire* (saying). With vision normally ascribed to knights and words to clerks, the rhyme links these traits to the characters in a way that makes them difficult to separate. For, as already evident, the *Fountain* does not simply contain a knight capable of composing poetry equal to that of a skilled clerk, as he does this night, but also a clerk who dares to profess his own melancholic yearnings for the lady of his desires. The hierarchy separating sight and speech, love and writing, knight and clerk, consequently intermingles, and while the duke who writes or the poet who loves may not on their own be worth a handful of straw, together they create an antiphrastic clerkly knighthood/knightly clerkliness that will come to define the status of the self—of the *I*—within Machaut's work.

In this interplay of self and other, Machaut's use of *mire(r)*, which primarily signifies in Middle French the act of looking into a mirror, proves essential. For, such gazing upon reflective surfaces, invoked twice within the same verse (*qui se vuet mirer si se mire*), establishes within the *Fountain* the traditional narcissistic structure of desire where a specular other comes to define the self. Such a structure, coming through the language (the *dire*, the speech) of the nocturnal poetry, juxtaposes clerk and knight as mirrored images of one another in this joint creation of the lyric cycle. The *I* subsequently has not a singular but a plural identity, simultaneously assumed by clerk and prince. *Mire* and *dire* (vision and speech), coming together to explore the tortured visual and verbal desire of the fifty poems, usurp any autonomy these characters might profess to have over their individual aspirations, joining them in such a way where their voice, vision, and desire cease to be their own but rather operate in service to the other.

In the poetry of Machaut's text, speech and writing blend together into a written speech and a spoken writing, where the *speaking I* of the knight exists through the clerk who composes the book containing his lament. At the same time, the clerk's *writing I* is possible solely because of the knight's speech received through the open window. Due to this, each part of the *I* that emerges—spoken *and* written, clerk *and* knight—works with and through the other, with its mirrored simulacrum, in a way that forms the divisive subjectivity of each in connection to the other. In this manner, vision (*mire*) establishes the construct through which the language (*dire*) of the work marks a self (the *I*) that emerges in its exploration of the language of love—the goal of the literary *dit* (tale). In the need to attest to the effects of love upon the formation of the human subject, the *Fountain* assumes for its aim, as the poet-narrator professes, to *tesmongnier et dire*—to testify and speak—testimony that will be directed toward the lady of his affection as he relates the truth of his experience.

The need for testimony takes on a certain urgency in the text for this *I* constructed through *dire* (speech), and this is due to the fact that the speech he professes is the only thing capable of outlasting him that might also serve as evidence to the passion he feels for his lady. His oft-referenced death thus spurs him on toward a record that will survive his impending annihilation. In this manner, testimony takes on a performative function in the *Fountain*—mirroring the fact that testimony, as Felman argues, neither offers a "completed statement, a totalizable account" nor does it "possess itself as a conclusion, as the construction of a verdict or the self-transparency of knowledge."[11] As a vow to be truthful, testimony always takes the form of "a *speech act* rather than [the formulation of] a statement."[12] To testify, therefore, is to promise to transmit a truth exceeding the language attempting to contain it and, because of this, as I point out in the introduction to this chapter, carries with it the seeds of its own limitations. Testimony, in other words, is *always potential*, never finalizing. Such limitations are quite evident in the *Fountain* whenever the *testimonial I* appeals to the lady to recognize the lover and respond, through her own longing gaze and speech—her own *mire* and *dire*—to his desperate message. In the unknowability of such reciprocity, the lover's tortured yearning enters a profound crisis where any attempt to witness becomes a simultaneous attempt to control the melancholy that, in this failure of reciprocity, inflicts his heart with a sundering blow:

> Si ne me say, ne puis, ne vueil deffendre,
> Eins me couvient vostre merci attendre,
> Se je ne vueil vous ou Amour offendre,
>   Si attendrai
> Tant que Pitez pour moi en vous engendre
> Grace et merci, et que vo face tendre
> Deingne seur moy son dous regart descendre.
>   Mais je ne say
> Quant ce sera, dont je suis en esmay,
> Car trop long sui de vos cointe corps gay[.]

I do not know how to, nor can I, nor do I want to defend myself; I must, on the contrary, wait for your mercy, if I do not want to offend you or Love. I will therefore wait until Pity produces within you grace and mercy for me, and that your sweet face deigns to have its sweet gaze descend upon me. But I do not know when this will be, and this troubles me, for I am too far from your happy and gracious body.[13]

Having no access to her gaze, that marker of what he believes would indicate recognition and a mutual exchange of desire, the *testimonial I* is incapable of knowing if his lady loves him in return. In this vacuum, he suffers from the clichéd language of love; he is wounded as the arrow from her vacant gaze irreparably lacerates his heart, he weeps and sighs, he thinks of despair and remains worried she may choose another man in this absence of visual exchange that might come to him from without. For, as with Dané and Narcissus from the Old French lay (Chap. 2) and René's Heart (Chap. 4), the *testimonial I* of Machaut's *Fountain* remains trapped within the double bind of a bilocational loss, at once external/*dehors* (from the lacking gaze of the lady) and internal/*dedenz* (from a lacking subjective integrity). Possessing a desire-as-lack that possesses him, the faulty *mire* (vision) that does not return a gaze from the longed-for phantasm of the lady quickly becomes a faulty *dire* (speech) as well. With this lack speaking through him, the *testimonial I* expresses a desire shot through with the anxiety that his words will fall upon deaf ears: "Pour ce mes cuers gemist, pleure et se teint./Mais ma dame ne puet oïr son plaint/Ne moy compleindre" [This is the reason why my heart sighs, weeps and darkens, but my lady cannot hear its plaint, nor me complaining].[14]

This crisis of desire stemming from unreciprocated speech brings with it another fear, for the obstacle to fulfillment may not lie solely within the beloved's resistance to return her *dire* (speech) to the lover; there may be a more frightening problem with speech from its inception. Reflecting this, the verses begin to express a building angst over the fact that the lady will not hear him, not because she fails to receive his message, but rather because his testimony *may not have the outcome he intends for it*. The discourse of wounding within the *Fountain* consequently moves from being the result of a failed mutual gaze into the realm of speech, which has the capacity to sunder the lover due to the antiphrastic nature of any language intended to transmit his desire to the beloved lady. His testimony, in other words, may be found lacking in the same way vision has already been. And the real possibility for this failure, that his words may not have the performative effect he wills for them, is precisely what lies at the heart of this crisis coming to the fore in Poem 19 of the plaint:

Et se j'envoy devers ma chiere dame
Dire qu'elle mon cuer mine et entame,
Et que s'amours l'art sans feu et sans flamme

> Et le martyre,
> Et que Desirs de plus en plus l'enflame,
> Elle dira que je ten a son blame
> Et que ne doy dire a home n'a fame
>   Mon grief martyre.
> Et s'il avient que je li vueille escrire,
> Ne say s'elle vorra ma lettre lire.
> Et de si long ne li porroie dire
>   Qu'elle m'affame
> Des tres dous biens amoureus[.]

And if I send a message to my dear lady saying that she wears down and cuts into my heart, and that her love consumes it without fire and without flames, martyring it, and that Desire enflames it more and more, she will say I am aiming for her disapproval and that I should not tell, not men or women, about my painful martyrdom. And if it happens that I want to write to her, I do not know if she will want to read my letter, and from such a distance I could not tell her she makes me hungry for love's sweet goods.[15]

Such linguistic disintegration consequently threatens to upset the entire purpose for this lyric cycle, because if the woman, even in receiving an account of her lover's woes, can still interpret it differently from how he intends, the entire plaint may be irreparably in vain. This alternate implication that will cause her to reject his request is subsequently already present in the language of his appeal from the start—*she will say I am aiming for her disapproval*—an otherness haunting and working against the testimonial agenda of these poems. Accordingly, all the beloved lady has to do is simply return the lover's own language back to him, revealing that his desire for reciprocity is *the very thing* spurring her on to reject him. For, in his words, she will encounter a divergent meaning that will deny him the acoustic reciprocity capable of conferring upon him a supposed end to his suffering. In this manner, testimony, in its attempt to promise truth, finds itself already shot through with deceit, something that Derrida— echoing what Guillaume's lover already knows—explains when he says that

> there is no testimony that does not structurally imply in itself the possibility of fiction, simulacra, dissimulation, lie, and perjury—that is to say, the possibility of literature, of the innocent or perverse literature that innocently plays at perverting all these distinctions. If this possibility that it seems to prohibit were effectively excluded, if testimony thereby became proof, information, certainty, or archive, it would lose its function as testimony.[16]

The "possibility of literature" of which Derrida speaks, this possibility inherent to testimony, infecting and potentially dispossessing it of truth, is the polyvocal nature of literary speech that finds itself at the heart of all linguistic exchanges. This confrontation with speech working against itself, undoing its construction to the point where coherence and mutuality are denied, has a textual precedent in Ovid's myth of Narcissus with the figure of Echo who embodies the "possibility of literature" that comes to shape the testimonial nature of the *Fountain*. As many critics point out, Echo is probably Ovid's most vital contribution to the myth, for what had been primarily a fable about the visual dangers of desire now becomes, thanks to her inclusion, a narrative exploring the libidinal properties of speech as well. Looking at the Latin tale though, it might appear that Echo should not cause any problems for Narcissus; only capable of repeating what she hears, she should simply confirm whatever he directs toward her in an acoustic mirror of reciprocated intention and meaning. The drama between the two characters, however, reveals something quite different when one day Narcissus finds himself alone and, looking around to see if his companions might be nearby, calls out "ecquis adest?" [Is anyone nearby?].[17] Echo's reply—"adest" [nearby]—a seemingly simplistic mimicry of his final word, nonetheless reveals her power to alter meaning through iteration.[18] For she not only transforms a question into a statement but also repeats selectively, taking the speaker's words and altering them so they come back with a *difference in meaning*. When, for instance, Narcissus expresses interest in seeing her and shouts "huc coeamus" [let's meet], a statement that—on his part—does not have any romantic overtones, Echo's response, "coeamus," assumes the form of a sexual request— *let us conjoin and copulate*.[19] Echo, in other words, forces Narcissus to speak a desire he never intended. And this desire *of and from the other*, this *alternate signification* of Narcissus's language coming to him from Echo, is not something coming from without, but is rather a meaning finding itself already present within his words the moment he utters them, conjoined together with them from the start:

> *Coeamus* mixes a request to meet with a request to copulate, to "intertwine." It illustrates and defines the linguistic intermingling that is an echo. A word's various meanings do not simply shatter it and disperse: they intermingle, mate, and couple with each other, a linguistic coupling as troubling, serpentine and confused as sexual copulation.[20]

Such is the polyvocal and, evident in its actions, *narcissistic* nature of the echo, for it is *dire* (speech) acting as *mire* (vision) or, as Ovid refers to it in his myth, a "deceptus imagine vocis," a deceptive *image of the voice*.[21] In this conflation of speech and vision, such an auditory image functions exactly as the simulacrum Narcissus beholds in the fountain, as this is yet an additional instance of an *other* coming in to upset a self that might want to claim dominion over its integrity. For, if Echo can couple with Narcissus's speech and make him profess a desire that goes against his will, if the echo can conjoin with the speech of the *testimonial I* and render the message to the beloved woman—one that returns as a rejection, who is speaking the moment the *I* opens its mouth? If anything, the force of Echo, *of the echo*, calls into question the idea of "original intent." If speech cannot mean what "I say it means," if my speech—infiltrated with the repeated and unavoidable alterity of the echo—works *against itself* and *against my "self,"* how can a unified, self-knowing *I* exist in the first place?

The echo consequently has implications not simply for the relationship between the *testimonial I* and the beloved lady, but rather haunts its formation as clerk and knight join together in their own *coeamus*. This is why, for instance, the poet-narrator's writing of the poetry is not simply a "recording of speech" originating with the knight, for, from the moment he opens his mouth, he does not—cannot—speak with his "own" voice, but rather with one already infected by the echo of polyvocality that undoes any intention he may have. This echo of the other's desire intermingling with his speech, in other words, cites an entire written tradition of love stemming from troubadour poetry. The poems of the knight's spoken lament are thereby infiltrated, in the moment of their inception, with *written* citations—and this is unavoidable. Consequently, the knight *speaks the writing of the poet*, while the poet *writes the speech of the knight*, and, in this conflation of spoken writing and written speech, language alienates any possession the jointly created *testimonial I* might claim to have over its "own" intent, desire, or linguistic production.

Such alienation becomes evident as the lover's plaint, incarnating the echo of polyvocality, forces the *testimonial I* to speak a language it never intended and that may never reach the lady. This *testimonial I*, in other words, divided against itself through language, ceases to be a unified entity, and is sundered—from the force of the echo that (dis)embodies it—into a wounded singular plurality and plural singularity, the definition of a *desiring subject*. The fact, therefore, that the poetry within the *Fountain* is a fusion of the written speech and spoken writing of two conjoined characters merely illustrates that its citational language does not come—cannot come—from one source, but is rather the product of a pluralized subject rent asunder by linguistic copulation. The poet's *writing I* and the knight's *speaking I* subsequently come to mirror one another through the *imago vocis*, the echo's voice that blocks any fulfillment through verbal reciprocity. Such is the reason why the clerk is able to compose poetry in the voice of the knight's otherness because his speech *already emerges in the voice of the other* as soon as he professes it. For now, the lover who wants to hear his own erotic intentions will forever be a frustrated subject alienated by the only language he can employ. This is no longer an *I* speaking, but rather a non-*I*, a non-self, an other speaking in place of the *I*. And because language destroys the speaking/writing self in the moment of the self's construction, the witnessing supposedly taking place with the plaint's *testimonial I*, infected from its inception by the echo's calamitous properties, has the potential to fail as well. In its attempt to witness to the linguistic crisis of the *imago vocis*, the *I* immediately loses its ability to testify. (The poet-narrator, it turns out after all, had a legitimate cause to be frightened by the sounds coming to him from the adjoining room!) Testimony in the *Fountain* witnesses to its own inability to testify, and such is the "truth" of this testimony, a truth escaping the *testimonial I* the moment it is professed.

6.2   The Testimony of Martyrdom

The internal divisiveness within testimonial speech has serious implications for the remainder of the *Fountain of Love*. When the *testimonial I*, for instance, laments the inherently divisive nature of his language in Poem 19, he fears this language will return to sunder him by exterminating his heart. At the same time, he realizes he must try to stem the fallout the echo causes and ensure his message reaches its destination unaltered. How might the image of his beloved, who at this point embodies the echo of his language, reciprocate his speech without difference while conferring wholeness upon him as well? For the *I*, witnessing to his tortured state so the beloved lady might recognize him, naturally desires that she will, even in the face of certain impossibility, acknowledge his message and return it to him as a faithful repetition with no change. Concurrently though, the echo, represented by the idealized phantasm of the woman, cannot originate any speech of its own, but will always return by dispossessing him of univocality with a lacerating polyvocality already present within his own speech. Such wounding is the sole possible response from the echo, and the *testimonial I* knows this, for the words the beloved alters cease to be "his" as they come back to annihilate him—and this annihilation, in turn, becomes, within the logic of the echo's power, the *perceived desire* of the lady. For, if the lady-as-echo appears to want the destruction of the lover, if this is the response he seems to get from her, the *testimonial I*, hoping to conform to these wishes, can thereupon attempt to give her what he thinks she wants. It is at this tension between a lover's desire for univocal integrity and the beloved's perceived desire for polyvocal wounding, that the *I* begins a discourse of witnessing to his love in terms of *martyrdom*, mentioning it first in Poem 19 (*mon grief martyre*). Coming from the Greek for firsthand witness, martyrdom (μαρτυς, *martus*) denotes a drastic *testimony-unto-destruction* and *self-destruction as testimony* that becomes central to a hoped-for solution to the lover's divided state. For, where the personal experience of the lover's self-sacrifice has the potential to transmit the lengths to which he is willing to go for recognition from the woman, she (because she is but a phantasmatic image) has no eagerness—or even ability—to reciprocate anything to the suffering lover.

Nonetheless, this does not stop the lover in his drive for libidinal fulfillment, and his martyrdom becomes a testimonial appeal for mutual witnessing—because, if the woman seems to want something of him, even if it is his destruction, she must be real, and her desire for him authentic. Her *mire* (vision) and *dire* (speech) may not be lacking at all! Ready to sacrifice himself for the woman and give her the self-destruction she seems to demand of him, the lover hopes she will in turn acknowledge the performative intention of his actions, *even if* intent proves problematic due to its polyvocal nature. In the face of the echo infiltrating his subjectivity with the voice of another's desire, the solution appears simply to be willing to accept the echo's destructive polyvocality; such is the reason why *martyre* (martyrdom) in Poem 19 is continuously put in context with language, rhyming with *escrire* (writing), *dire* (speech), and *lire* (reading). The martyrdom of the *testimonial I* is thus *martyrdom for language*, for the *imago vocis*—that image of the voice embodied by the echo—in the hopes that its power can be undone in the face of his self-erasure. Because, if his language has the capacity to wound him, incapable of transmitting his intentions unaltered, he is perpetually in a bind where his language consistently demands his silence—his *infant*—by depriving him of "his" voice. Running this risk, the *testimonial I* endures the martyrdom of witnessing to the echo, which speaks through and with him, "replying" by silencing him in his destruction.

This is the reason why Simon Gaunt, when discussing the prevalence of self-sacrifice in troubadour poetry, notes that witnessing-unto-death is the only process capable of guaranteeing "the subject the recognition [he] craves" because such an act "conceals the possibility that the [woman-as-Other] does not have the power the subject imagines to confer recognition, and the trauma that the [woman herself] may be lacking. Sacrifice denies this trauma because it presupposes that the [woman] does exist, and that [she] lacks nothing."[22] In this manner, martyrdom challenges the echo's catastrophic power by transforming the woman's lack and her inability to reciprocate desire into something that "can be read from within the logic of sacrifice as [the lover's] failure to appease the Other."[23] Failing to appease the woman—precisely because it *can only be* a failure— nonetheless furthers the fiction of her agency. For, even if the echo deprives the lover of an acceptable response from her, this does not imply, under the "logic of sacrifice," that a response can never come. If anything, it simply pushes him further into martyrdom with the testimonial appeal of "look at what I am doing *to myself for you*." In the fantasy created through testimonial martyrdom, the *I* destroys himself—again and again—attempting to prove that the woman might reciprocate his speech and confer upon him the integrated selfhood he craves. Continuous self-sacrifice consequently becomes the sole means the lover has to prove his fidelity to the desire he hopes to receive from the phantasmatic image. As such, martyrdom becomes a simultaneous attempt to undergo *and* circumvent the echo's wounding effects, and, because of this, results in a precarious liminality between wanting integrity and destruction, reciprocated love and suicidal isolation. It is at this nexus between desired fulfillment and desired annihilation that the *testimonial I* ironically finds himself seeking wholeness through self-wounding and erasure. The echo, like the Diamond Mirror of René's *Love-Smitten Heart*, represents that "law of eros," reminding the lover that to love is to remain faithful to the tension arising from the self's synchronous construction and destruction. This fidelity subsequently entails submitting to the reality of language—of "my" language—and the unavoidable wounding it inflicts upon me as I seek to support the fantasy that it can still fulfill. Destroying himself through testimonial martyrdom in order to constitute himself through the same testimonial martyrdom, the lover of the *Fountain* finds himself in an endless cycle of language shot through with the endless repetition of the echo's alterity.

For the *testimonial I* to exist, he really has no choice but to maintain his martyrdom and its fidelity to eros. In this manner, self-sacrifice proves to be "symptomatic of the subject's attempt to retain that which it never had, and this returns us to the trauma that sacrifice seeks to occlude."[24] In the melancholic turn self-sacrifice takes, where distinctions between possession and loss collapse, testimonial martyrdom, far from upholding and transmitting "truth," begins to promote a fantasy—because, as I have already discussed—to exist in the first place, it is already infiltrated with what Derrida terms the "possibility of literature." From within this "possibility of literature," martyrdom denies, even as it calls attention to, the destructive forces of the *imago vocis*. Attempting to hold on to the fantasy, the *testimonial I* seeks to expand the reach of his martyrdom in Poem 30 by turning *to literature*, looking for means other than through "his" language, where he might be capable of alerting the lady to his suffering. For, if his language has been shot through by its own alterity, maybe another— any other—can echo in place of him. Searching for such a figure who might join him to his beloved, the *I* turns to Ovid's *Metamorphoses* and its tale of Morpheus, the god of sleep, who, capable of assuming any form in dreams, can speak any language and make any sound (the literal embodiment of polyvocality). The hope is that Morpheus can visit the beloved in her sleep and, in the form of testimony by proxy, let her know of the martyrdom the *testimonial I* continuously endures for her:

> Pour ce prier vueil au dieu de sommeil
> Que Morpheüs face son appareil
>   Tel qu'a briés mos
> Le gentil corps qui n'a point de pareil
> Sache mon cuer, ma tristece, mon dueil,
> Et qu'il le tient par son dous riant oueil
>   Pris et enclos.

I want to ask the god of sleep to have Morpheus accomplish his mission with simply a few words. In this way, the noble lady who has no equal might know my heart, my sadness, my pain, and might keep my heart, through her sweet and bright gaze, enclosed and hidden.[25]

The reliance of the *testimonial I* upon Morpheus is linked to the text's reliance upon literature to testify, for this persona first appears in the lyric cycle as part of a retelling of the tale concerning Ceyx and Alcyone, the spouses from *Metamorphoses* whose affection for one another creates such a powerful unity that it links them in life and death. For, as Machaut recounts, Alcyone learns about her husband's death because Somnus, the god of sleep, chooses his son Morpheus to appear as Ceyx in her dreams and inform her about her loss. Coming from the same mythical cycle as that of Narcissus in Book Three of Ovid's text, Garth Tissol has argued the story of these inseparable lovers—itself an exploration of singularity and duality—mirrors, in quite overt ways, that of the *infant* before the fountain. Alcyone's dream of her husband's simulacrum, like the image Narcissus sees before him, involves a figurative repetition that presents a truth based on its "verisimilitude, as becomes clear with Somnus's choice of Morpheus as the dream best qualified to take on the task of representing Ceyx. Morpheus's name defines his power to become the perfect appearance of shape [...], in his case human shape."[26] Morpheus, transforming into a copy of Ceyx in the *Metamorphoses*—and subsequently into one of the *testimonial I* in the *Fountain*—must become, to be taken as authentic, an identical simulacrum of the person he represents. This must happen to such an extent that neither Alcyone nor the beloved lady will be able to distinguish between the truth and fantasy of his testimonial intervention. For Alcyone ends up welcoming and embracing, during Morpheus's visit, her husband's image, this copy of a copy with no discernable distinction, which is identical to Narcissus's own confusion of a body for a shade.[27] The appeal to Morpheus, however, has the potential to present the same tension martyrdom brings the *testimonial I*, albeit now under a new guise. For, by allowing himself to be replaced by a simulacrum in a dreamt vision, the *testimonial I* signals his complete surrender to a self-erasure marking the effects his desire has had on him from the start. Nonetheless, his call for the god's help allows him the opportunity to solidify the fantasy that, despite his destruction, unification with the beloved image is possible:

> Mais s'en son cuer tient secretement close
> De Morpheüs la parole et enclose,
>   Et le matin,
> Au resveillier, l'en souveigne et la glose
> Et qu'elle dongne a chascun mot sa glose,
> Certes, je tien que mon fait se repose
>   En dras de lin.

But if she holds Morpheus's words secretly enclosed and gripped in her heart, so that in the morning, upon awakening, he makes her remember them and their proper meaning so that she gives each word its proper meaning, I think my concerns will certainly sleep in linen sheets.[28]

The oneiric encounter between Morpheus as the lover's double and the image of the woman, to whom the god will speak in dreams, represents the longed-for reciprocity the *testimonial I* craves, albeit now enmeshed all the more in an illusory world where simulacra interact with one another in perfect symbiosis. And such fantasy can humanize the lady all the while conferring, as Žižek states, "upon the hitherto impossible/unattainable object a body, which gives the untouchable thing a voice and makes it speak—in short, which *subjectivizes* it."[29] For, in this subjectivization, the *testimonial I* claims that the lady-as-image will be able to use her acumen for linguistic interpretation, rendering unto each word of Morpheus's message its proper meaning or *glose* ("gloss" in English). Coming from the Greek for *tongue*, gloss (γλώσσα, *glóssa*) implies that, upon remembering the god's oneiric intervention the following day, she can make each word received from him "speak correctly" and that, despite the repetition this recall will necessitate, a repetition which might be shot through with an echo of difference, no such alteration will occur. The goal of the *testimonial I*, through its reliance upon Morpheus, is to outdo language by using language, a fantastic search for a strict univocality that will destroy the inherent echo of language's polyvocal nature:

> Que tout d'un fait
> Songier souvent ne doit mie estre fable,
> Einsois chose doit estre veritable,
> Quant elle n'est muant ne variable.
>   Aussi de fait
> Elle verra les maus qu'elle me fait,
> Se Morpheüs a droit me contrefait,
> Et que je l'aim de loial cuer parfait,
>   Ferme et estable,
> Et qu'elle m'a par le riant attrait
> De son dous oueil droit parmi le cuer trait.
> Mais ne sont l'arc, la saiette et le trait
>   D'if ne d'erable.

Dreaming often about the same event should not be a fable, but rather true since it does not change or vary. Also, in truth, if Morpheus imitates me justly, she will see the pains she gives me and that I love her with a true and loyal heart that is firm and stable and, by the pleasant attraction of her sweet eyes, that she has struck me right in the heart, but the bow, the arrow and the shot are not made of yew or maple wood.[30]

The request is remarkable, for in this disregard for polyvocality, the *testimonial I* entrenches himself in the ambiguities of fiction and truth where, evident in the paired rhyme of *fable* (fantasy) and *veritable* (truth), he proclaims dreams must be authentic. This is an authenticity that can somehow withstand the *variable* nature of the iterations required because, as Morpheus imitates and repeats the form and message of the *testimonial I*, he instills the message within the woman who, recalling it the next day, shall be expected to understand everything seamlessly, with no deviation at all from the "original" intended meaning. *Fable*—literature—in the fantastic world of the *Fountain*, carries with it just as much testimony as *veritable*, as truth.

A similar blurring of *fable* (fantasy) and *veritable* (truth) haunts the attempt of the *testimonial I* to undo the echo through Morpheus's verisimilitude, for, in the wished-for dream, a like encounter of phantasms will take place as the god assumes the form of the lover. The *I* though comes to know fulfillment, not through any physical coupling that might occur after his beloved receives the message through this somnial delivery system, but rather solely through her image:

> Douce dame dont je porte l'empreinte
> Dedens mon cuer figuree et empreinte,
> Que fine amour y a mis et empreinte
>   A un pincel
> De Souvenir, mais tout entour enseinte
> De loyauté l'a qui garde l'enseinte,
> Qu'autre n'i soit figuree ne peinte,
>   Dont trop m'est bel,
> Par Souvenir vois tost a son appel,
> Quant je l'aeur, mon dieu terrien l'apel.
> Sans li muer, morray en ceste pel,
>   Car joie mainte
> M'ont fait si oueil qui ne sont fier ne fel.

> Souvent li di, souvent li renouvel,
> En lieu de vous, quant je sui en revel,
>   Ceste complainte.

Sweet lady whose imprint I carry etched and depicted within my heart that fine love put and inscribed there with Memory's brush, surrounding it with loyalty and keeping it enclosed so no other imprint could be depicted or painted there, this is something that suits me well. Thanks to Memory, I rush to its call, and when I adore it, I call it my earthly god, without changing it, I will die in this body, for its eyes, which are neither arrogant or treacherous, have given me much joy. Often, when I am joyful, I say and repeat this complaint to the imprint instead of you.[31]

With all the overtones of religious zealotry, the *testimonial I* in this poem lays it on the line. The image (imprint), held within his heart, is permanent, protected by sweet memories that will propel him to martyrdom simply for the chance of her bountiful gaze. This confrontation with the beloved's simulacrum, a waking dream reflecting the nocturnal vision he hopes to relay to his beloved, shall be the fulfillment of his quest and undo, not simply the problems *dire* (speech) has caused him, but will also serve as the undoing of *mire* (vision), of the destructive and lacking gaze Narcissus experiences at the fountain. For in this hoped-for seamless transmission from lover to Morpheus to beloved, there shall apparently be no alteration, nothing shall be *variable*. And if the *testimonial I* succeeds in this literary venture, he shall also succeed in his *testimony*, where no lack exists, the longed-for mutual gaze comes to fruition, and happiness prevails: "Car de joie n'arai, bien le tesmong,/Jamais deffaut" [For, so I testify, I will never lack joy].[32]

6.3   MUTE WITNESS: TESTIMONY AT THE FOUNTAIN

The desire for reciprocity within the poetic cycle of the *Fountain* comes to fruition at daybreak when the poet seeks out the prince whose lament caused him so much happiness during the night. After meeting, the two enter a garden where they walk toward an ornately constructed fountain atop an ivory pillar. The first thing the poet notices about this fountain—even before seeing its twelve-headed golden serpent watering a lavishly illustrated marble basin—is that the story of Narcissus has been hewn into its ivory pillar. This tale *par excellence* of phantasmatic desire, the longing that haunts him and his companion so much they stay awake the entire night, makes such an impression upon him that he is overtaken, for the story strikes him as something alive, living right there upon the fountain: "Que par ma foy! y m'estoit vis,/Quant je le vi, qu'il estoit vis" [By my faith it seemed to me, when I saw it, that it was alive].[33] And yet, despite the mention of the classical myth, the sole time it will appear in Machaut's text, the poet does not expound on it, quickly moving on to a discussion of the finely rendered images in and around the marble bowl depicting scenes from the story of the Trojan War.

Leaving aside for a moment the slightness of this reference to Narcissus's story, it is important to point out that critics have noted that these textual references, a hark back to the Greek and Latin cultural past of the Middle Ages, render this marble and ivory construct in the center of the garden a veritable *fountain of literature*, a symbol of the intertextual nature literary production necessitates, and a textual inheritance in turn irrigating Machaut's entire work. As such, the *Fountain of Love*, like the aquatic source from which it derives its name, is a text, in the true spirit of *translatio studii*, conscious of its debt to that which precedes it, telling the various tales—sometimes more than once—that support and testify to its narrative thrust. Ceyx and Morpheus, for instance, have already made their appearance during the nocturnal poetic lament, depictions of the story of the Trojan War emerge at the fountain and later again, while the ancient myth of the Sybil has its own importance yet to be revealed. The *Fountain of Love*, in other words, is a work that deliberately incorporates such source material, witnessing to its enduring power while repeating it in a new context that is unique and innovative. The fountain, the recipient of this nourishing legacy of classical provenance, rightly finds itself at the heart of the work as the primary symbol of a polyvocal ensemble echoing these tales of melancholic desire and struggles for erotic and physical dominance.

In addition to this Greek and Latin inheritance though, the fountain, with its inscription of the Narcissus story upon its ivory column, also places Machaut's work within a medieval tradition, drawing inspiration (like René's *Love-Smitten Heart*) from Guillaume de Lorris's *Romance of the Rose*. This text, with its own version of Ovid's tale carved into the stone of the fountain at the center of its garden, transforms the classical myth into an exemplum of *fin'amor*, for this is *the* pool, its readers learn, where Narcissus died. His story, the only thing surviving him in the *Rose*, serves as a visual and linguistic memorial to his fate. The same might be assumed of the parallel circumstances with Machaut's fountain, especially when the poet-narrator claims that he finds the story to be alive (*y m'estoit vis* [...] *qu'il estoit vis*) in a statement that, due to the ambiguity of the masculine pronoun *il* ("it" or "he"), conflates text and character in a move that potentially eliminates any distinction between the two. The fountain appears to bring the *infant* forth—as if alive—in his own literary text, inscribing him upon the ivory in a way that stands in *for* him as a testament *to* him. As a tale basing itself in speech and vision, *dire* and *mire*, the pillar should have a direct testimonial function, an assumption furthered by the poet-narrator's use of the expression "y m'estoit vis," typically rendered into English as "it seemed to me." However, in the original Latin—"mihi est visum" (to me is seen)—from which the phrase originates, there is a direct link to visual perception, where a speaker expresses certainty over what he or she *is seeing* and uses the phrase to express such truth to others. The poet-narrator, relating that the living story causes Narcissus to appear as alive, gives his own accurate account of what he witnesses here. There is, nonetheless, one catch, for instead of using the opportunity to testify about this story that seems alive, revivifying its central character to an audience which might also be suffering from melancholic eros, he instead shrouds it in silence. Narcissus's tale, in other words, is *there* and *not there*, obvious enough for the poet-narrator to recognize it but seemingly not important enough to relay as he does with the myths of Ceyx and Morpheus or Paris and Helen. What is the purpose of a memorial bringing its readers right to the edge of testimonial language—for the story is just right there on the column—and yet remaining mute as to what it relates?

Machaut's fountain is quite a perplexing memorial, for while apparently testifying to Narcissus's story, it does not serve as a deterrent to subsequent lovers, who still come here to repeat the horror that befell their mythic predecessor. The fact that such a fate inscribed on the fountain does not hinder these lovers is, I argue, related to the poet-narrator's reticence surrounding any narration of it, for this is a story that *resists* testimony, a story where Narcissus, a (non-)self, dies and where Echo, the only witness to this event, cannot speak of her own volition. All that remains is silence, a deadly muteness annihilating any witnessing that were to take place, even if it could:

> The specific circumstances of Narcissus's death signal the impossibility of knowing and narrating Narcissus's story. They cut the story from any narrative voice, from any subjective source. In fact, this cut contextualizes Narcissus's story as a traumatic event. It is suspended, outside of memory, radically foreign to any story that "I" might want to tell.[34]

This is a tale sundered within itself, a *wounded narrative of wounding* where witnessing, speech, and truth cannot coincide. No person can give a firsthand account of this rupture, for in its unknowable trauma, incapable of being told even as it emerges, it comes to be the place where testimony itself breaks down, silencing all who might dare speak of its impossible nature. With a story that attempts to speak of the stillborn character of human subjectivity, the question should turn from exploring why the poet-narrator shrouds it in silence (because he has no choice) to rather—how can it exist in the first place? For the story tells of and embodies the *infant* of the echo, the *infant* coming to silence all through their "own" words, the *infant* that has already silenced the *testimonial I* during the poetic cycle as well as the poet-narrator at the fountain. As with all traumatic narratives, the myth of Narcissus contains what Felman refers to as "the paradoxical story of an inherent resistance to storytelling. Every trauma includes not only a traumatic story but a *negative story element*, an *anti-story*."[35] And because such tales undo themselves in their own telling, they embody "the difficulty of articulation and the tragic unnarratability of the ungraspable disaster and its immeasurably devastating, unintelligible drama. The impossibility of telling is not external to this story: it is the story's heart."[36]

This incapability to relate Narcissus's anti-story consequently poses a problem for these characters trying to relay any truth about the fountain, and this is despite the fact that the poet-narrator claims he has *already related* to his readers "le voir sans fable/De la fonteinne delitable" [the truth, without fables, about the delightful fountain].[37] Such a statement opens up various questions regarding truth, the witness's agency, and the potential for testimony to take place when confronted with a silencing trauma that has no witness. In order to address these concerns, I shall turn toward an exploration of the fountain itself, whose construction reveals some answers—for it does have a message it decrees—as the poet states when he sits down in the garden "[p]our escouter et pour vëoir/L'ordenance de la fonteinne" [to listen to and see the fountain's ordinance].[38] So, what does the fountain have to say? The ivory pillar and the marble basin may be the place to start, for these contain the fountain's language and imagery, the aural and visual aspects most readily available to the onlooking listener. Acting exactly as the jasper and black marble columns of the *Love-Smitten Heart*, the pillar and basin give the appearance of having petrified the words and images upon them, seemingly stabilizing any meaning they contain. This permanence, though, is but a fiction, a mirage resembling the phantasm of the marble-like statue Narcissus beholds upon the fountain's waters, which is, in truth, ephemeral and devoid of all stability. The fountain's waters subsequently work to counterbalance the false petrification housed by the ivory and marble, liquefying all notions of univocality, of coherent selfhood, of *testimony*, and replacing them with a divisive polyvocality haunting the entire construct. The multiheaded snake ceaselessly irrigating the fountain embodies this quality, for the water, coming from twelve separate mouths in a polyphonic chorus related to the *coeamus* of Ovid's fable, dissolves any univocal narratibility of Narcissus's tale. Such is the fountain's decree—its *ordenance*—a term which, as Alexandre Leupin claims, "seems to accord to writing the power to say anything and everything. This mastery and this confidence are summed up in a single word: *ordenance*, the Law of discourse, the nature of fiction."[39] It is *ordenance*, the thing the poet-narrator sits down to observe and hear, that undoes him and his companion, for "[t]hey are both subjected to the nature of language, to its felicities, to its desires. This nature [...] permits poetry to make and un-make them. Language: that which subverts every appropriation of place by whatever subject, if only in order to there define itself by a fundamental usurpation."[40] Derrida's "possibility of literature" is always there, a testimonial anti-testimony, which becomes, in truth, the only possibility for testimony. Speech, in other words, is always and already infiltrated by *ordenance*, and the wounding of narcissistic desire denies speech the possibility to transmit "my" truth.

That the language of anti-testimony silences these characters, making testimony impossible, has haunted the text from the start, only reaffirmed in the garden as the lover tries to give voice to his martyrdom at the fountain. Continuing the lament from the previous night, he informs the poet-narrator that he has unrequited desires for a lady unaware of his feelings, and that he will most likely die and be erased from her memory. Attempting to speak of what he believes to be his impending death, he fears his testimony will fail, and any wish he might have to send her a message shall become hindered by the fact that such a declaration of love might displease her. The echo remains the fundamental barrier blocking him from what he wants, for it is always there, refracting his intentions and destroying his testimony. Even though Echo cannot speak of her own accord, she nonetheless can witness, through any speaker, to the divided subjectivity occurring at the fountain; all I have to do is open my mouth and she, infiltrating my speech, testifies to the annihilation of selfhood—of my selfhood—through the unavoidable polyvocality of "my" language. This permeability between self and other, however, is already at the heart of testimony for, as Felman posits, the witness, although bearing a "radically unique, noninterchangeable and solitary burden," paradoxically also "transgress[es] the confines of that isolated stance, to speak *for* others and *to* others."[41]

The *Fountain of Love* attests to this permeability when the poet, writing in the first person of the *testimonial I*, composes a series of verses *for another*. It is at the fountain that the lover tells the poet he would like some proof of his love and asks his companion, who knows the art of love, to compose a testimonial on his behalf that will survive his death. The poet, producing the poems from the night before, surprises the lover, who thought his martyrdom was hidden from everyone. In this manner, the poet testifies by inhabiting the lover's voice, and the lover receives "his" testimony written with the poet's hand—testimony that relates the impossibility of testimony because of its infiltration by otherness. As already evident with the poetry, the literary references present at the fountain are also markers of the voice of the other haunting all works. For Machaut's appropriation of Ovid's story—even if the *Fountain of Love* never contains a concrete narrative of it—testifies to Echo's strength inscribed at the heart of "his" book that speaks of her mute witnessing. For such literature reveals the intertextual nature of Machaut's literary creation by threatening the coherence of any authorial voice he may claim to have. The echo of alterity becomes the only way within the *Fountain* that witnessing is possible, providing the space necessary for the work's creation while simultaneously problematizing its very nature. In this sense, it is impossible for the *I* to testify when the echo has already destroyed it the moment it brings forth language. And, as such, any speech transformed by the echo—in truth, *all language*—becomes a generalized testimony to the echo already inhabiting my speech, testifying on its behalf through me. Each speech act I make testifies to Echo's memory of Narcissus's disaster and to the radical alienation any self experiences from its sense of "self." Speech, as a generalized testimony to this division, always references the divisiveness of desire as well—for, when I speak, I speak the language of my wounding, the language of eros, the language of desire. The lover and poet-narrator have no choice but to submit, like Narcissus before the fountain or like Heart before the Diamond Mirror, to this divisive power. To be in love is to testify to this division and to want, like the lover of the *Fountain*, this testimony to be true, an accurate account of the wounding my libidinal speech inflicts upon me. This is why, for instance, the woman's gaze that the lover imagines to receive from her is not a look of consolation but rather one of violence—and welcomed violence at that—when her sweet eyes shoot an arrow right into his heart and tear his integrity asunder. Such consistent self-destruction, as evident with the lover's perpetual martyrdom, is, in truth, the joy of eros, the joy—in a real sense—of the echo itself, and this is where the garden scene of Machaut's *Fountain* leads, as it contemplates the pleasure to be gained from this precarious state of being wounded by desire and failing to achieve satisfaction.

6.4   Echo's Response: The Joy of Narcosis

The wounding speech of the echo's mute powers, even as it speaks to his desire, is the central problem that the *testimonial I* has tried to keep at bay since the start of the *Fountain*. This is no more evident in the way the narrator makes use of the term for *word* (*mot* in the singular and *mos* in the plural), that basic linguistic element finding itself at the center of so much of these characters' anxieties. Each time *mot* or *mos* appears in the *Fountain*, a total of twelve times, it designates either a desire to keep silent (speaking no words), to control signification (each word should have a "proper meaning"), to speak as few words as possible, or to emphasize that meaning has not been disturbed (texts are copied, for instance, word for word—*mot a mot*—to ensure no corruption in the transfer).[42] Words, *mos*, present a primary threat within Machaut's work, and language itself, the means by which the text that the poet-narrator composes exist, is shot through with its own potential undoing. For, even when he claims to have identically replicated a text, as he does with the lover's nocturnal lament in the garden, this does not necessarily safeguard against the fact that additional meanings can still escape his grasp. His work of *simply repeating* language already carries with it the threat of the echo's alteration, and such inadvertent consequences bring with them harrowing implications. The fantasy over linguistic control that an *exact copy* of speech brings may be most pertinent when the poet, in composing the knight's lament as he bemoans the fact that he must endure his wounds—his *maus*—writes: "[s]i me couvient mes maus souffrir et taire" [I must suffer and silence my pains].[43] Naturally, the echo orchestrates this torture, for any request directed toward the beloved may return as a rejection, the *mos* (words) of the amorous appeal, reflecting back upon him as grievous lacerations—as *maus*. The verse exposes the duality of meaning here, for in the near homonym of *mos* and *maus* ("words" and "pains," *mots* and *maux* in contemporary

French orthography but with an identical pronunciation), a similarity not visible but, nonetheless, audible, the written, and spoken aspects of the poetic cycle diverge, no longer coinciding with one another. An "exact" copy—*mot a mot* (word for word)—loses any ability the narrator might have professed to contain and confine meaning, while the *mos/maus* (words/pains) returning do not simply cause the *testimonial I* to suffer but also silence him, his words, his *mos*, and, along with it, the narrator's authorial acumen.

At the locale where the silenced literary inscription upon the ivory column mingles with the words and wounds—*mos* and *maus*—of the *testimonial I*, the poet and lover lie on the grass and, with their heads resting upon one another, fall asleep near a stream emanating from the fountain. The poet then immediately enters into the world of oneiric fantasies, relating a dream that he, now a *dreaming I*, claims to testify to truth: "En mon dormant songay un songe/Que je ne tien pas pour mensonge" [In my sleep I dreamt a dream that I do not consider a lie].[44] At the start of this vision, told entirely from the poet-narrator's perspective, Venus appears and, speaking about the lover, states that although she has recognized his suffering and inexperience with love, he is partly to blame, for, by claiming to be constantly dying because of "les maus d'amer" [the pains (*maus*) of love], he has never asked for her assistance.[45] Despite this, she takes pity on him, bringing with her the knight's beloved lady, who has come to console the suffering knight: "Conforte toy et plus ne pleure,/Car je vueil, ordonne et devis/Qu'aies merci et ton devis" [Take comfort and do not cry any more, for I want, order and hope that you have mercy and what you desire].[46]

The answer to this longed-for fulfillment at the heart of the nocturnal lyric cycle comes in twenty poems where that entity previously feared as capable of destroying the lover with her words of rejection—the beloved woman—finally speaks. Already in the first poem, it is clear all will be well, as she exhorts the lover to abandon his suffering and accept the relief her words bring to him:

> Amis, je te vieng conforter
> Et joie et solas aporter
> Et de ces tenebres oster
>   Ou je te voy
> Et aussi te vien j'enorter
> Que tu te vueilles deporter

De faire dueil et toy getter
  De ceste anoy.
Et je te promés, par ma foy,
Que m'amour et le cuer de moy
Aras toudis aveques toy,
  Et sans fausser,
Seray tienne, faire le doy;
Et se tu ne prens cest ottroy,
Jusqu'a mort me verras, ce croy,
  Desconforter.

> Lover, I come to comfort you, to bring you joy and consolation, and to remove this darkness I see you in, and also I come to exhort you to please leave behind this mourning and these troubles. And I promise you, by my faith, that you will always have my love and my heart with you, without betrayal, I will and must be yours; and if you do not accept this gift, you will see me, I believe, hopeless until death.[47]

Affirming that her gaze *does* exist and recognize the forlorn lover, she completes the one-sided glance he before projected toward her, transforming him into the object of her vision and, consequently, her desire as well. It is not, however, simply the gaze she reciprocates, but also all his pain, because if he does not cease with his suffering, his death will become hers, as she joins him in a self-sacrificial ritual aimed at proving that the joyous desire of this "other"—now *him*—prevails.

The problem all along, it would appear, has lain with him; *he* has been blind to the reality of her affection for him and to the lengths she would go to demonstrate the veracity of this mutual yearning. In this manner, the text introduces the dream—fiction—as testimony, testimony as haunted by Derrida's "possibility of literature," testimony that *undoes the very premise of testimony*. There is no need to martyr the self to prove the desire of the other because, in the poetic language put forth from the woman's mouth, her desire for the lover is shot through with the hope that it *already does* and *will continue*. Her words construct an entire host of "future memories" that promise a joyful permanence for this erotic satisfaction: "Et loing et pres, ou que je soie,/T'aim et desir/Et ameray sans repentir" [And near or far, wherever I am, I love and desire you, and will love you without repenting].[48] For him to continue his martyrdom no longer serves any purpose, since the lady assures a new reality of what is to come, concretizing what the previously uncertain future might bring. The lover's self-sacrifice, his testimonial martyrdom, has worked, obscuring any deficient qualities the lady might have had and, much like melancholy, making the fantasy of reciprocal desire into a seeming reality. And this *will not change* due to the fact that their lives are now intertwined in a coupling that suffers no loss or abandonment: "tu es miens et je suis toie,/Sans retollir" [you are mine and I am yours with nothing lacking].[49] The lady brings in her response a desire fulfilled, and a fulfillment devoid of lack—*sans retollir*—for the once-dreaded echo has, in essence, answered, and it has altered nothing, as the lover's amorous hopes, inscribed in the lady's own speech, rebound back with all fears erased and all wishes realized.

The mutuality occurring in the lady's poetry subsequently comes to fruition when, upon concluding, she kisses the lover and, looking at him and holding out her hand, exchanges rings with him—placing on his finger her ruby ring and taking from him his diamond ring. Venus, overjoyed by the transaction, departs with her companion just before the lover and poet awaken to discover two miraculous occurrences: they have shared the same dream and the lover bears on his finger the ruby ring his lady has given him. Events in dreams, normally housed solely within the realm of oneiric visions, have now traversed their confines and, in this collapse of reality and fantasy, emerge into what is now a generalized fantastic reality/realistic fantasy. Testimony, haunted by the literariness of language, speaks to the reality of fantasy, and this is precisely why the poet can assuredly state that this dream is not a lie—not a *mensonge*. Such a collapse between reality and fantasy, however, does not bring with it any of the confusion one might expect, but rather a radicalized univocality where fulfillment now reigns supreme—desires have been attained and lover and poet, whose speech and writing earlier did not conform to one another in exact similitude, now come together by the fountain in their experience of the same dream—*mot a mot* (word for word).

After these post-oneiric realizations, the lover thanks not only Venus but Morpheus as well, this god who replied to his request and, because of this, the woman knows he loves her. This dual invocation of love and fantasy housed within the personae of the two gods thus come together, as their symbolic manifestations work as one on behalf of the erotic fulfillment he experiences. For, Venus is capable of serving as his lady's guide within the world of dreams, and Morpheus, as the *testimonial I* professes during the nocturnal lament, is able to render images, such as the one created by Pygmalion, real:

> Pymalion fist l'image d'ivoire
> Que moult pria et ama sans recroire,
> Mais il n'ot pas si tres noble victoire
>   Ne tel eür
> Comme j'aray, se Morpheüs avoire
> Ce que je tieng qui sera chose voire.

Pygmalion made his image of ivory that he greatly loved and ceaselessly prayed to, but he did not have such a noble victory nor the happiness that I will have, if Morpheus renders this true, as I hope he does.[50]

What though is this *voire*, this truth, for which the lover yearns here? During the dream, for instance, the lady chastises those, like the lover, whose desires transcend the bounds of what fantasy will not allow:

> Mais qui autre mercy desire
> Et qu'il dit qu'il pleure et soupire,
> Dont il le couvient a martyre
>   Vivre et manoir,
> Il a tort et assés s'empire.
> Venus scet bien ceste matyre.
> Pour ç'ose bien devant li dire
>   Qu'on doit savoir
> Qu'il ne fait mie son devoir,
> Eins vuet sa dame decevoir
> Qui autre mercy vuet avoir.

But he who desires another favor, saying he weeps and sighs for it, must live and remain in martyrdom. He is wrong and worsens his case. Venus knows this story all too well, and this is why I dare to say before her, as it is obvious, that he does not act as he should, but wants to deceive his lady as he seeks another favor.[51]

Desire, born out of a phantasmatic process, must remain centered upon the image for it to function as it sustains and prolongs itself. Quite simply, without the image, as the *Fountain* tells us, desire can neither exist nor serve any purpose. For, while the lady warns the knight that any attempt to move from fantasy into reality will signify negative intentions on his part, she knows that to keep him happy, to maintain the longing he has for her, she has to move the discourse back into a space where the fantasy of fulfillment can occur. Fantasy, in this sense, must infiltrate any sense of the real in order for desire to succeed. This is why, before exchanging rings, the woman orchestrates an exchange of images, because in such reciprocity, his happiness can be hers as well. In this manner, the two become mirror images of each other's desire in an idealized mutuality:

> Mais ton ymage je porteray
> > Et ta figure
> En mon cuer que je garderay
> Pour le mien que je te lairay[.]

But I will carry your image and likeness in my heart, this I will keep, in exchange for mine that I will leave for you.[52]

The blurring of fiction into reality that the dream creates opens a space for the image to survive, as it is this phantasm that will sustain the knight, even in his lady's absence and his distance from her: "Mais mon fin cuer en porteras/Et mon ymage/En quoy tu te conforteras" [But you will take my pure heart and my image, in which you will find comfort].[53] The image, in other words, transcends all barriers that deceptive fiction may try to impose upon it, and becomes, for all intents and purposes, *real* in the assurance of a joyous future.

The dream, in the realization of the image, acts as a meta-fantasy, for fantasy is made real *through* fantasy as it reconfigures the echo whose destructive forces earlier decimated any hope of reciprocal desire. As such, the dream sequence fulfills its function as fantasy should, the purpose of which, as Žižek posits, is to answer the "unbearable enigma of the desire of the Other, of the lack of the Other; but it is at the same time fantasy itself which, so to speak, provides the co-ordinates of our desire—which constructs the frame enabling us to desire something."[54] Without fantasy, desire would not be possible, and if, as I have argued throughout this study, that desire is what constitutes the self (as the myth of Narcissus purports), it is fantasy that creates human subjectivity. For it is *fantasy as desire*—through a desire for intersubjectivity, for reciprocity with an imaginary other—in all its precariousness, that preserves selfhood, created through the destructive forces of a desire that simultaneously destroys it through its creative forces. It is fantasy that allows for this maintenance of the desire that sustains in annihilation and annihilates in sustenance one's sense of self:

in the fantasy-scene the desire is not fulfilled, "satisfied" but constituted (given its objects, and so on)—*through fantasy, we learn "how to desire."* In this intermediate position lies the paradox of fantasy: it is the frame co-ordinating our desire, but at the same time [...] a screen concealing the gap, the abyss of the desire in the Other. Sharpening the paradox to its utmost—to tautology—we could say that desire itself is a defence against desire: the desire structured through fantasy is a defence against the desire of the Other, against this "pure," trans-phantasmatic desire.[55]

For, as Žižek outlines here, fantasy does not really cause wishes to come true, but, as evident in the *Fountain*, the desire satisfied in the dream sequence, the desire continuing on after the dream has ended, shapes the reality of these characters. At the same time, it also combats any of the painful divisiveness that the echo previously caused as well as any of the conscious self-sacrifice the knight might endure to prove himself worthy of the lady's gaze. Through the reveries of the dream sequence, he learns, in a real sense, *how to desire*, mastering the fact that desire can only be linked to fantasy and experienced through fantasy. For it is the image (and the imaginative properties it suggests) that propels desire forward while covering over all notions that it lacks the ability to reciprocate any longing projected onto it. The lady and the knight can complete one another through the images they keep, and this will be *sans retollir*, without alteration.

Accordingly, sleep is necessary—for the poet-narrator and prince repose here not simply because they were kept awake the night before, and not simply because Morpheus has cast his spell over them either. For in the garden where Narcissus suffered his fate, where the waters of melancholic narcissism—in a literal sense—permeate the entire locale, those who enter are naturally *bound to sleep* due to the fundamental sedation produced by the mythic story carved into the fountain. As Pierre Hadot points out, for instance, the narcissus flower remaining by the fountain after Narcissus's liquefaction, due to its strong scent, dulls and stupefies.[56] In this manner, it has, as its popular etymology indicates, a *narcotic* effect (νάρκη, nárke > numbness; νάρκωσις, nárkosis > narcosis). And the text attests to this due to the fact that, in the narcotic slumber of the dream, the knight is able to ignore the error committed by his mythic predecessor. Nonetheless, such a coma-like effect is also necessary for the constitution of selfhood through desire. For, as the knight and poet might understand the divisive powers of the echo, of the image, of their *"own" desire upon them*, the somnifacient effect of narcissistic reveries helps them maintain the façade that the self can be complete. In order for the self to maintain the illusion of its wholeness and integrity, to maintain the desire in and through the "reality" presented by the image, the narcotic stupor cast upon the poet and lover in the garden undoes any potential harm inflicted by the echo and image, and it is the fantastic reality/realistic fantasy of the dream, where such wounds can be ignored and overcome, that provides the ideal space for the testimony of such a joyful experience.

That fantasy has the ability to make the image appear real in this dream is, however, not the first time images have seemed authentic within the *Fountain*. Pygmalion, as the *testimonial I* recounts during the nocturnal lyric cycle, carved an image of ivory—an *image d'ivoire*—a creation he wished were real with such intensity that Venus, according to the account in Ovid's *Metamorphoses*, makes it alive, much like the oneiric sequence with the goddess and the knight's beloved lady. Apart from extratextual references, however, Pygmalion also created at Venus's request the Fountain of Love, the aquatic source at the heart of Machaut's text, carving into the ivory pillar the story of Narcissus, the story that the poet-narrator claims to look *vis*, alive. Intertextually, ivory proves important to the structure of such illusions, for this material is central to an extensive literary tradition, stretching back to Homer, in which dreams enter into the sleeper's imaginative faculties through a Gate of Ivory; ivory—*ivoire*—is consequently the substance that causes images to become true—*voire*—through fantasy, as Machaut attests, in the rhyme *ivoire/voire* employed in the *Fountain*.[57] Through the ivory that brings a fantastically true testimony, this fantasy of fantasy, this desire as a defense against desire, comes the joy of narcosis, that exhilaration numbing any negative forces that alteration, lack, or division might inflict upon the self. For satisfaction is always there, just waiting in fantasy, where the *I* can believe that what it conjures up in imaginative fancy is in fact real. This is why the lover exclaims at the end of the dream that the somnial vision heightens its own veracity and maintains his desire:

> Comment joie li aporta
> En disant que l'impression
> Par douce ymagination
> Devoit avoir de sa figure
> Contre tous maus qu'amans endure[.]

> How she brought him joy by telling him he should have, thanks to sweet
> imagination, the imprint of her image, useful against all the pains a lover
> endures.[58]

Such is the reason, for instance, that the text is called the *Fountain of Love*,
a title the lover announces at its midpoint, for this is a piece of literature
irrigated by the phantasmatic properties its aquatic source embodies.
However, this is not the work's sole title—and, perhaps not surprisingly
for a text steeped in the discourse of duality and divided selfhood—there
is a second title: the *Book of Morpheus*, a title to which Machaut attests in
his *Book of the True Poem* (*Livre du Voir Dit*).[59] One singular work that
bears two titles referencing two distinct personages, Narcissus at the fountain and Morpheus in the dream, twinned characters who come together
(much like the *writing I* and *speaking I* at the text's start) to direct the
entire work and to lull its characters into a stupor where images of ivory
achieve authenticity, a stupor that is not only narcotic, but morphinic as well.

This joint somniferous effect has larger implications within the
Fountain, for ivory images are not simply linked to Morpheus and
Narcissus, but also to the process of writing itself; the poet's desk upon
which he composes the nocturnal lament is "entaillie d'ivoire" [sculpted
from ivory].[60] Language, in this sense, does not simply wound, but also
transmits the dulling effects of its wounding. Just as the erotic image has
the power to become real through fantasy, the linguistic image as the
phantasm does as well. And the image (or phantasm) is not simply the
source of desire, memory, and dreams, but also finds itself central to language. For, as Aristotle outlines in *On the Soul*, a word is the combination
of a mental image and the sound to which it is linked: "Not every sound
[…] made by an animal is voice […]; what produces the impact must have
soul in it and must be accompanied by an act of imagination, for voice is a
sound *with a meaning*."[61] Agamben, expounding upon this Aristotelian
notion and its influence upon medieval phantasmatic theory, explains that:
"only those [sounds] accompanied by a phantasm [are words,] because
words are sounds that signify. The semantic character of language is thus
indissolubly associated with the presence of the phantasm."[62] In this manner, words, based within and emanating from the image, join together
with desire and the dream, as all three operate within the tension of realistic fantasy and fantastic reality that the image represents. For the
Fountain, unreservedly playing up this ambiguity, is all about the authenticity of the image, as literature, quite plainly, comes alive on its pages as

figures from classical texts interact with the poet-narrator and knight at the pool, itself inspired by Ovid and the *Romance of the Rose*, where Narcissus met his fate. To combat any doubts as to the truthfulness of such literature, the poet uses the *Book of the Sibyl*—recounting the story of one hundred senators who had the same dream—to demonstrate that because this text *says so*, it is possible for multiple people to have identical oneiric visions, and for those visions *to be true*.[63] Literature consequently testifies to the accuracy of dreams as dreams simultaneously testify to the truth of literature, and the phantasm, at the center of all this, creates a closed system where fantasy works to create its own realistic appearances in a "reality" where language becomes miraculously self-evident. In this manner, writing makes the fantasy real, since, as Jacqueline Cerquiglini-Toulet points out, "art has a connection to *necromancy*. Magic [*magie*] is the anagram of *image*. Art is metamorphosis. It gives life and voice to the inanimate."[64] As such, writing, by making the image appear real, functions like desire, which similarly renders the longed-for phantasms, as in the poet and lover's dream, alive: "in order to write, [Machaut] creates himself with his tools, the quill, the paper or parchment, an object worthy of being loved, even if this object is an 'image,' a linguistic being that writing makes stable. The laws of love are in truth the laws of grammar."[65]

Through the image, desire and writing emerge to sustain the actualization of the image, which in turn produces more desire and more writing; this is, in truth, a concretization of the fantasy, of the fantasy *through* fantasy. The fixation on the beloved lady's phantasm, in other words, is the genesis for the original fifty poems, which in turn cause further obsessive thoughts leading to the production of twenty more as fantasy compounds upon itself, and through all this, lover and poet find a place where the image seems capable of being appropriated. Because, if it worked for Ceyx and Pygmalion, why can it not work here as well? The fountain in the garden, as that place of the phantasm, naturally finds itself at the center of all this, for those who drink from its waters do so to sustain the enticing reflections that appeal to their longing for erotic permanence. Not surprisingly, there is a strong impetus in the text to fulfill the melancholic imperative the aquatic source puts in motion and to make the image also alive—*vis*—in reality. In this sense, Machaut's *Fountain* looks ahead to later works like Cervantes's *Don Quixote*, whose own knight has the audacity to commit the "error" of living the fantasy, of living literature, as if it were true—and to the point where reality becomes unthinkable without the fantasy that informs and directs it.

And literature *does not stop* infiltrating the reality of the *Fountain*! For just before taking his leave at the text's conclusion, the knight opens his mouth and sings a rondeau:

> *En païs ou ma dame maint*
> *Pri Dieu qu'a joie m'i remaint.*
> Se j'ay heü peinne et mal maint,
> *En païs ou ma dame maint,*
> Espoir ay qu'en aucun temps m'aint,
> S'en dit mes cuers qui siens remaint[.]

> I pray that God will joyfully bring me back to the country where my lady lives. If I have had a lot of sorrow and pain in the country where my lady lives, I have hope that the time will come when she loves me, my heart that remains hers tells me so.[66]

Such a melodious outburst, emanating from the exuberance carried within *his heart*, connects back to the power that desire and language have to render the phantasm authentic. For it is the heart, as the lady explains during the dream, that houses her image and that, in its beating, speaks here—in the rondeau—letting loose an energetic current that passes through the throat and out the mouth. This process of poetic composition, as Agamben explains, links "eros and poetry, desire and poetic sign", where the poetic sign

> arises in the spirit of the heart [and] can immediately adhere both to the dictation of that "spiritual motion" that is love, and its object, the phantasm impressed by phantastic spirits. [...] [Such a process], uniting phantasm, word and desire, opens a space in which the poetic sign can appear as the sole enclosure offered to the fulfillment of love and erotic desire in their roles as the foundations and meaning of poetry.[67]

The lover, in other words, sings this rondeau already infiltrated by the voice of the phantasm, of the image-as-echo housed within him, of this other he hopes is real, of this other that lives within him, directing his "own" speech to profess his "own" desire for it. This is what it is to love, to accept the echo that deprives me of my voice, to allow it to speak the language of love for me and through me:

One must welcome the other that is already at work in one's so-called "own" voice in order to learn how to put it to work and transform it. The poet most certainly occupies Narcissus's place, but does so in order to accomplish what Narcissus is incapable of doing: recognizing, loving, embracing the other directly in the voice. Instead of fleeing like Narcissus […], I must—this is the Ovidian law which is also the law of poetry—move toward it, mating with that which has already mated with me.[68]

The entirety of the *Fountain* becomes a testament to the power of this image-as-echo and the connection it establishes between language and fantasy, and how both operate together in a way to shape the lived experiences of these characters. For the rondeau, identical to the dream, speaks to that which is yet to come, the hope for happiness and fulfillment—just right there if believed and accepted—as a *lived future* concretized in the memory of the heart. According to the poet, everything is going well as the lover leaves, secure in his love and armed with all the weaponry needed to combat desire, sighs, and tears: "Venus, lui, s'ymage et sa gent/Et son rubis que point n'oubli" [Venus, himself, her image and nobility, and her ruby that I cannot forget].[69] The ruby ring, that object which broke the barrier between sleep and wakefulness, seems to be the clincher, for this is the culminating proof, on top of all the literary evidence the narrator provides, that proves the veracity of the dream, the image, and the lady's overwhelming reciprocal affection for the knight.

Then, upon the lover's departure, the narrator, in the closing words of the *Fountain*, exclaims: "Dites moy, fu ce bien songié?" [Tell me, was this well dreamed?].[70] Everything, it would seem, is thrown up in the air. What exactly is dreamed here? The entire text? A dream somewhere that did not announce itself as such as it was happening? In this address to the audience, we are forced to rethink everything that came before, to work through, to *repeat* the entire text, and this time potentially with an understanding of the text that *differs in its repetition* from what we first thought. These concluding words retroactively dissolve any stability the *Fountain* may have had with the mute directive of this echo that has been there all along, bringing an altered interpretation to every word, an interpretation to which we were oblivious as we read and which, nonetheless, was right there, reverberating throughout all its pages. For, it would appear that the entire narrative is told from within the dream, within the image, within the fantasy, a fantasy we did not know we were experiencing, a fantasy announcing itself *as real*, as a *testimonial experience* from the start. And this testimony is, of course, related to language, to writing, to the ivory desk upon which the poet-narrator composes his work, repeating his ability—like Pygmalion's story upon the ivory column—to make images and words appear as alive. As such, the poet does not need to retell the story of Narcissus when he sees it at the fountain, for he has already retold it—*is already retelling it*—throughout the entire text. The *Tale of the Fountain of Love*, the *Dit de la fontaine amoureuse*, as its name reveals, already *tells* the story of the echo, of the phantasm, of the construction and dissolution of selfhood through imagery and language, through *mire* (vision) and *dire* (speech).

The fact that Machaut's work substitutes itself for Pygmalion's inscription does not in any way diminish the testimonial silence so central to the Narcissus myth inscribed upon the ivory column, even if the final line of the *Fountain* appears to send the exact opposite message. For it begins with an appeal to its audience to speak—*tell me*—and then a question, imploring us to witness to the beauty, efficacy, and authenticity of what we have just experienced, and just experienced *as a dream*. We, however, can give no answer to this question—for where and to whom would we direct such a reply? The text's appeal for our speech, in fact, has the opposite effect, as it silences us in its muting appeal. Any response we might be able to render has already been undercut by the echo, so evident in this final line, that forces us to go back and reconsider all the language that *will have already* preceded our own, a reconsideration that radically alters any intention we may have read in it, a reconsideration that radically alters any intention we may have in our own speech as well. The concluding verse dissolves the stability we might find in our own speech, as this echo of the text bears its multivocal imprint upon us, upon what has come before us. For in this now generalized dream, which we unknowingly approach on our first reading of the text, the text collapses any distinction between wakefulness and sleep. We enter into the text *as if asleep*, into a generalized morphinic narcosis, as its words dissolve any ownership we might claim over our desire to direct its "intention," to direct our intention in its interpretation, in short, to *testify*. And this is a fate already foretold at its start in the anagram containing the "names" of narrator and knight. Because this anagram dissects each name, each identity, weaving every letter of both personages into the words of the text, and to such a point that they lose their individuality, their very "self." For although many have taken up Machaut's game, trying to reconstitute these names from the letters of the words in these verses, each attempt, each repetition, fails to arrive at an "original wholeness" of the name—the best one can arrive at are "names" bearing the mark of alteration, of difference, of "something else" either added or taken away. Language dissolves and changes the self, and such is the silence of the echo speaking through me and beyond my control, testifying to the stupor that the image, this text, and language itself hold over me as my self conforms to and is dissolved by the linguistic image—the *imago vocis*—that constitutes me. In this waking dream, we want to believe that reality can guarantee the promise of the phantasm, identical to the promise housed by the reflection Narcissus sees upon the fountain's waters, identical to the promise Morpheus holds out to the lover in his oneiric visions. The closest we can get though, the closest to which we can testify, always comes through fantasy, through writing, through literature. Machaut's *Fountain of Love* teaches us that it is not reality that informs literature, but rather the reverse, as it is language and its literary production that informs our reality. Life, in this sense, becomes a generalized dream, a generalized fantasy, in truth, a generalized testimony to the literary experience.

NOTES

1. Guillaume de Machaut, *Le Livre de la fontaine amoureuse*, ed. Jacqueline Cerquiglini-Toulet (Paris: Editions Stock, 1993), v. 132; 40. Quotations in Middle French, with verse and page numbers cited, are taken from this edition. English translations are my own.
2. Giraut de Borneil, "Razon e leuc" in *The "Cansos" and "Sirventes" of the Troubadour Giraut de Borneil: A Critical Edition*, ed. and trans. Ruth Verity Sharman (Cambridge: Cambridge University Press, 1989), vv. 35–40 and 52, 131, 133, translation modified.
3. R. Howard Bloch, *The Anonymous Marie de France* (Chicago: University of Chicago Press, 2003), 36–38.
4. This is evident in the *Story of the Grail*, "l'estoire ensi le tesmoigne,"—as the story *testifies* or *makes known*. See: Chrétien de Troyes, *Le Roman de Perceval ou le conte du Graal*, ed. William Roach (Geneva: Librairie Droz, 1959), v. 2807, 82.
5. Shoshana Felman, "Education and Crisis, or the Vicissitudes of Teaching" in *Testimony: Crises of Witnessing in Literature, Psychoanalysis, and History*, by Shoshana Felman and Dori Laub (New York: Routledge, 1992), 5.
6. Scholars have arrived at different spellings of these names in this anagram (all derivations of "Guillaume de Machaut" and "Jean de Berry et Auvergne"), but none form *exact* spellings of either name. Laurence de

Looze argues the genius of Machaut's anagram lies precisely in its problematic solvability. See: "'Mon nom trouveras': A New Look at the Anagrams of Guillaume de Machaut—The Enigmas, Responses, and Solutions" in *Romanic Review* 79.4 (1988), 537–57. For a discussion of how Machaut constructs his authorial persona in his works, see: Elizabeth Eva Leach, *Guillaume de Machaut: Secretary, Poet, Musician* (Ithaca, NY: Cornell University Press, 2011), 82-131.

7. Guillaume, *Fontaine*, vv. 45–47 and 49–51, 36.
8. Ibid., vv. 229–39, 46, 48.
9. Jacqueline Cerquiglini-Toulet, *"Un engin si soutil": Guillaume de Machaut et l'écriture au XIVe siècle* (Paris: Honoré Champion, 2001), 113.
10. Guillaume, *Fontaine*, vv. 131–35, 40.
11. Felman, "Education," 5.
12. Ibid.
13. Guillaume, *Fontaine*, vv. 347–56, 54.
14. Ibid., vv. 456–68, 60.
15. Ibid., vv. 523–35, 66.
16. Jacques Derrida, *Demeure: Fiction and Testimony*, trans. Elizabeth Rottenberg (Stanford: Stanford University Press, 2000), 29–30.
17. Ovid, *Ovid's Metamorphoses, Books 1–5* (Norman: University of Oklahoma Press, 1997), v. 3.380, 97; Ovid, *The Metamorphoses of Ovid* (New York: Harcourt Brace, 1993), 92.
18. Ibid.; Ibid.
19. Ibid., vv. 3.386–87, 97; Ibid.
20. Nouvet, *Enfances narcisse* (Paris: Galilé, 2009), 38. My translation of: "'*Coeamus*' entremêle une demande de rencontre à une demande de copulation, c'est-à-dire d''entrelacement' [...]. Il illustre et définit l'entremêlement linguistique qu'est un écho. Les divers sens d'un mot ne se contentent pas de le faire éclater et de le disperser: ils s'entremêlent, s'accouplent, et couplent les uns avec les autres, couple linguistique aussi troublante, serpentine, et confuse que la copulation sexuelle." For more on the use of Echo in Medieval French literature, see: Miranda Griffin, *Transforming Tales: Rewriting Metamorphosis in French Medieval Literature* (Oxford: Oxford University Press, 2015), 68-101.
21. Ovid, *Metamorphoses*, v. 3.385, 97.
22. Simon Gaunt, *Love and Death in Medieval French and Occitan Courtly Literature: Martyrs to Love* (Oxford: Oxford University Press, 2006), 30.
23. Slavoj Žižek, *Enjoy Your Symptom!: Jacques Lacan in Hollywood and Out* (New York: Routledge, 1992), 64.
24. Gaunt, *Love*, 35.
25. Guillaume, *Fontaine*, vv. 708–13, 78.

26. Garth Tissol, *The Face of Nature: Wit, Narrative, and Cosmic Origins in Ovid's Metamorphoses* (Princeton: Princeton University Press, 1997), 78. For a reading of this rewriting of the myth of Morpheus in the *Fountain*, see the conclusion to Griffin's *Tales*, 211-35.
27. Ibid., 83.
28. Guillaume, *Fontaine*, vv. 756–62, 80, 82.
29. Žižek, *Enjoy*, 66.
30. Guillaume, *Fontaine*, vv. 782–94, 82, 84.
31. Ibid., vv. 1003–18, 96, 98.
32. Ibid., vv. 801–02, 84.
33. Ibid., vv. 1311–12, 114.
34. Nouvet, *Enfances*, 150. My translation of: "Les circonstances spécifiques de la mort de Narcisse signalent l'impossibilité de connaître et de narrer l'histoire de Narcisse. Elles coupent l'histoire de toute voix narratrice, de toute source subjective. Cette coupure inscrit de fait l'histoire de Narcisse dans la parenthèse qu'est l'événement traumatique. Elle est suspendue, hors mémoire, radicalement étrangère à toute histoire qu'un 'je' pourrait vouloir se raconter."
35. Shoshana Felman, *The Juridical Unconscious: Trials and Traumas of the Twentieth Century* (Cambridge, MA: Harvard University Press, 2002), 240.
36. Ibid., 159. I do not agree with those who claim Machaut does not include Narcissus's story because it is already so well known during the fourteenth century. Machaut includes his own version of the myth elsewhere, most famously in his Motet VII, and obviously understands that it explores themes related to desire, language, and human subjectivity. See: Guillaume de Machaut, *Poésies lyriques, Vol. II*, ed. V. Chichmaref (Paris: Honoré Champion, 1909), 495–96.
37. Guillaume, *Fontaine*, vv. 1421–22, 120.
38. Ibid., vv. 1372–73, 118.
39. Alexandre Leupin, "The Powerlessness of Writing: Guillaume de Machaut, the Goron, and Ordenance" in *Yale French Studies* 70 (1986), 137.
40. Ibid., 136.
41. Felman, "Education," 3.
42. Consider seven of the eight times *mot* appears here: "Et qu'elle dogne a chascun mot sa glose" [and may she give to each word its proper meaning], v. 760, 82; "je nul mot ne sonne" [I speak not a word], v. 979, 96; "Que mot ne dist" [saying not a word], v. 1036, 100; "Onques n'i fist arrest ne doute/Qu'escripte ne fust mot a mot" [He did not stop and did not doubt that it was written word for word], vv. 1522–23, 126; "Mais ci l'ay mot a mot escript,/Si com veü l'ay en escript" [But I wrote it word for word just as I saw it written], vv. 1993–94, 152. The eighth use juxtaposes *mot* with the tortures of love: "Mais qui scet bon mot, se le die./Si vous

dirai la maladie/Qui me perse le cuer de l'ame" [But he who knows a good word, let him say it. I will tell you about the malady piercing my heart and soul], vv. 1443–45, 122. The plural form, *mos*, appears twice in the phrase "briés mos" or "in few words." See: v. 710, 78; v. 2109, 158.

43. Guillaume, *Fontaine*, v. 397, 58.
44. Ibid., vv. 1565–66, 128.
45. Ibid., v. 2152, 160.
46. Ibid., vv. 1622–24, 132.
47. Ibid., vv. 2207–22, 164.
48. Ibid., vv. 2229–31, 164.
49. Ibid., vv. 2225–26, 164. In Middle French, the verb *retollir* implies that nothing is removed or lacking in this relationship.
50. Ibid., vv. 963–68, 94.
51. Ibid., vv. 2335–45, 172.
52. Ibid., vv. 2257–60, 166.
53. Ibid., vv. 2241–43, 166.
54. Slavoj Žižek, *The Sublime Object of Ideology* (London: Verso, 1989), 118.
55. Ibid.
56. Pierre Hadot, "Le mythe de Narcisse et son interprétation par Plotin" in *Narcisses*, ed. Jean-Bertrand Pontalis (Paris: Gallimard, 2000), 84.
57. On the connection between ivory and dreams, see: Frederick Ahl, *Metaformations: Soundplay and Wordplay in Ovid and Other Classical Poets* (Ithaca: Cornell University Press, 1985), 261–64. The rhyme of *ivoire* and *voire* in the *Fountain* occurs in vv. 1395–96: "Et Venus le marbre et l'ivoire/Fist entaillier, c'est chose voire" [And Venus had the marble and ivory sculpted, this is true]. See: Guillaume, *Fontaine*, 118.
58. Guillaume, *Fontaine*, vv. 2616–20, 188.
59. Guillaume, in his *Book of the True Poem* (*Livre du Voir Dit*), twice references this second title: "Je vous fais escrire l'un de mes livres que j'ai fait derrainement, que on appelle *Morpheus*" [I am going to have copied for you one of my books I recently wrote, it is called *Morpheus*] and "Je vous envoie mon livre de *Morpheus*, que on appelle *La Fontaine Amoureuse*" [I am sending you my book *Morpheus*, called *The Fountain of Love*]. See: Guillaume de Machaut, *Le Livre du Voir Dit*, ed. Paul Imbs (Paris: Librairie Générale Française, 1999), 124, 126, and 186, my translations.
60. Guillaume, *Fontaine*, vv. 229–30, 100.
61. Aristotle, *On the Soul* in *The Basic Works of Aristotle*, trans. Richard McKeon (New York: Modern Library, 2001), 573.
62. Giorgio Agamben, *Stanzas: Word and Phantasm in Western Culture*, trans. Ronald L. Martinez (Minneapolis: University of Minneapolis Press), 76–77.
63. This tale is known as the *Book of Sybil*. See: Josiane Haffen, *Contribution à l'étude de la sibylle médiévale* (Paris: Les Belles Lettres, 1984).

64. Cerquiglini-Toulet, *Engin*, 210. My translation of: "L'art est en rapport avec la nigromance. Magie est l'anagramme de l'image. L'art est métamorphose. Il donne vie et voix à l'inanimé."
65. Ibid., 226. My translation of: "Pour écrire, [Machaut] se forge avec ses outils, la plume, le papier ou le parchemin, un objet digne d'être aimé, même si cet objet est une 'image,' un être de mots que l'écriture fixe. Les lois de l'amour sont bien des règles de grammaire."
66. Guillaume, vv. 2825–30, 200.
67. Agamben, *Stanzas*, 128.
68. Nouvet, *Enfances*, 70. My translation of: "Il faut accueillir l'autre qui est déjà à l'œuvre dans la voix soi-disant propre afin d'apprendre à le mettre à l'œuvre et à en faire quelque chose d'autre. Le poète s'occupe certes la place de Narcisse, mais afin d'accomplir ce dont Narcisse est incapable: reconnaître, aimer, embrasser l'autre à même la voix. Au lieu de le fuir comme Narcisse [...], je dois donc—telle est la loi ovidienne qui est également la loi lyrique—m'avancer vers lui, m'accoupler à lui qui s'est déjà accouplé à moi."
69. Guillaume, *Fontaine*, vv. 2842–43, 200.
70. Ibid., v. 2848, 200. For how this concluding line speaks to the problematic nature of interpretation in the *Fountain*, see: Daisy Delogu, "'Laisser le mal, le bien eslire': History, Allegory, and Ethnical Reading in the Works of Guillaume de Machaut" in *A Companion to Guillaume de Machaut*, ed. Jennifer Bain and Deborah McGrady (Leiden: Brill, 2012), 269.

REFERENCES

Agamben, Giorgio. 1993. *Stanzas: Word and Phantasm in Western Culture*. Trans. Ronald L. Martinez. Minneapolis, MN: University of Minneapolis Press.

Ahl, Frederick. 1985. *Metaformations: Soundplay and Wordplay in Ovid and Other Classical Poets*. Ithaca, NY: Cornell University Press.

Aristotle. 2001. *On the Soul*. In *The Basic Works of Aristotle*. Trans. Richard McKeon, 535–606. New York: Modern Library.

Bloch, R. Howard. 2003. *The Anonymous Marie de France*. Chicago: University of Chicago Press.

Cerquiglini-Toulet, Jacqueline. 2001. *"Un engin si soutil": Guillaume de Machaut et l'écriture au XIVᵉ siècle*. Paris: Honoré Champion.

Chrétien de Troyes. 1959. *Le Roman de Perceval ou le conte du Graal*. Ed. William Roach. Geneva: Librairie Droz.

de Looze, Laurence. 1988. "Mon nom trouveras": A New Look at the Anagrams of Guillaume de Machaut—The Enigmas, Responses, and Solutions. *Romanic Review* 79 (4): 537–557.

Delogu, Daisy. 2012. "Laisser le mal, le bien eslire": History, Allegory, and Ethical Reading in the Works of Guillaume de Machaut. In *A Companion to Guillaume de Machaut*, ed. Jennifer Bain and Deborah McGrady, 261–275. Leiden: Brill.

Derrida, Jacques. 2000. *Demeure: Fiction and Testimony*. Trans. Elizabeth Rottenberg. Stanford, CA: Stanford University Press.

Felman, Shoshana. 1992. Education and Crisis, or the Vicissitudes of Teaching. In *Testimony: Crises of Witnessing in Literature, Psychoanalysis, and History*, by Shoshana Felman and Dori Laub, 1–56. New York: Routledge.

———. 2002. *The Juridical Unconscious: Trials and Traumas of the Twentieth Century*. Cambridge: Harvard University Press.

Gaunt, Simon. 2006. *Love and Death in Medieval French and Occitan Courtly Literature: Martyrs to Love*. Oxford: Oxford University Press.

Giraut de Borneil. 1989. Razon e leuc. In *The "Cansos" and "Sirventes" of the Troubadour Giraut de Borneil: A Critical Edition*. Ed. and Trans. Ruth Verity Sharman, 130–135. Cambridge: Cambridge University Press.

Griffin, Miranda. 2015. *Transforming Tales: Rewriting Metamorphosis in French Medieval Literature*. Oxford: Oxford University Press.

Guillaume de Machaut. 1909. *Poésies lyriques, Vol. II*. Ed. V. Chichmaref. Paris: Honoré Champion.

———. 1993. *La Fontaine amoureuse*. Ed. Jacqueline Cerquiglini-Toulet. Paris: Editions Stock.

———. 1999. *Le Livre du Voir Dit*. Ed. Paul Imbs. Paris: Librairie Générale Française.

Hadot, Pierre. 2000. Le mythe de Narcisse et son interprétation par Plotin. In *Narcisses*, ed. Jean-Bertrand Pontalis, 127–160. Paris: Galimard.

Haffen, Josiane. 1984. *Contribution à l'étude de la sibylle médiévale: étude et édition du MS. BN., F. FR 25 407 fol. 160v-172v: le livre de Sibile*. Paris: Les Belles Lettres.

Leach, Elizabeth Eva. 2011. *Guillaume de Machaut: Secretary, Poet, Musician*. Ithaca, NY: Cornell University Press.

Leupin, Alexandre. 1986. The Powerlessness of Writing: Guillaume de Machaut, the Goron, and Ordenance. Trans. Peggy McCracken. *Yale French Studies* 70: 127–149.

Nouvet, Claire. 2009. *Enfances narcisse*. Paris: Galilée.

Ovid. 1997. *Ovid's Metamorphoses, Books 1–5*. Ed. William S. Anderson. Norman: University of Oklahoma Press.

Tissol, Garth. 1997. *The Face of Nature: Wit, Narrative, and Cosmic Origins in Ovid's Metamorphoses*. Princeton, NJ: Princeton University Press.

Žižek, Slavoj. 1989. *The Sublime Object of Ideology*. London: Verso.

———. 1992. *Enjoy Your Symptom!: Jacques Lacan in Hollywood and Out*. New York: Routledge.

CHAPTER 7

Epilogue: Between *Je me plaing* and *Iste ego sum*

The thirteenth-century trouvère Thibaut de Champagne begins one of his songs by praising the qualities of *fin'amor*—love, wisdom, and goodness—that have trodden a path through his heart. His love is so strong, he proclaims, that it lights up the night, and when he beholds the sweet gaze of his beloved lady, her countenance makes the brightest day in summer appear dark. Unfortunately, though, she has not reciprocated his inclinations, and, because of this, he has lost any sense of who or where he is:

> Or n'i voi plus mes qu'a lui me conmant,
> Que toz pensers ai laissiez por cestui:
> Ma bele joie ou ma mort i atent,
> Ne sai le quel, des que devant li fui.
> Ne me firent lors si oeil point d'anui,
> Ainz me vindrent ferir si doucement
> Dedens le cuer d'un amoureus talent
> Qu'encor i est le cous que j'en reçui.
> Li cous fu granz, il ne fet qu'enpirier;
> Ne nus mires ne m'en porroit saner
> Se cele non qui le dart fist lancier,
> Se de sa main i voloit adeser.
> Bien en porroit le cop mortel oster
> A tot le fust, dont j'ai tel desirrier;
> Mes la pointe du fer n'en puet sachier,
> Qu'ele brisa dedenz au cop douner.
> Dame, vers vos n'ai autre messagier

© The Author(s) 2019
N. Ealy, *Narcissism and Selfhood in Medieval French Literature*, The New
Middle Ages, https://doi.org/10.1007/978-3-030-27916-5_7

Par cui vos os mon corage anvoier
Fors ma chançon, se la volez chanter.

I no longer see except for this one thing, to entrust myself to her, for I have forgotten all other thoughts than this: since I was in her presence I wait either for my death or my beautiful joy, I do not know which of the two. Her eyes did not cause me any torment, on the contrary, so sweetly they came to strike me with an amorous desire, right in my heart: the blow that I received from them is still there. This blow was deep, it does not stop worsening; and no doctor could heal me except she who shot the arrow, if she deigned to touch the wound with her hand. She could heal the deadly blow, something I want so much, by removing all the wood from the arrow's shaft; but the iron tip, she will not be able to remove because when it struck me it shattered inside. Lady, I have no other messenger with whom to send my heart other than my song, if you are willing to sing it.[1]

Thibaut's song, reflecting the state of a *lyric I* caught within a matrix of desire where the options are death or life, pain or joy, positions his self-hood as one that is mortally wounded since he does not—cannot—know whether this lady's gaze can truly heal him. The trouvère, nonetheless, seems to contradict himself, for although he likens his beloved to a doctor who might be able to cure him through her touch, she remains incapable of making his body whole, as the arrow's sharp tip irretrievably broke within him as it pierced his flesh. He may want the wound healed, but even if his lady were to reciprocate his affection, desire has forever altered his corporeal integrity. Having opened himself up to her, he learns precisely what Narcissus comes to experience, that a beloved other, no matter what she might do, lacks any ability to render him complete and to satisfy his longing. No amount of self-sacrifice on his part can do the trick, and even the lyric's ending, in the appeal he makes to his heart to send the song to her, demonstrates his impotence. In his suffering, there is no guarantee she will receive the song, sing it in return, and echo back his speech with the intention he believes to have inscribed in it. Consequently, the song, as an object housing his desire, acts as an instrument prolonging his suffering, wounding him in return, and permits the lack it carries in its words, this estrangement from his own self, to act as his sole reality.

As evident in Thibaut's song, selfhood, as I have explored throughout this study, is perpetually divided by desire—by love—if we can conflate the two terms here, and, as Derrida states, always operates within a framework of narcissism, of instability, of alterity:

Narcissism! There is no narcissism and non-narcissism. There are narcissisms that are comprehensive, generous, open, and extended. What is called non-narcissism is the economy of a much more welcoming hospitable narcissism, one that is much more open to the experience of the other as other. I believe that without a moment of narcissistic reappropriation, the relation to the other would be destroyed [...] in advance. The relation to the other—even if it is asymmetrical, without possible reappropriation—must trace a movement of reappropriation in the image of oneself for love to be possible. Love is narcissistic.[2]

Here, Derrida puts forth the idea that all intersubjective relations, even those seemingly one-sided, must be based on "narcissistic reappropriation," or the appropriation of the Other into the self, as a prerequisite for their existence. And, accordingly, there is no alternative, no other definition of selfhood. The Other, in this sense, must come into and define the self through a process of wounding that maintains the wound of subjectivity open because it is the desire of the self, in order to keep the hope alive for eventual completeness, to see his or her own libidinal yearnings returned, just like Narcissus, in the gaze of the other. The desire to desire, to be fulfilled, *to be human*, according to Derrida, is narcissistic, and, as such, is the only thing that renders love possible. As we saw with Ovid's tale, the mythic adolescent burns with impossible desire for the image he sees on the fountain's surface, first, because he comes to realize that the "other" he beholds is the representation and definition of the "self," and he wants to know that the desire he feels is aimed at an acknowledgment of himself in the love of this other. Derrida's exclamation that "love is narcissistic" is continuously reinforced whenever the human self, as in the manifestations of narcissistic desire studied throughout the medieval literature of this book, longs to see his or her own idealized image reflected in and through the desire of an other. As I have striven to explain in each chapter, such is the definition of selfhood, where the other of desire, language, the echo, the unconscious, the *self*, comes in to destroy any notion of integrated subjectivity.

I quote from Thibaut and Derrida because I find both, although separated by nearly 800 years, to be speaking with a similar outlook regarding love, narcissism, and their effects upon the self. At the start of this book, I began by stating that its central theme was to be about selfhood, or, more precisely, how we can understand the process of coming into our selfhood and of what this selfhood might consist. Together, these two give us an answer—that selfhood is always infiltrated by otherness, that subjectivity is always intersubjective in nature. Throughout this book, I have explored how literary texts use Ovid's myth of Narcissus as a means of understanding such notions of selfhood. To these ends, I have made reference to *je me plaing* ("I lament myself"), Narcissus's exclamation from the Old French lay bearing his name, as the key to comprehend how selfhood emerges in each of the literary texts I examine, as well as the various psychoanalytic discourses I employ as a means of exploring how each arrives at its own theories of selfhood in ways relating to this plaint. As I state in Chap. 2, *je me plaing*, stemming from the divisiveness that Narcissus undergoes when he realizes the image can neither see nor desire him, establishes him through its grammar as an *I* (je) and *myself* (me), reflecting the separation of his selfhood between subjective and objective statuses. His subjectivity, in other words, comes forth in the desire to be the image's *object of affection*, something which, of course, can never happen. His pain consequently invokes the etymology of *plaing* which, coming from the Latin verb *plangere*, instills a self-beating, a self-wounding, a definition of the self as a wound, all of which resonate across the subsequent chapters of this book. For Alain de Lille's *Plaint of Nature*, whose title links it etymologically to *je me plaing* (*planctus, plangere*), positions itself as an attempt to close through mourning the open wound desire has inflicted upon humanity. René d'Anjou's *Book of the Love-Smitten Heart*, which also begins as a plaint, works toward maintaining the wound of *je me plaing* open so the main character can revel in the melancholy that collapses his beloved lady's absence with her imagined presence. The temporality of *je me plaing*, occurring as Narcissus tries to rectify his already divided self, launches a discussion of Chrétien de Troyes's *Story of the Grail*, where repeated woundings call out for an understanding of the traumatic origins of the self. Finally, the appeal of *je me plaing*, an endeavor to comprehend and heal the wound of desire through language, serves as the basis for an exploration of testimonial speech in Guillaume de Machaut's *Fountain of Love*.

Each text, in its own way, has to grapple with how to transmit the force of this wound, of this *je me plaing*, due to the fact that any retelling of the myth inevitably causes its own narcosis, its own forgetting of the horrors of the human condition—that the self always emerges, unalterably, irrevocably, inevitably as still-born. For, as Claire Nouvet purports:

> Neatly separating "I" from "other" is an attempt to simplify the "I" by "purifying" it of the difference that constitutes and humiliates it at the same time. For the "I," the other in "me" is in fact proof of an original victimiza-

tion that the self, through prideful affirmation, strives to forget and, above all, deny. The "I" is asserted by excluding the other so that it does not know, and especially does not feel, the difference it carries from within, even as it remains powerless to suppress or understand it. Even though the "I" is asserted through this exclusion, it goes numb, desensitizing itself to the narcissistic wound that strikes it and from which it emerges: this wound of the other in the self that, from the start, jeopardizes any pretense the self might have at claiming to be itself. Narcissistic narcosis. Avoidance behavior.[3]

It is such *narcissistic narcosis*, such *avoidance behavior*, that causes so much urgency in all the texts I discuss in this book, an urgency reflected in their attempts to reinscribe selfhood as something that might be rectified and made whole. For, if only we might avoid loving as Narcissus loves, if only Nature's plaint could set humanity back on a path of divine plenitude, if only Sweet Mercy accepted René's Heart, if only Perceval had spoken and healed the Fisher King's wound, if only the beloved lady truly could give her ruby ring to Machaut's lover. If only .... if only .... if only, the self could be made whole, desire could be fulfilled. And who, as it turns out, would not want such a happy ending? In this sense, the Narcissus myth contains its own anti-story, its own undoing that references the impossibility, even as I say it, to speak about the truth regarding "my" selfhood. Each retelling of the myth, including the five texts contained herein, can only but fail, as a result, to speak to the truth of the myth.

What are the implications of such an impossibility to speak to this truth, of an impossibility, ultimately, of testimony? If selfhood is so precarious, if our selfhood puts itself, its integrity, its existence, into question at every step, where are we to go? What, ultimately, are the implications of coming into one's selfhood? As I discuss at the end of Chap. 6, the answer may lie within fantasy, within *literature*. And, because this literary discourse has already entered and shaped our realities, the narratives of our own selfhood, desires, and loves have *already been written*, the script has *already been laid out for us*, thanks to Narcissus and those who have taken up his story, appropriating it to their own highly personal and yet universal narratives of love, desire, and selfhood, which, in turn, come to be ours as well. If all accounts of the Narcissus story fail in their attempt to state what happens to the self, then somewhere, within the mute echo of each retelling, lies, uncovered, incomprehensible, but still nonetheless *there*—even as it undoes itself—the story of our self as well. In this sense, as Roland Barthes professes, all I can do is "repeat (and fail to achieve)" my own love story that has *already taken place*. And it has already taken place because "only the Other could write my love story," has already written it.[4] I repeat this story as I live out my own selfhood, my own life, my own desire. All I can be, as a result, is a reenactment of the echo who repeats "my" own story, the echo depriving me of any ownership of my own story even as I tell it because it is simply an iteration of what has already come, of what has already been told.

The wound of desire can then, through literature, be its own redemption. If the death of the self is the only possibility for selfhood within the structure that narcissism imposes on it, fantasy—and the narcosis it brings with it, the mechanism seeking to deny the sundered self—serves a dual function. Although fantasy attempts to undo the wound and create the illusion that fulfillment is possible, there would be no need for it were the self not divided and thus, as I explore throughout this entire book, desire would be impossible. It is the wound that creates desire and these texts that explore desire, even as they attempt to rectify the lacerations that selfhood continuously endures. For, when all is said and done, this is, as Judith Butler posits, our sole reality when it comes to love, when it comes to our own selfhood: "Let's face it. We're undone by each other. And if we're not, we're missing something. [...] One does not always stay intact. It may be that one wants to, or does, but it may also be that despite one's best efforts, one is undone, in the face of the other, by the touch, by the scent, by the feel, by the prospect of the touch, by the memory of the feel."[5] To be wounded by the other is to love, to desire, to be, in truth, *fully human*.

As I hope to have demonstrated throughout this book, the wounding within the self that obliges us to look toward an other in an attempt to heal our self is precisely what defines our subjectivity. Narcissus serves as the primary example of this in the literature I have explored because it is he who illustrates our inextricable link with the desire of and for another, a concept which in turn has come to shape philosophical, theological, and psychoanalytic discourses in their attempts to delineate the human experience as one in relation to others. If we are to take, as Lacanian psychoanalysis purports, that selfhood and desire are synonymous terms, for "there cannot be a subject without a concept of desire" because "desire [creates] the subject," the goal of examining selfhood is, in fact, an attempt to understand desire.[6] A self, in other words, is fully a self only when it experiences the narcissistic wounding of desire through an other, a process that takes place, as Julia Kristeva reminds us, through love itself. For solely when in love can the "'I' be an *other*," something which, she argues, "suggests a state of instability in which the individual is no longer indivisible and allows himself to become lost in the other, for the other." This experience becomes the "fragile crest where death and regeneration vie for dominance," quite simply, because "love is the time and space in which 'I' assumes the right to be extraordinary. Sovereign yet not individual. Divisible, lost, annihilated; but also, through imaginary fusion with the loved one, equal to the infinite space of super-human psychism. [...] I am, in love, at the zenith of subjectivity."[7] Ultimately, if the medieval literature examined in this book teaches us anything, it is that the unavoidable imperative to deny Narcissus as our reality is the only way we can accept him, accept our desire, accept our very self. *Iste ego sum!*

NOTES

1. Thibaut de Champagne, "Chanson d'amour" in *Chansons des trouvères*, ed. Marie-Geneviève Grossel et al. (Paris: Librairie Générale Française, 1995), vv. 25–40, 588, 590, my translation.
2. Jacques Derrida, "There Is No *One* Narcissism" in *Points...: Interviews, 1974–1994*, ed. Elizabeth Weber and trans. Peggy Kamuf (Stanford: Stanford University Press, 1995), 199.
3. Claire Nouvet, *Enfances Narcisse* (Paris: Galilée, 2009), 155. My translation of: "Séparer purement et simplement le 'moi' de l'autre, c'est tenter de simplifier le 'moi' en le 'purifiant' d'une altérité qui le constitue et l'humilie tout à la fois. Pour le 'moi,' l'autre en 'moi' est en effet l'épreuve d'une victimisation originelle qu'une fière affirmation de soi s'efforce d'oublier, et, surtout, de dénier. Le 'moi' s'affirme en excluant l'autre afin de ne pas savoir, et surtout de ne pas sentir, l'altérité qu'il porte en lui sans parvenir à la contenir ou à la comprendre. Alors même qu'il s'affirme par exclusion, il s'engourdit, s'insensibilise à la blessure narcissique qui le frappe et dont il émerge: la blessure de l'autre en lui qui d'origine met à mal toute prétention d'être lui-même. Narcose narcissique. Conduite de fuite."
4. Roland Barthes, *A Lover's Discourse: Fragments*, trans. Richard Howard (New York: Hill and Wang, 1978), 93–94.
5. Judith Butler, *Undoing Gender* (New York: Routledge, 2004), 19.
6. Patrick Fuery, *Theories of Desire* (Melbourne: Melbourne University Press, 1995), 16.
7. Julia Kristeva, *Tales of Love*, trans. Leon S. Roudiez (New York: Columbia University Press, 1987), 4–5.

REFERENCES

Barthes, Roland. 1977. *A Lover's Discourse: Fragments*. Trans. Richard Howard. New York: Hill and Wang.

Butler, Judith. 2004. *Undoing Gender*. New York: Routledge.

Derrida, Jacques. 1995. There Is No *One* Narcissism (Autobiographies). In *Points...: Interviews, 1974–1994*. Ed. Elisabeth Weber and Trans. Peggy Kamuf, 196–215. Stanford, CA: Stanford University Press.

Fuery, Patrick. 1995. *Theories of Desire*. Melbourne: Melbourne University Press.

Kristeva, Julia. 1987. *Tales of Love*. Trans. Leon S. Roudiez. New York: Columbia University Press.

Nouvet, Claire. 2009. *Enfances narcisse*. Paris: Galilée.

Thibaut de Champagne. 1995. Chanson d'amour. In *Chansons des trouvères*, ed. Marie-Geneviève Grossel et al., 586–591. Paris: Librairie Générale Française.

Index[1]

A

Agamben, Giorgio, 10, 19, 35, 112, 116, 127n7, 214, 216
Ahl, Frederick, 54n16
Alain de Lille
  Anticlaudianus, 69, 90, 94
  Plaint of Nature/De planctu Naturae, 16, 52, 60, 228; antiphrasis in text, 72, 75 (*see also* Liberal Arts); Concept of human subjectivity, 60; God, 78, 80, 86, 87, 90, 93; God as fountain, 86, 98n72; Hermaphroditus, 66; humanity (human soul), 86, 87; logic of substitution, 77, 79; macrocosm and microcosm, 81; nature, 60, 62, 74, 76, 77, 81, 83, 85, 91 (*see also* Plaint); the plaint (planctus), 61; polyvocal nature of language, 83, 84, 91 (*see also* Liberal Arts); role of

Narcissus, 64, 65, 70, 71, 73, 79, 88, 93; Venus, 67, 75, 78, 79, 81
"Sermon on the Intelligible Sphere," 91 (*see also* Alain)
Aristotle, 214

B

Barthes, Roland, 229
Bartsch, Shadi, 96n20
Bernart de Ventadorn, 3–5, 8
Bloch, R. Howard, 54n22
Brown, Raymond E., 176n63
Butler, Judith, 230

C

Camille, Michael, 54n25, 175n41
Caruth, Cathy, 137–139, 141, 158, 159, 171, 177n79
  See also Trauma

[1] Note: Page numbers followed by 'n' refer to notes.